Contributions to Differential Psychology

Centennial Psychology Series

Charles D. Spielberger, *General Editor*

Anne Anastasi *Contributions to Differential Psychology*
William K. Estes *Models of Learning, Memory, and Choice*
Hans J. Eysenck *Personality, Genetics, and Behavior*
Irving L. Janis *Stress, Attitudes, and Decisions*
Neal Miller *Bridges Between Laboratory and Clinic*
Brenda Milner *Brain Function and Cognition*
O. Hobart Mowrer *Leaves from Many Seasons*
Charles E. Osgood *Psycholinguistics, Cross-Cultural Universals, and Prospects for Mankind*
Julian B. Rotter *The Development and Applications of Social Learning Theory*
Seymour B. Sarason *Psychology and Social Action*
Benton J. Underwood *Studies in Learning and Memory*

Contributions to Differential Psychology
Selected Papers

Anne Anastasi

PRAEGER SPECIAL STUDIES • PRAEGER SCIENTIFIC

Library of Congress Cataloging in Publication Data
Main entry under title:

Contributions to differential psychology.

  (Centennial psychology series)
  Bibliography: p.
  Includes index.
  1. Difference (Psychology) 2. Personality.
3. Psychological tests. 4. Factor analysis. 5. Nature
and nurture. I. Anastasi, Anne, 1908-   . II. Series.
BF697.C585 1982   155   82-9845
ISBN 0-03-059044-2   AACR2

Published in 1982 by Praeger Publishers
CBS Educational and Professional Publishing
A Division of CBS, Inc.

© 1982 by Praeger Publishers

23456789 052 987654321

Printed in the United States of America

Contents

Editor's Introduction

The founding of Wilhelm Wundt's laboratory at Leipzig in 1879 is widely acclaimed as the landmark event that provided the initial impetus for the development of psychology as an experimental science. To commemorate scientific psychology's one-hundredth anniversary, Praeger Publishers commissioned the Centennial Psychology Series. The general goals of the Series are to present, in both historical and contemporary perspective, the most important papers of distinguished contributors to psychological theory and research.

As psychology begins its second century, the Centennial Series proposes to examine the foundation on which scientific psychology is built. Each volume provides a unique opportunity for the reader to witness the emerging theoretical insights of eminent psychologists whose seminal work has served to define and shape their respective fields, and to share with them the excitement associated with the discovery of new scientific knowledge.

The selection of the Series authors was an extremely difficult task. Indexes of scientific citations and rosters of the recipients of prestigious awards for research contributions were examined. Nominations were invited from leading authorities in various fields of psychology. The opinions of experienced teachers of psychology and recent graduates of doctoral programs were solicited. There was, in addition, a self-selection factor: a few of the distinguished senior psychologists invited to participate in the Series were not able to do so, most often because of demanding commitments or ill health.

Each Series author was invited to develop a volume comprising five major parts: (1) an original introductory chapter; (2) previously published articles and original papers selected by the author; (3) a concluding chapter; (4) a brief autobiography; and (5) a complete bibliography of the author's publications. The main content of each volume consists of articles and papers especially selected for this Series by the author. These papers trace the historical development of the author's work over a period of forty to fifty years. Each volume also provides a cogent presentation of the author's current research and theoretical viewpoints.

In their introductory chapters, Series authors were asked to describe the intellectual climate that prevailed at the beginning of their scientific careers, and to examine the evolution of the ideas that led them from one study to another. They were also invited to comment on significant factors—both scientific and personal—that stimulated and motivated them to embark on their research programs and to consider special opportunities or constraints that influenced their work, including experimental failures and blind alleys only rarely reported in the literature.

In order to preserve the historical record, most of the articles reprinted in the Series volumes have been reproduced exactly as they appeared when they were first published. In some cases, however, the authors have abridged their original papers (but not altered the content), so that redundant materials could be eliminated and more papers could be included.

In the concluding chapters, the Series authors were asked to comment on their selected papers, to describe representative studies on which they are currently working, and to evaluate the status of their research. They were also asked to discuss major methodological issues encountered in their respective fields of interest and to identify contemporary trends that are considered most promising for future scientific investigation.

The biographical sketch that is included in each Series volume supplements the autobiographical information contained in the original and concluding chapters. Perhaps the most difficult task faced by the Series authors was selecting a limited number of papers that they considered most representative from the complete bibliography of the author's life work that appears at the end of each volume.

The Centennial Psychology Series is especially designed for courses on the history of psychology. Individual volumes are also well-suited for use as supplementary texts in those areas to which the authors have been major contributors. Students of psychology and related disciplines, as well as authorities in specialized fields, will find that each Series volume provides penetrating insight into the work of a significant contributor to the behavioral sciences. The Series also affords a unique perspective on psychological research as a living process.

Anastasi's Contributions

Although general guidelines were suggested for each Series volume, each author was encouraged to adapt the series format to meet his or her individual needs. For this volume, Professor Anastasi has selected 20 papers that reflect her broad interests and wide-ranging contributions to differential psychology. An abiding concern with the role of environmental, cultural, and experiential factors in psychological development underlies most of her research and writings.

In the Preface and the introductory chapter, Professor Anastasi reviews the criteria for selecting the papers for this volume, and she identifies the major themes that have characterized her life work. The individual papers, which cut across several substantive areas of psychology, are organized according to three major themes: interpretation of test scores; factor analysis and traits; and heredity and environment. Introductions for each chapter provide cogent information about the reprinted papers and about how the research findings are related to the major themes and to the research literature. The historical context, the salient theoretical issues, and the settings and the people that have stimulated and influenced the research are also examined.

Throughout her highly productive career, Professor Anastasi has been vitally concerned with applications of statistical procedures to the measurement of mental traits. The seven papers in Chapters 2 and 3, on the interpretation of test scores, reflect the author's influential contributions to psychometric theory and the assessment of individual differences, and her continuing efforts to identify shortcomings and pitfalls in the use and interpretation of psychological tests. Her early interest in the measurement of components of memory is expressed in the papers in Chapter 4. The papers in Chapters 5 and 6 report investigations of the role of experience in determining the nature and origins of traits and applications of factor analysis to investigating the organization of traits.

The papers included in Chapters 7 and 8 present the author's views on complex theoretical and methodological issues relating to how heredity and environment influence behavioral development and trait formation in a field that has been characterized by intense controversy. In Chapter 9, Professor Anastasi examines and evaluates a number of current trends in differential psychology. She notes with approval a growing concern with the formulation of relevant theory and a movement away from the blind empiricism of earlier decades.

In August 1981, Professor Anastasi was the recipient of the American Psychological Association's Distinguished Scientific Award for the Applications of Psychology. An eloquent testimony to the significance, scope, and enduring impact of her many scientific contributions to differential psychology can be found in the citation that accompanied this award:

For persistently seeking to clarify the nature and origins of psychological traits and facilitating their valid measurements. She has been a major force in the development of differential psychology as a behavioral science, having illuminated the ways trait development is influenced by education and heredity and the ways trait measurement is affected by training and practice, cultural contexts, and language differences. Her texts, *Differential Psychology* and *Psychological Testing,* being both integrative and probing, do not simply summarize the groundwork in these fields, but provide impetus for further work. Ever watchful for misleading generalizations and misconceptions, she displays unusual perceptiveness in her timely emphasis on key issues and unusual critical acumen in her timely undercutting of spurious issues.

Acknowledgments

The interest and enthusiasm of all with whom we have consulted concerning the establishment of the Series have been most gratifying, but I am especially grateful to Professors Anne Anastasi, Hans J. Eysenck, and Irving L. Janis for their many helpful comments and suggestions and for their early agreement to contribute to the Series. For his invaluable advice and consultation in the conception and planning of the Series, and for his dedicated and effective work in making it a reality, I am deeply indebted to Dr. George Zimmar, psychology editor for Praeger Publishers.

The Series was initiated while I was a Fellow-In-Residence at the Netherlands Institute for Advanced Study, and I would like to express my appreciation to the director and staff of the Institute and to my NIAS colleagues for their stimulation, encouragement, and strong support of this endeavor.

Charles D. Spielberger

Preface

In selecting papers for this book, I was faced with conflicting criteria. Should priority be given to historical interest or to currently applicable substantive content? How should theoretical discussions and broad literature surveys be weighted relative to research reports? Within the available space, would it be better to include short papers in their entirety or excerpts from longer papers? Not surprisingly, I could formulate no simple, generalizable answers to these questions but had to confront each dilemma anew in choosing individual papers. As I look over the final choices, it appears that I gave about equal weight to historical interest and viable substantive content. I leaned more heavily toward theoretical discussions and broad literature coverage than toward research reports. And I included both excerpts and short papers, letting other variables determine the decisions in individual cases. None of the listed criteria was completely discarded; they were only sampled with varying degrees of concentration. As a result, the selected papers reflect a wide diversity of type and content; in length, they range from a half-page comment in the *American Psychologist* to excerpts from a 111-page monograph; and in publication dates, they extend from 1930 to 1981.

The 20 selected papers have been classified under three major themes, with two or three chapters covering the subdivisions of each theme. Within each theme, the papers are arranged chronologically, except in two instances where the order was changed in the interest of topical continuity. An opening chapter (Ch. 1) provides the background, setting, and climate for the papers. It considers what was happening in the particular area of psychology at the time the individual research projects were conducted and the papers were written. A concluding chapter (Ch. 9) is concerned with the current status of the major topics sampled in the book. An effort was also made to identify conspicuous developments in these areas that seemed to be gaining momentum in the late 1970s and early 1980s. As in other books in this series, an autobiographical sketch (Ch. 10) and a complete list of my publications are also included.

It is a pleasure to acknowledge the contributions of the General Series Editor, Charles D. Spielberger, and the publisher's psychology editor, George P. Zimmar. I am indebted to them for convincing me to undertake the preparation of such a book in the first place; for some stimulating, productive, and thoroughly enjoyable discussions on many matters about the book, with digressions into psychology in general; and for their intellectual flexibility and their receptiveness to my idiosyncracies.

A. A.

Contributions to
Differential
Psychology

1
A Fifty-Year Span: Context and Climate

Chronologically, the papers reproduced in this collection extend from 1930 to 1981. With only minor exceptions, my complete publication list falls within a fifty-year period. This span defines the time during which I have been a participant observer in American psychology. For the young science of psychology, it was a period of emerging self-concept, rapid expansion, and significant growth in both theoretical and applied fields. There were important breakthroughs and an increasing involvement in societal problems. Every American psychologist who lived and worked through this period was undoubtedly influenced by its evolving scientific and social climate and—to varying extents—contributed to this evolution.

I came into psychology when there were still a few generalists in the field, and I was influenced by personal contact with some notable examples. My own interests remained broad, as evidenced in my teaching, my textbooks, and my research (see Ch. 10). In selecting papers for this book, however, I tried to identify major themes recurring in my work over the years, and to choose the clearest examples of these particular themes. One pervasive interest was in psychometrics, covering the assessment of individual differences, test development methodology, and the interpretation of test performance. The selected papers in this area are reproduced in Chapters 2 and 3, and their background is discussed in the first section of this chapter. The second section is concerned with factor-analytic studies and the nature and origin of psychological traits. The related papers are included in Chapters 4, 5, and 6. The theme underlying the third section, and illustrated in Chapters 7 and 8, is that of heredity and environment.

Although these three themes are clearly recognizable in the selected papers, the grouping represents an a posteriori classification, and the distinctions are not sharp. Individual papers could be classified under two or even all three themes, although each falls predominantly under one of them. Moreover, there are certain subthemes running through several papers; these subthemes will be described at the appropriate places in the following sections. In the last section of this chapter, we shall take a quick look at the conditions under which psychological research and writing were conducted during the early years of this fifty-year span. What were the available facilities, opportunities, and limitations, as viewed from the perspective of the 1980s?

INTERPRETATION OF TEST SCORES

As psychology emerged from the laboratory and began to grapple with problems of societal interest, it encountered frequent methodological pitfalls. With the increasing complexity of both the behaviors under investigation and the natural contexts in which they occurred, the control of conditions and the isolation of variables met with unprecedented difficulties. Procedural and interpretive hazards were especially evident in the application of tests and other observational techniques to the assessment of individuals and groups. The rapid development of group tests and their premature popularization in the 1920s and 1930s led to some hasty conclusions and overgeneralizations. The testing boom that followed World War I may have done as much to retard the progress of psychological testing as to advance it.

In the preface to the first edition of my *Differential Psychology,* I wrote:

> Throughout the present book, special emphasis has been placed upon the examination of common sources of error and pitfalls in the interpretation of obtained facts. We have thus hoped to provide the student with certain tools whereby he may evaluate for himself a set of data with which he is confronted. (Anastasi, 1937, p. vii)

The same statement, with only minor rewording, was repeated in the preface to subsequent editions. In the third edition, I added: "The development of critical ability and of a dispassionate and objective attitude toward human behavior is more urgently needed today than ever before" (Anastasi, 1958a, p. vii). I can say the same in the 1980s.

The quest for pitfalls represents a subtheme appearing early in my writings and occurring not only in connection with the interpretation of test scores but also in the conclusions drawn from other types of behavioral observations. The latter can be illustrated by the interpretation of data gathered through clinical interviews and case histories, and in the analysis of spontaneous drawings and other artistic productions. Although the pitfall-questing subtheme is most clearly illustrated in the critical papers included in Chapter 2, it also underlies the other psychometric papers given in Chapter 3. In fact, this subtheme can be recognized in at least some papers reproduced in nearly all chapters; and it thus overlaps all three major themes.

My research and publications in psychometrics also include more positive contributions, involving the development and evaluation of tests and biographical inventories for specific purposes (e.g., Anastasi, Foley, & Sackman, 1954; Anastasi, Meade, & Schneiders, 1960; Schaefer & Anastasi, 1968), as well as some work with relevant statistical techniques (e.g., Anastasi, 1934, 1953; Anastasi & Drake, 1954). In selecting papers for inclusion in this book, however, I have given preference to broadly oriented discussions, rather than research reports, because of the more general interest of the former. With regard to psychometrics in particular, I have concentrated on the critical evaluations because of their continuing relevance.

FACTOR ANALYSIS AND TRAITS

From its earliest beginnings, differential psychology has been concerned with the nature of intelligence and the organization of mental traits. An important milestone in this area was the publication in 1904 of an article by the British psychologist, Charles Spearman. Representing a first attempt to approach the problem through empirical, quantitative methods, this article presented both a theory and a new method of investigation. According to Spearman's theory, which he called the "two-factor theory," all intellectual activities share a single common factor, the general factor (g). In addition, the theory postulated numerous specific factors (s), each strictly specific to a single activity. Although in modern terminology this theory would be described as a single-factor theory, since the one common factor accounts for all correlation, the original "two-factor" label has persisted.

In a later book, *The Abilities of Man,* Spearman (1927) elaborated on the theory, reported available evidence, and described the further development of his statistical procedures. Beginning as an in-

spectional analysis of certain relationships within a table of intercorrelations, the procedure had by this time evolved into the application
of the *tetrad equation*. Even before the publication of this book,
however, Spearman and his followers recognized the inadequacy of a
single general factor in accounting for all correlation among test
scores. More and more research was beginning to reveal group factors, narrower in scope than *g* but broader than *s* factors. Although
Spearman and other British psychologists identified a few subsidiary
group factors in their own studies, the intensive investigation of such
group factors has been more characteristic of American research. In
a book entitled *Crossroads in the Mind of Man,* published only a year
after Spearman's book, Truman L. Kelley (1928) outlined a method
for using tetrad equations to locate group factors, and presented
evidence for five such factors in addition to a general factor. The five
factors, which he identified in samples of seventh-grade, third-grade,
and kindergarten children, were described as verbal, number, memory, spatial, and speed factors.

Shortly after the publication of Kelley's book, Henry E. Garrett
initiated a long-term project at Columbia University designed to investigate Kelley's five factors at different age levels and with more
extensive sets of specially developed tests. This research was conducted chiefly by Garrett's doctoral students in a series of dissertations that he directed. The first dealt with the verbal and number
factors (Schneck, 1929). The second was my dissertation on the
memory factor (Anastasi, 1930). Upon completion of this first
study, I carried out further studies designed principally to test the
hypothesis that there are not one, but several memory factors (Anastasi, 1932). Excerpts from my two published monographs on both
sets of studies are reproduced in Chapter 4. Dissertations on the
speed factor (DuBois, 1932) and on the spatial factor (Schiller,
1934) followed.

Other studies in the project were concerned with special problems, such as the relative importance of test form and content in the
organization of abilities (Smith, 1933) and age changes in factor
structure (Asch, 1936; Bryan, 1934; Clark, 1944; Garrett, Bryan, &
Perl, 1935; Reichard, 1944). The latter studies were designed to test
Garrett's differentiation hypothesis regarding the development of
intelligence. On the basis of research on groups ranging from five-
year-olds to college students, Garrett (1946) concluded that intelligence is relatively undifferentiated in early childhood and becomes
increasingly specialized with age until maturity. Relevant data were
provided by a comparison of separate studies employing subjects at
different age levels, as well as by both cross-sectional and longitudinal studies covering multiple age levels.

Several investigations published after Garrett's 1946 paper reported contradictory results, which called the differentiation hypothesis into question. A detailed examination of these studies, however, led Cyril Burt (1954) to the conclusion that the contradictory findings arose from inappropriate choice of subjects, tests, or statistical techniques of factor analysis, as well as from other methodological weaknesses. In the same paper, Burt cites evidence for the differentiation hypothesis, which he had formulated during his early research on the mental and scholastic abilities of English schoolchildren, conducted while he was serving as Psychologist to the London County Council. On the basis of his reanalysis of intervening published studies, Burt reaffirmed his original differentiation hypothesis.

While recognizing the possible role of accumulating experience and diverging interests, both Burt and Garrett attributed the differentiation of abilities chiefly to maturation. My own reading of the relevant literature, including the more extensive literature appearing after the 1950s, led me to question the maturational explanation and to propose, instead, educational and other experiential variables to account for the varying degrees of factorial differentiation found in different populations. The two papers reproduced in Chapter 6 summarize the pertinent findings. Even while still working on the organization of memory, in fact, I had become aware of the possible role of experiential background in factorial organization. Accordingly, I conducted a study to demonstrate the experimental alteration of factorial structure through interpolated experience (Anastasi, 1936). This study is excerpted in Chapter 5. Its results led to a minor skirmish with Louis Leon Thurstone, which was typical of the controversies on trait organization and factor analysis that enlivened the journals of the period (Anastasi, 1935, 1938; Thurstone, 1938b).

During the 1930s, the methodology of factor analysis had been making dramatic progress, leaving the simple tetrad equation far behind. And the later Columbia studies (including my 1936 monograph) had been keeping up with the times in their application of available statistical techniques. Within a single decade, Hotelling (1933) developed the method of principal components, Kelley (1935) the method of principal axes, and Thurstone (1935) the centroid method of factor analysis. Thurstone's procedures, including orthogonal and oblique rotation of axes, were more fully developed in his 1947 book, *Multiple-Factor Analysis.* Although the centroid method was offered as a convenient approximation of more precise procedures, it remained the most common method used in research for a couple of decades, until the availability of high-speed computers made more elaborate procedures practicable.

The 1930s and 1940s also ushered in Thurstone's primary mental abilities, including empirical research identifying some ten factors, as well as a battery of specially developed tests to measure them (Thurstone, 1938a, 1948). Some of these tests were employed in the later Columbia studies on age changes in factorial organization.

HEREDITY AND ENVIRONMENT

Theoretical Considerations

The question of what is inherited and what is acquired in human behavior has been a persistent theme in differential psychology. At the turn of the century, Karl Pearson (1904), Edward L. Thorndike (1905), and other students of individual differences reacted against a naive environmentalism that regarded the mind as a blank tablet (Locke's *tabula rasa*) upon which experience writes. But in its place, they substituted an equally naive hereditarianism, which permeated psychological thought for nearly half a century (Cravens, 1978). The earliest attempts to investigate human heredity were based on the analysis of family resemblances. Although many forms and variants of this procedure have been utilized, interpretation of results is usually difficult. The chief source of confusion is that the family is a cultural as well as a biological unit. Related persons usually live together, sharing a common environment. Although the psychological environment is by no means uniform for all members of a family, their environments nevertheless have many broad features in common, such as socioeconomic level and cultural milieu. In general, the closer the degree of hereditary relationship, the greater are these environmental similarities.

In addition, family members constitute a part of each other's environments. Family interaction thus provides many opportunities for mutual influence. A third source of influence is social expectancy. Children are often reminded of the talents and defects of their forebears, and any chance display of similar traits on their part will be augmented by such references. What is expected of an individual helps to shape his or her self-concept, which, in turn, is likely to affect subsequent development.

It follows that to demonstrate familial resemblances in a psychological trait does not in itself constitute proof of its hereditary origin. In the effort to disentangle the contributions of hereditary and environmental factors to behavior development, special familial relations have been investigated, including twins and foster children.

Even this approach, however, is limited by various methodological weaknesses. Major studies on foster children conducted between the 1920s and the 1950s yielded conflicting results and ambiguous conclusions (see Anastasi, 1958a, Ch. 9). Twin studies, dating back to Galton (1883), are still being conducted today. Although their methodology has steadily improved, the interpretations of results remain controversial.

While still differing in the primary focus of their research procedures and interpretations, however, psychologists have gradually come to recognize that the relation between heredity and environment is far more complex than the early extremist views indicated. The 1950s ushered in a period of enhanced theoretical sophistication in research and discussions on the "nature-nurture" question (Cravens, 1978, pp. 269–274). This shift in orientation is illustrated in an article by Hebb (1953), in which he observed that, as usually formulated, questions about heredity and environment may be meaningless and unanswerable. He went on to point out "that all behaviour is dependent both on heredity and on environment, and all non-reflex behaviour at least involves the special effects of environmental stimulation that we call learning" (Hebb, 1953, p. 44). As for the proportion of behavioral *variance* determined by heredity and by environment, Hebb recognized that this is a meaningful question but of limited use, particularly when applied to individuals. The matter was further explored in my 1958 paper (Anastasi, 1958b—reproduced in Chapter 8). In that article, I proposed that a more appropriate question is "How?"—that is, what are the specific etiological mechanisms or chains of events whereby hereditary and environmental conditions influence behavior?

The operation of environmental, cultural, or experiential factors in psychological development is a major theme underlying most of my research and writing. This theme can be recognized not only in the papers reproduced in Chapters 7 and 8, but also in several papers included in earlier chapters, such as the previously cited factor-analytic research on trait formation. Several papers pertaining to the interpretation of test scores, especially those concerned with the effects of training and of cultural background on test performance, also exemplify this theme. The papers reproduced in the two chapters specifically labelled "heredity and environment" were selected because they deal explicitly either with theoretical discussions of heredity and environment in the etiology of behavioral differences or with research designed to assess the contributions of a particular experiential variable to individual differences. In exploring such experiential contributions, a wide diversity of approaches was followed.

Studies of Artistic Production

One approach is illustrated by studies of artistic production, broadly defined. These studies, conducted in collaboration with my husband, John Porter Foley, Jr., reflected our jointly developing avocational interest in art, which began with museums and progressed to art galleries, art books, and personal collecting. This interest led to several projects concerned with children's art, with the artistic productions of self-taught "Sunday painters," and with cultural differences in artistic expression (Anastasi & Foley, 1936, 1938, 1940a). Our visits to art galleries also contributed to our decision to embark on a long-term project on the relations of art and abnormality (Anastasi & Foley, 1940b, 1941a, 1941b, 1941c, 1943, 1944). In the late 1930s and early 1940s, several New York art shows featured psychotic art, as well as the art products of children and of primitive cultures. At least one gallery provided a copy of Prinzhorn's (1923) classic book on psychotic art as a handy reference source for its visitors.

The unbridled psychologizing in the writings of certain artists and art critics augmented our mounting dissatisfaction with the unsupported claims by some psychiatrists and clinical psychologists about the meaning of "pathological" signs in art products. These claims ranged from far-fetched personality interpretations of paintings by eminent artists to the unvalidated use of various projective drawing tests for clinical assessment. A subtheme underlying our psychotic art project can be described simply as a "debunking" enterprise. Our own research on alleged indices of pathology, conducted with control groups and uniform data-gathering procedures, demonstrated that many such indices tended to be related not to pathology but to educational, occupational, and socioeconomic backgrounds (Anastasi & Foley, 1944, 1952).

Psychological writings of the 1920s and 1930s were also characterized by frequent overgeneralizations about human behavior on the basis of data gathered within a single culture. Such overgeneralization is illustrated by descriptions of developmental stages, especially as applied to children's drawings. For instance, the Goodenough (1926) Draw-a-Man Test was originally designed as a nonverbal intelligence test suitable for use with children from different cultural and subcultural populations. When it was subsequently administered to a variety of ethnic and national groups, however, performance was found to depend much more on specific cultural background than had originally been supposed (Dennis, 1966). In a review of the research on this test published between 1928 and 1949, Goodenough and Harris (1950, p. 399) expressed the opinion that "the search for a culture-free test, whether of intelligence, artistic ability, personal-social characteristics, or any other measurable trait is illusory." This view was reaffirmed by Harris (1963) in discussing his revision of the Goodenough test.

Against the psychological climate of the 1930s, my husband and I became interested in examining children's drawings from different cultures (e.g., Anastasi & Foley, 1936). One of these studies, reported in Chapter 7, was an analysis of drawings by Indian children of the North Pacific Coast (Anastasi & Foley, 1938). These drawings had been collected in the field by Franz Boas, then professor of anthropology at Columbia University.[1] Boas generously turned over the drawings to us for analysis and report. Although readily discussing with us any points we raised regarding the study, he declined co-authorship. We were fortunate in having closer contact with Boas than would have resulted simply from being in the same university, because my husband served as research associate in two studies that were part of an extended project, directed by Boas, on the influence of race and environment on bodily development and on behavior (Efron & Foley, 1937; Foley, 1937a, 1937b).

Creativity Research

At the 1950 convention of the American Psychological Association, Guilford (1950, p. 444) opened his presidential address with the remark, "I discuss the subject of creativity with considerable hesitation, for it represents an area in which psychologists, whether they be angels or not, have feared to tread." Within a decade, the tread had become nearly a stampede! Bolstered by the demand for high-level creative talent in science and engineering, research on creativity at all levels reached a peak in the 1960s. The principal contributions of Guilford's own research were, first, the development of many new types of tests to measure different aspects of creativity and, second, the identification of several creativity factors through factor analysis. Initiated as a study of creativity, Guilford's project developed during the next 20 years into a comprehensive reformulation of the structure of intelligence as a whole. Within this structure, creative aptitudes fell chiefly under the category of "divergent thinking" (Guilford, 1959; Guilford & Hoepfner, 1971).

---

[1] See Cravens (1978, pp. 89–105) for an account of Boas' historical impact.

Although Guilford's tests were originally designed for adults, other investigators soon adapted some of his divergent-thinking tests for use at younger ages. A study that attracted wide attention at the time, especially among educators, was conducted by Getzels and Jackson (1962) with high school students. Because of methodological flaws, however, this study tended to exaggerate the contrast between intelligence test performance and creativity (R. L. Thorndike, 1963). This was also true of a similar study by Torrance (1959) with schoolchildren. Torrance's study was part of a long-term project on creativity, covering many age levels, using a variety of procedures, and giving considerable attention to personality problems and to the role of educational practices in stifling or stimulating creativity.

Other approaches to creativity employed individual case studies of persons who had attained eminence through their creative achievements (e.g., MacKinnon, 1962; Roe, 1951; Taylor, Ellison, & Tucker, 1966). Although traditional psychological research on creativity had concentrated chiefly on ways of identifying creative persons, there was a growing awareness that creative talent should be, not only identified, but also developed. Increasing attention was given to training procedures, to the working styles of creative producers, and to the situational conditions conducive to creative achievement.

My own interest in the role of experiential factors in the development of creative thinking is reflected in a long-term research project conducted in collaboration with several students and former students (Anastasi, 1970). This research utilized three basic procedures. First, the personal characteristics and experiential backgrounds of highly creative high school students were investigated through biographical inventories and tests. Second, an exploratory study was conducted of the home environments and child-rearing practices associated with creativity among elementary schoolchildren. Third, an intensive program of creativity training for the elementary school ages was developed and evaluated through follow-up studies. One of the published papers from the first part of this project is reproduced in Chapter 7.

Intelligence Test Performance

Discussions of the heredity-environment problem in differential psychology have traditionally focused on the sources of individual differences in intelligence. Some of the hereditarian excesses promulgated in the early decades of the twentieth century represented misinterpretations of the intelligence test performance of various ethnic and national groups (Cravens, 1978). The influence of certain environmental factors upon intelligence test performance was a primary concern in a set of studies of black and Puerto Rican children in New York City, conducted jointly with some of my graduate students (Anastasi & Cordova, 1953; Anastasi & D'Angelo, 1952; Anastasi & deJesús, 1953). The study of black preschool children included an analysis of variance of test scores with reference to race, sex, and type of neighborhood (uniracial versus interracial). The results revealed some significant interactions among these three variables. The Puerto Rican studies provided data on the nature and effects of bilingualism. Having been exposed to Spanish at home and to English at school, the Puerto Rican children in our sample had not learned either language adequately and were thus handicapped in both. Consequently, administering a test with English or with Spanish instructions yielded no significant difference in their performance. This fact has now been repeatedly demonstrated in research on bilingual minorities.

A question that has long interested human geneticists is that of the relation between intelligence and family size (Anastasi, 1954, 1956, 1959). Differential fertility in various subgroups of the population was recorded as early as the seventeenth century. Demographic data subsequently collected in the United States and in several European countries demonstrated a significant inverse relationship between family size and such variables as income, occupational level, and amount of education. These findings led to some highly pessimistic predictions of a steady decline in the intellectual level of the human species.

Instead of the predicted decline, however, the administration of intelligence tests to large, comparable samples of various populations after lapses of 10 to 20 years revealed significant rises in performance. The assessment of the nature and consequences of the reported relations between intelligence and family size presents an awesome array of statistical and methodological pitfalls (Anastasi, 1956). Publication of the findings of the follow-up testing studies led to extensive reanalyses of the implications of fertility differentials. The widespread concern with this problem in the 1950s is illustrated by the convening of a special working group by UNESCO to prepare a statement on the issue, which was submitted to the World Population Conference in 1954. This Conference, held in Rome under United Nations auspices, included a session on "methods of research on relations between intelligence and fertility." A paper I presented at that session was published in the *Eugenics Quarterly* and is reproduced in Chapter 7 (Anastasi, 1954).

THE RESEARCH ENTERPRISE

The fifty-year period spanned by the papers in this volume was characterized, not only by a mounting accumulation of psychological knowledge and a rapid expansion of fields of application, but also by major changes in the way research was carried out and disseminated. Some of these changes are illustrated by the papers from successive decades in this collection.

Computing Facilities

Unquestionably, the most conspicuous innovation in research procedures is associated with the introduction of computers. For his Columbia dissertation on verbal and numerical abilities, Schneck (1929) computed all his correlations on a hand-operated Monroe desk calculator. The task was accomplished at the cost of many weeks of concentrated labor and considerable eye strain. The psychology department gradually acquired some electrical Monroes and one or two Marchants. My own dissertation (Anastasi, 1930) was the first in the trait project that utilized the services of a newly opened "computing center" located in the basement of Hamilton Hall, the Columbia College academic building. The equipment consisted of a Hollerith tabulator, available for test scoring as well as for computing Pearson correlations. For all other computations, of course, I too used a desk calculator.

   With the advent of successive models of computers—and especially the introduction of high-speed computers—the effects on psychometric research were clearly evident. The impact of computers was manifested, not only in unprecedented gains in speed and ease of data analysis, but also in the widespread adoption of sophisticated statistical techniques, whose use was not heretofore feasible. This effect was clearly demonstrated in the evolution of methods of factor analysis, mentioned earlier in this chapter.

Research Funding

The practice of awarding sums of money to support a research project is not so modern as might be supposed. In the report of his pioneer investigation of sibling relationships in physical and psychological traits, Pearson (1904) acknowledges financial support received from both governmental and private sources. This is undoubtedly one of the earliest recorded instances of such grants for research in differential psychology. The identity of one of Pearson's sponsors, however—the Worshipful Company of Drapers—does sound more picturesque than the agencies and foundations familiar to to-day's researchers!

Several of the early Columbia University projects cited in this chapter, including Garrett's trait project, were supported by an in-house source, the Columbia University Council for Research in the Social Sciences. A number of my own subsequent studies were also funded directly by grants from this council. This funding continued for a few years after I had left Barnard for Queens College, through the completion of our psychotic art research. Sources of funding for my later research included the U.S. Air Force, the College Entrance Examination Board, the National Institute of Mental Health, and the Center for Urban Education (on a subcontract from the U.S. Office of Education). The period of the large, long-term grants began shortly after World War II and rose to a crescendo in the 1960s. Conditions in psychometrics research and in my own experience par-alleled what was occurring in psychology in general, as in all scien-tific research in America.

Support Services

The Depression of the 1930s yielded some positive side effects for academic researchers. Several psychological studies—small by today's standards but nonetheless significant—were aided or even made pos-sible by the availability of assistants provided through the WPA (Works Progress Administration). Draftsmen, clerks, translators, and other persons with varying kinds and amounts of training and ex-perience were assigned to universities, and their services could be requested by individual researchers for particular projects. Still more relevant were the support services made available by the NYA (Na-tional Youth Administration). This agency provided modest hourly fees for students who assisted in faculty research within their own college. In several studies conducted in the 1930s, I availed myself of the services of both WPA and NYA assistants.

Another example of a relevant WPA activity was the establish-ment of the Children's Federal Art Gallery (Foley & Anastasi, 1938). One of the many undertakings sponsored by the highly productive Federal Art Projects of the WPA, this gallery not only exhibited chil-dren's art to child and adult audiences but also conducted several other educational and recreational projects for children. Because my husband was then teaching at George Washington University and I visited Washington frequently, we served as research advisers to this gallery and benefited from the contacts it afforded with the spon-taneous art products of children.

Publication

In the 1930s, Ph.D. candidates in the Columbia University Psychology Department were required to deposit 75 copies of their published dissertation in the library, before the degree could be awarded. This requirement was not as unrealistic as it now sounds. Its fulfillment was facilitated by the availability of the *Archives of Psychology,* a monograph series edited by R. S. Woodworth and managed by Enrica Tunnell, who was also librarian of the Psychology Reading Room. After the student had passed the final "orals" and had made any changes recommended by the examining committee and the adviser, the dissertation could appear in the *Archives* within one or two months. These dissertations were published in their entirety, with no deletions or editorial changes. The *Archives* also published monographs by faculty and postdoctoral students and were not limited to Columbia researchers. The series continued until 1945.

Other available monograph series, such as *Psychological Monographs* and *Genetic Psychology Monographs,* were utilized extensively as research outlets, because page costs were modest. It is also noteworthy that psychological journals of the period accepted much longer articles than they do today. In the 1930s and 1940s it was not unusual for a 25- to 50-page article to appear in such publications as the *Journal of General Psychology,* the *Journal of Experimental Psychology,* or the *Journal of Educational Psychology.* Examples can be found in the reference list appended to this chapter.

In earlier decades, journal articles were still longer. Pearson's 1904 report of his sibling study covered 60 pages in *Biometrika;* Spearman's classic paper on the organization of intelligence in the 1904 *American Journal of Psychology* was 93 pages long. It is clear that, for better or for worse, the published reports of psychological research have been growing shorter since the turn of the century.

REFERENCES

Anastasi, A. A group factor in immediate memory. *Archives of Psychology,* 1930, No. 120. Pp. 61.
——.[a] Further studies on the memory factor. *Archives of Psychology,* 1932, No. 142. Pp. 60.
——. The influence of practice upon test reliability. *Journal of Educational Psychology,* 1934, 25, 321–335.

[a]When multiple publications by the volume author are included in a chapter reference list, the author's name has not been repeated.—Ed.

——. Some ambiguous concepts in the field of "mental organization." *American Journal of Psychology*, 1935, *47*, 509–511.

——. The influence of specific experience upon mental organization. *Genetic Psychology Monographs*, 1936, *18*(4), 245–355.

——. *Differential psychology*. New York: Macmillan, 1937.

——. Faculties *versus* factors: A reply to Professor Thurstone. *Psychological Bulletin*, 1938, *35*, 391–395.

——. An empirical study of the application of sequential analysis to item selection. *Educational and Psychological Measurement*, 1953, *13*, 3–13.

——. II. Tested intelligence and family size: Methodological and interpretive problems. *Eugenics Quarterly*, 1954, *1*, 155–160.

——. Intelligence and family size. *Psychological Bulletin*, 1956, *53*, 187–209.

——. *Differential psychology* (3rd ed.). New York: Macmillan, 1958.(a)

——. Heredity, environment, and the question "How?" *Psychological Review*, 1958, *65*, 197–208. (b)

——. Differentiating effect of intelligence and social status. *Eugenics Quarterly*, 1959, *6*, 84–91.

——. *Correlates of creativity in children from two socioeconomic levels* (Final Proj. Rep. CUE Subcontract No. 2, Contract No. OEC-1-7-062868-3060). New York: Center for Urban Education, November 1970. Pp. 76.

—— & Cordova, F. A. Some effects of bilingualism upon the intelligence test performance of Puerto Rican children in New York City. *Journal of Educational Psychology*, 1953, *44*, 1–19.

—— & D'Angelo, R. Y. A comparison of Negro and white preschool children in language development and Goodenough Draw-A-Man IQ. *Journal of Genetic Psychology*, 1952, *81*, 147–165.

—— & deJesús, C. Language development and nonverbal IQ of Puerto Rican preschool children in New York City. *Journal of Abnormal and Social Psychology*, 1953, *48*, 357–366.

—— & Drake, J. D. An empirical comparison of certain techniques for estimating the reliability of speeded tests. *Educational and Psychological Measurement*, 1954, *14*, 529–540.

—— & Foley, J. P., Jr. An analysis of spontaneous drawings by children in different cultures. *Journal of Applied Psychology*, 1936, *20*, 689–676.

—— & Foley, J. P., Jr. A study of animal drawings by Indian children of the North Pacific Coast. *Journal of Social Psychology*, 1938, *9*, 363–374.

—— & Foley, J. P., Jr. The study of "populistic" painters as an approach to the pyschology of art. *Journal of Social Psychology*, 1940, *11*, 353–368. (a)

—— & Foley, J. P., Jr. A survey of the literature on artistic behavior in the abnormal: III. Spontaneous productions. *Psychological Monographs*, 1940, *52*(6, Whole No. 237). (b)

—— & Foley, J. P., Jr. A survey of the literature on artistic behavior in the abnormal: I. Historical and theoretical background. *Journal of General Psychology*, 1941, *25*, 111–142. (a)

—— & Foley, J. P., Jr. A survey of the literature on artistic behavior in the abnormal: II. Approaches and interrelationships. *Annals of the New York Academy of Sciences*, 1941, *42*, 1–112. (b)

—— & Foley, J. P., Jr. A survey of the literature on artistic behavior in the abnormal: IV. Experimental investigations. *Journal of General Psychology,* 1941, *25,* 187–237. (c)

—— & Foley, J. P., Jr. An analysis of spontaneous artistic productions by the abnormal. *Journal of General Psychology,* 1943, *28,* 297–313.

—— & Foley, J. P., Jr. An experimental study of the drawing behavior of adult psychotics in comparison with that of a normal control group. *Journal of Experimental Psychology,* 1944, *34,* 169–194.

—— & Foley, J. P., Jr. *The Human-Figure Drawing Test as an objective psychiatric screening aid for student pilots* (Proj. No. 21-37-002, Rep. No. 5.) Randolph Field, Tex.: USAF School of Aviation Medicine, October 1952. Pp. 30.

——, Foley, J. P., Jr., & Sackman, H. *An empirical evaluation of the SAM Personality-Sketch Test.* (Proj. No. 21-0202-0007, Rep. No. 6.) Randolph Field, Tex.: USAF School of Aviation Medicine, April 1954. Pp. 51.

——, Meade, M. J., & Schneiders, A. A. The validation of a biographical inventory as a predictor of college success. *College Entrance Examination Board Research Monographs,* 1960, No. 1. Pp. 81.

Asch, S. E. A study of change in mental organization. *Archives of Psychology,* 1936, No. 195. Pp. 30.

Bryan, A. I. Organization of memory in young children. *Archives of Psychology,* 1934, No. 162. Pp. 56.

Burt, C. The differentiation of intellectual ability. *British Journal of Educational Psychology,* 1954, *24,* 76–90.

Clark, M. P. Changes in Primary Mental Abilities with age. *Archives of Psychology,* 1944, No. 291. Pp. 30.

Cravens, H. *The triumph of evolution: American scientists and the heredity-environment controversy, 1900–1941.* Philadelphia: University of Pennsylvania Press, 1978.

Dennis, W. Goodenough scores, art experience, and modernization. *Journal of Social Psychology,* 1966, *68,* 211–228.

DuBois, P. H. A speed factor in mental tests. *Archives of Psychology,* 1932, No. 141. Pp. 38.

Efron, D., & Foley, J. P., Jr. Gestural behavior and social setting. *Zeitschrift für Sozialforschung,* 1937, *6*(1), 152–161. (Reprinted in T. M. Newman & E. L. Hartley (Eds.), *Readings in social psychology.* New York: Holt, 1947. Pp. 33–40. Only original journal article contains introduction by Franz Boas.)

Foley, J. P., Jr. An experimental study of the effect of occupational experience upon motor speed and preferential tempo. *Archives of Psychology,* 1937, No. 219. Pp. 40. (a)

Foley, J. P., Jr. Factors conditioning motor speed and tempo. *Psychological Bulletin,* 1937, *34,* 351–397. (b)

Foley, J. P., Jr., & Anastasi, A. The work of the Children's Federal Art Gallery. *School and Society,* 1938, *48,* No. 1253, 859–861.

Galton, F. *Inquiries into human faculty and its development.* New York: Macmillan, 1883.

Garrett, H. E. A developmental theory of intelligence. *American Psychologist,* 1946, *1,* 372–378.

Garrett, H. E., Bryan, A. I., & Perl, R. E. The age factor in mental organization. *Archives of Psychology,* 1935, No. 176. Pp. 31.

Getzels, J. W., & Jackson, P. W. *Creativity and intelligence: Explorations with gifted students.* New York: Wiley, 1962.

Goodenough, F. L. *Measurement of intelligence by drawings.* Yonkers, N.Y.: World Book Co., 1926.

Goodenough, F. L., & Harris, D. B. Studies in the psychology of children's drawings: II. 1928–1949. *Psychological Bulletin,* 1950, *47,* 369–433.

Guilford, J. P. Creativity. *American Psychologist,* 1950, *5,* 444–454.

Guilford, J. P. Three faces of intellect. *American Psychologist,* 1959, *14,* 469–479.

Guilford, J. P., & Hoepfner, R. *The analysis of intelligence.* New York: McGraw-Hill, 1971.

Harris, D. B. *Children's drawings as measures of intellectual maturity: A revision and extension of the Goodenough Draw-a-Man Test.* New York: Harcourt, Brace and World, 1963.

Hebb, D. O. Heredity and environment in mammalian behaviour. *British Journal of Animal Behaviour,* 1953, *1,* 43–47.

Hotelling, H. Analysis of a complex of statistical variables into principal components. *Journal of Educational Psychology,* 1933, *24,* 417–441, 498–520.

Kelley, T. L. *Crossroads in the mind of man: A study of differentiable mental abilities.* Stanford, Calif.: Stanford University Press, 1928.

Kelley, T. L. *Essential traits of mental life.* Cambridge, Mass.: Harvard University Press, 1935.

MacKinnon, D. W. The nature and nurture of creative talent. *American Psychologist,* 1962, *17,* 484–495.

Pearson, K. On the laws of inheritance in man. II. On the inheritance of the mental and moral characters in man, and its comparison with the inheritance of the physical characters. *Biometrika,* 1904, *3,* 131–190.

Prinzhorn, H. *Bildnerei der Geisteskranken: ein Beitrag zür Psychologie und Psychopathologie der Gestaltung* (2nd ed.). Berlin: Springer, 1923. Pp. 361.

Reichard, S. Mental organization and age level. *Archives of Psychology,* 1944, No. 295. Pp. 30.

Roe, A. A psychological study of eminent biologists. *Psychological Monographs,* 1951, *65*(14, Whole No. 331).

Schaefer, C. E., & Anastasi, A. A biographical inventory for identifying creativity in adolescent boys. *Journal of Applied Psychology,* 1968, *52,* 42–48.

Schiller, B. Verbal, numerical, and spatial abilities of young children. *Archives of Psychology,* 1934, No. 161. Pp. 69.

Schneck, M. M. R. The measurement of verbal and numerical abilities. *Archives of Psychology,* 1929, No. 107. Pp. 49.

Smith, G. M. Group factors in mental tests similar in material or in structure. *Archives of Psychology,* 1933, No. 156. Pp. 56.

Spearman, C. "General intelligence" objectively determined and measured. *American Journal of Psychology*, 1904, *15*, 201–293.

Spearman, C. *The abilities of man.* New York: Macmillan, 1927.

Taylor, C. W., Ellison, R. L., & Tucker, M. F. *Biographical information and the prediction of multiple criteria of success in science.* Greensboro, N.C.: Richardson Foundation, 1966.

Thorndike, E. L. Measurements of twins. *Archives of Philosophy, Psychology, and Scientific Method*, 1905, No. 1.

Thorndike, R. L. Some methodological issues in the study of creativity. *Proceedings, 1962 Invitational Conference on Testing Problems, Educational Testing Service*, 1963, 40–54.

Thurstone, L. L. *Vectors of mind: Multiple-factor analysis for the isolation of primary traits.* Chicago: University of Chicago Press, 1935.

Thurstone, L. L. Primary mental abilities. *Psychometric Monographs*, 1938, No. 1. (a)

Thurstone, L. L. Shifty and mathematical components: A critique of Anastasi's monograph on the influence of specific experience upon mental organization. *Psychological Bulletin*, 1938, *35*, 223–236. (b)

Thurstone, L. L. *Multiple-factor analysis.* Chicago: University of Chicago Press, 1947.

Thurstone, L. L. Psychological implications of factor analysis. *American Psychologist*, 1948, *3*, 402–408.

Torrance, E. P. Current research on the nature of creative talent. *Journal of Counseling Psychology*, 1959, *6*, 309–316.

2
Interpretation of Test Scores: In Quest of Pitfalls

In the search for interpretive pitfalls, the papers in this chapter explored several areas in which warning signs were needed. The first two selections address principally the early attempts to design "culture-free" tests for use with persons from different cultures or subcultures. The first paper was presented at the 1949 Invitational Conference on Testing Problems, sponsored by Educational Testing Service. The second was part of a symposium entitled "Psychological Tests: Uses and Abuses," held at the 1961 meeting of the American Psychological Association. The symposium was chaired by Kenneth B. Clark, and the other participants were Joshua Fishman, Goodwin Watson, and Otto Klineberg. The papers, none of which had a separate title, were solicited for publication by Edward J. Shoben, then editor of Teachers College Record. *Although by the 1960s the term "culture-free" was beginning to give way to more moderate terms, such as "culture-fair," the purposes and procedures of cross-cultural testing were still the subject of lively debate—a debate that lingers on in the 1980s.*

The brief note on age changes in adult test performance was motivated by David Wechsler's conclusions about the decline in adult intelligence with age—a conclusion based on cross-sectional comparisons within test standardization samples. This note represents an early statement of a subsequently well-established fact, namely, that such comparisons confound age changes with cultural changes.

The need for behavioral norms even when interpreting nontest data was the subject of a paper presented at a colloquium on "Relations between Psychology and Psychopathology," held at the International Congress of Psychology in Bonn, Germany, in 1960. The colloquium chairman, José Germain, was also editor of Revista de Psicologia General y Aplicada, *in which Spanish translations of the colloquium papers were soon published. My own paper was also published in French in* Revue de Psychologie Appliquée, *whose editor had attended the colloquium. Both references are included in my 1960 and 1961 publications listed at the end of this volume. The original English version, however, has not heretofore been published.*

The last paper in this chapter was prepared at a time when popular criticisms of psychological tests and hostility toward testing were beginning to reach significant proportions. Its main thesis is that test developers and test users need to give more attention to the psychological interpretation of test scores, which has lagged behind the advances in test construction technology.

Some Implications of Cultural Factors for Test Construction

Any discussion of the influence of cultural background on test performance involves at least two distinct questions. First, to what extent is test performance determined by cultural factors? Second, what shall we do about it?

In considering the first question, it is important to remember at the outset that culture is not synonymous with environment. Although this distinction should be obvious, some writers apparently forget it when drawing conclusions about heredity and environment. For example, environmental factors may produce structural deficiencies that in turn lead to certain types of feeblemindedness. Research on microcephaly, hydrocephaly, and several other varieties of mental deficiency associated with brain damage has yielded a growing body of evidence for the role of prenatal environmental factors in the development of these conditions. Yet these types of mental deficiency would certainly not be classified as cultural in their etiology. Nor are they remediable in the individual case by education or by the manipulation of other cultural factors. Of course, the environmental factors leading to the development of these structural deficiencies may themselves be culturally influenced in the long run. Some day, we may know enough about them to control them through maternal nutrition, prenatal medical care, and the like. But such factors would represent an *indirect* cultural influence on behavior, mediated by organic deficiencies. Moreover, any such improvement in cultural conditions could have only a long-range effect, and would not help the individual in whom the organic deficiency is already present.

Cultural factors do, however, affect the individual's behavior in many direct ways. Psychologists are coming more and more to recognize that the individual's attitudes, emotional responses, interests, and goals—as well as what he is able to accomplish in practically any area—cannot be discussed independently of his cultural frame of reference. Nor are such cultural influences limited to the more complex

Some implications of cultural factors for test construction. *Proceedings of the 1949 Invitational Conference on Testing Problems, Educational Testing Service,* 1950, pp. 13–17. (As reproduced in A. Anastasi, (Ed.), *Testing problems in perspective.* Washington, D.C.: American Council on Education, 1966. Pp. 453–457.) Reprinted by permission.

forms of behavior. There is a mass of evidence, both in the field observations of anthropologists and in the more controlled studies of
psychologists, to indicate that "cultural differentials" are also present in motor and in discriminative or perceptual responses.

Now, every psychological test is a sample of behavior. As such,
psychological tests will—and should—reflect any factors that influence
behavior. It is obvious that every psychological test is constructed
within a specific cultural framework. Most tests are validated against
practical criteria dictated by the particular culture. School achievement and vocational success are two familiar examples of such criteria. A few tests designed to serve a wider variety of purposes and
possibly to be used in basic research are, in effect, validated against
other tests. Thus when we report that a given test correlates highly
with the number factor, we are actually saying that the test is a valid
predictor of the behavior common to a group of tests. If we had no
number tests in the battery, we could not have found a number factor. The type of tests included in such a battery—however comprehensive the battery may be—reflects in part the cultural framework
in which the experimenter was reared. It is obvious that no battery
samples *all* possible varieties of behavior; and as long as a selection
has occurred, cultural factors are admitted into the picture.

In the construction of certain tests, special consideration has
been given to cultural group differences in the selection of test items.
The practices followed with regard to items showing significant
group differences may be illustrated, first, with reference to *sex differences.* Insofar as the two sexes represent subcultures with distinct
mores in our society, sex differences in item performance may be
regarded as cultural differentials. The Stanford-Binet (8, Ch. V)[a] is
probably one of the clearest examples of a test in which sex differences were deliberately eliminated from total scores. This was accomplished in part by dropping items that yielded a significant sex
difference in per cent passing. It is interesting to note, however, that
it did not prove feasible to discard all such items, but that a number
of remaining items that significantly favored one sex were balanced
by items favoring the other sex. The opposite procedure was followed in the construction of the Terman-Miles Interest-Attitude
Analysis (9), as well as in other similar personality tests designed to
yield an M-F Index. In these cases, it was just those items with large
and significant sex differences in frequency of response that were
retained.

---

[a]Numbers in parentheses refer to list of references at the end of the paper. For historical
authenticity, both style and numbering of references from original publications have been
retained.—Ed.

Another type of group difference that has been considered in the selection of test items is illustrated by the so-called *culture-free tests,* such as the International Group Mental Test (4), the Leiter International Performance Scale (7), and R. B. Cattell's Culture-Free Intelligence Test (1, 2). In these tests, a systematic attempt is made to include only content universally familiar in all cultures. In actual practice, of course, such tests fall considerably short of this goal. Moreover, the term "culture-common" would probably be more accurate than "culture-free," since at best, performance on such items is free from cultural *differences,* but not from cultural *influences.*

As a last example, let us consider *socioeconomic level* as a basis for the evaluation of test items. One of the objectives of the extensive research project conducted by Haggard, Davis, and Havighurst (3, 6) is to eliminate from intelligence tests those items that differentiate significantly between children of high and low socioeconomic status. On the other side of the picture, we find the work of Harrison Gough (5) in the construction of the Social Status Scale of the Minnesota Multiphasic Personality Inventory. In this scale, only those items were retained that showed significant differences in frequency of response between two contrasted social groups.

It is apparent that different investigators have treated the problem of cultural differences in test scores in opposite ways. An obvious answer is that the procedure depends upon the purpose of the test. But such an answer may evade the real issue. Perhaps it is the purpose of the test that should be more carefully examined. There seems to be some practical justification for constructing a test out of items that show the maximum group differentiation. With such a test, we can determine more clearly the degree to which an individual is behaviorally identified with a particular group. It is difficult to see, however, under what conditions we should want to study individual differences in just those items in which socioeconomic or other cultural group differences are lacking. What will the resulting test be a measure of? Criteria are themselves correlated with socioeconomic and other cultural conditions. The validity of a test for such criteria would probably be lowered by eliminating the "cultural differentials." If cultural factors are important determiners of behavior, why eliminate their influence from tests designed to sample and predict such behavior?

To be sure, a test *may* be invalidated by the presence of uncontrolled cultural factors. But this would occur only when the given cultural factor affects the test without affecting the criterion. It is a question of the *breadth* of the influence affecting the test score. For example, the inclusion of questions dealing with a fairy tale familiar to children in one cultural group and not in another would probably lower the validity of the test for most criteria. On the other hand, if one social group does more poorly on certain items because of poor facility in the use of English, the inclusion of these items would probably *not* reduce the validity of the test. In this case, the same factor that lowered the test score would also handicap the individual in his educational and vocational progress, as well as in many other aspects of daily living. In like manner, slow work habits, emotional instability, poor motivation, lack of interest in abstract matters, and many other conditions that may affect test scores are also likely to influence a relatively broad area of criterion behavior.

Whether or not an item is retained in a test should depend ultimately upon its correlation with a *criterion*. Tests cannot be constructed in a vacuum. They must be designed to meet specific needs. These needs should be defined in advance, and should determine the choice of criterion. This would seem to be self-evident, but it is sometimes forgotten in the course of discussions about tests. Some statements made regarding tests imply a belief that tests are designed to measure a spooky, mysterious "thing" which resides in the individual and which has been designated by such terms as "Intelligence," "Ability Level," or "Innate Potentiality." The assumption seems to be that such "intelligence" has been merely overlaid with a concealing cloak of culture. All we would thus need to do would be to strip off the cloak and the person's "true" ability would stand revealed. My only reaction to such a viewpoint is to say that, if we are going to function within the domain of science, we must have operational definitions of tests. The only way I know of obtaining such operational definitions is in terms of the criteria against which the test was validated. This is true whether a so-called practical criterion is employed or whether the criterion itself is defined in terms of other tests, as in factorial validity. Any procedure, such as the discarding of certain items, that raises the correlation of the test with the criterion, enables us to give a more precise operational definition of the test. But we cannot discard items merely on the basis of some principle that has been laid down a priori, such as the rule that items showing significant group differences must be eliminated. If this procedure should lower the validity coefficient of the test, it could have neither practical nor theoretical justification.

It is also pertinent to inquire what would happen if we were to carry such a procedure to its logical conclusion. If we start eliminating items that differentiate subgroups of the population, where shall we stop? We could with equal justification proceed to rule out items showing socioeconomic differences, sex differences, differences among ethnic minority groups, and educational differences. Any items in which college graduates excel elementary school graduates could, for example, be discarded on this basis. Nor should we retain items that differentiate among broader groups, such as national cultures, or between preliterate and more advanced cultures. If we do all this, I should like to ask only two questions in conclusion. First, what will be left? Second, in terms of any criterion we may wish to predict, what will be the validity of this minute residue?

REFERENCES

1. Cattell, R. B. A culture-free intelligence test: I. *Journal of Educational Psychology,* 1940, 31, 161–179.
2. Cattell, R. B., Feingold, S. N., & Sarason, S. B. A culture-free intelligence test: II. Evaluation of cultural influence on test performance. *Journal of Educational Psychology,* 1941, 32, 81–100.
3. Davis, A., & Havighurst, R. J. The measurement of mental systems (Can intelligence be measured?). *Scientific Monthly,* 1948, 66, 301–316.
4. Dodd, S. C. International Group Mental Tests. Unpublished doctoral dissertation, Princeton Univer., 1926.
5. Gough, H. G. A new dimension of status: I. Development of a personality scale. *American Sociological Review,* 1948, 13, 401–409.
6. Haggard, E. A., Davis, A., & Havighurst, R. J. Some factors which influence performance of children on intelligence tests. *American Psychologist,* 1948, 3, 265–266. (Abstract)
7. Leiter, R. G. *The Leiter International Performance Scale, Vol. 1.* Santa Barbara, Calif.: Santa Barbara State College Press, 1940.
8. McNemar, Q. *The revision of the Stanford-Binet scale: an analysis of the standardization data.* Boston: Houghton Mifflin, 1942.
9. Terman, L. M., & Miles, Catharine C. *Sex and personality: studies in masculinity and femininity.* New York: McGraw-Hill, 1936.

Psychological Tests:
Uses and Abuses

A common misuse of psychological tests arises from the confusion of measurement with etiology. No test can eliminate causality. Nor can a test score, however derived, reveal the origin of the behavior it reflects. If certain environmental factors influence behavior, they will also influence those samples of behavior covered by tests. When we use tests to compare different groups, the only question the tests can answer directly is: "How do these groups differ under existing cultural conditions?" This limitation of tests may appear so obvious as to be trite. But it needs to be made explicit, because it is still frequently forgotten in discussing the implications of test results.

DESCRIPTION

If, then, we are to apply tests across cultural groups, what can we do to obtain a maximum of information with a minimum of misinformation? First, for purely descriptive purposes, groups should be compared in as wide a *variety* of tests as possible. This recommendation follows from the empirically established fact that groups do not occupy the same relative positions when compared in different intellectual traits. No one position or rank order, established in terms of a single test score, is any "truer" or more "basic" than any other. Just as we have been moving from the global IQ to a profile of multiple aptitude scores in the description of individuals, so we need to follow a profile approach in the description of groups.

The factorial analysis of intelligence has revealed a number of differentiable aptitudes in each of which the individual may occupy a different position. True, different factor analysts have sliced intelligence in diverse ways. The handful of primary mental abilities identified by Thurstone (20) has been proliferating over the intervening thirty years. The hierarchical pattern favored by Vernon (21) and other British psychologists is an alternative way of organizing the multiplicity of narrower and narrower factors that have been emerg-

Psychological tests: Uses and abuses. *Teachers College Record*, 1961, *62*, 389–393. Reprinted by permission.

ing. The large number of factors systematically mapped out by Guilford (10, 11) is of special interest because of their extensive coverage of creativity and reasoning.

It is apparent at this stage that we cannot prescribe a well-formulated list of aptitudes to be covered for a comprehensive description of any group. Moreover, there is some evidence to suggest that the very categories in terms of which we slice intelligence may vary from one culture to another. The implication is clear, however, that no one test score, nor any small number of scores, can provide an adequate picture of the intellectual status of a group. The best we can do is to utilize as wide a variety of tests as is available to us and retain the separateness of their scores in any description of the group.

In this connection, we may also consider so-called culture-free tests. The objections that have been raised against the term "culture-free" are quite familiar, and while substitute terms have been proposed, such as "culture-fair" or "culture-common," "culture-free" seems to be easier to say and will probably survive. If we are to use this term, we must remember that the tests are not free from all cultural influences. No test can be culture-free in that sense. They are only free from the influence of those cultural factors that differentiate the groups to be compared. To put it differently, they reflect only those cultural influences *common* to the groups concerned.

A test that is culture-free in the comparison of groups A and B, therefore, may be highly culture-bound when used in comparing groups B and C. An entirely different test may be culture-free in the B-C comparison. A good example is provided by the verbal-nonverbal dichotomy into which intelligence tests are frequently classified. It has commonly been assumed that nonverbal tests are more nearly culture-free than verbal tests. Such an assumption is obviously correct in the case of persons who speak different languages. In the early testing of immigrants to this country, for example, the language barrier was paramount. It was in this connection that some of the first performance and nonlanguage tests were developed. But there are other cultural barriers besides language. There are groups speaking the same language whose cultures differ in other important respects. In the comparison of such groups, verbal tests may be less culturally loaded than tests of a predominantly spatial, numerical, or perceptual nature.

Cultural factors may influence relative performance on verbal and nonverbal tasks in a variety of ways. Interests, value systems, work habits, problem-solving attitudes, or emotional insecurity arising from cultural conditions may in turn stimulate or retard the development of certain aptitudes. When the California Test of Mental

Maturity was administered to university students in Ceylon, the Ceylonese greatly surpassed the American norms on the language part while falling far below the norms on the nonlanguage part (18, 19). This difference is the reverse of what might have been expected in the case of a bilingual population such as the Ceylonese. The investigator attributed the results to the value systems of the upper-class Ceylonese culture, which included rejection of manual tasks and attachment of high prestige to verbal scholarship. The nature of the Ceylonese educational system, with its emphasis upon feats of memory and upon learning by precept and rote, was also cited as a possible contributing influence.

As a result of a somewhat different combination of cultural pressures, Jewish children tested in America usually perform much better on verbal tests than on tests involving concrete objects and spatial relations. In a study of kindergarten children in Minneapolis public schools, the Stanford-Binet was administered to groups of Jewish and Scandinavian children equated in age, sex ratio, and socioeconomic status (4). The Jewish children were found to be superior on tests based upon general information and verbal comprehension, while the Scandinavian children excelled on tests requiring spatial orientation and sensorimotor coordination. Similarly, in an analysis of the scores of Jewish and non-Jewish college freshmen on the ACE, the Jewish students did relatively better on the linguistic than on the quantitative parts of the test, while the reverse was true of the non-Jewish students (13). The traditional emphasis placed in most Jewish families on formal education and abstract intelligence has often been cited as an explanation of such findings. It is also interesting to note that in a recent study of Jewish children and college students with the Wechsler scales, the difference between verbal and performance scores was not large enough to be significant at the .05 level at the time of school entrance, but reached the .001 level among school children and college students (15).

Investigations of the American Negro have generally revealed poorer performance on perceptual and spatial tasks than on most types of verbal tasks. On the California Test of Mental Maturity, Negroes scored higher on the language than on the nonlanguage part (12). Negro children do particularly poorly on such tests as the Minnesota Paper Form Board (3) and the Chicago Non-Verbal Examination (17). When Negro and white boys were matched on Stanford-Binet IQ and their performance on individual items was compared, the Negroes excelled on disarranged sentences, memory for sentences, and vocabulary, but were inferior on arithmetic reasoning, repeating digits backwards, and detecting absurdities in pictures (5). In several studies with the Wechsler scales, Negroes proved to be significantly poorer in Block Design, Digit Symbol, and Arithmetic than in most of the verbal tests (7, 8, 9). One factor that may account for some of these results is the greater emphasis put on speed in certain performance and nonlanguage tests. A second proposed explanation centers around problem-solving attitudes. Insofar as the social environment of the American Negro, especially in the South, may encourage attitudes of passive compliance rather than active exploration, it would be more conducive to rote verbal learning than to perceptual manipulation of stimuli and problem solving.

We thus find three groups—two of them bilingual and one with a relatively poor educational background—which for very different reasons perform better on verbal than on nonverbal tests. Glib generalizations can be very misleading in interpreting the test scores of different cultural groups.

ETIOLOGY

If we want to go beyond description and inquire into the *origins* of group differences, then we must look into antecedent circumstances leading up to the differences. Test scores do not provide such information. Nor are we any longer satisfied with a general answer that differences are due to "heredity" or to "environment." Heredity and environment are not entities; they refer to broad classes of factors. We need to identify the specific hereditary or environmental factors that are involved. We also need to ask the question "How?" We need to know the mechanisms whereby a given hereditary or environmental factor ultimately leads to the observed group difference in test score (2).

As an illustration, let us consider three environmental mechanisms that may produce differences in intelligence. Suppose three children obtain equally low scores on an intelligence test: one because neonatal anoxia led to brain damage; another because of inadequate schooling; and the third because he was reared in an intellectually underprivileged home where curiosity and active problem-solving attitudes were discouraged, inarticulateness was fostered, and motivation for academic achievement was low. All three deficiencies have an environmental origin, but the implications for the individual and the prognosis of progress are quite different in the three cases. We cannot simply attribute the condition to environment and apply a single solution reserved for environmentally caused conditions.

Nor can we say that it's "just an environmental difference and hence we can ignore it." Environmentally caused differences can be as pervasive, enduring, and basic in the life of the individual as those caused by heredity. To turn this around, the observation that a condition is pervasive, enduring, and basic does not in itself prove that the condition must be hereditary and cannot be used as an argument against improving the very environmental factors that brought it about. Such a circular argument represents one misuse of test findings.

PREDICTION

If we want to use test scores to *predict outcome* in some future situation, such as an applicant's performance in college, we must use tests with high predictive validity against the specific criterion. This requirement is sometimes overlooked in the development and application of culture-free tests. In the effort to include in such tests only activities and information common to many cultures, we may end up with content having little relevance to any criterion we may wish to predict (1). The fact that a test is culture-free certainly does not insure its validity for all purposes. Again it is trite to insist that in predicting a specific outcome, there is no substitute for predictive validity; but the point is sometimes forgotten in discussions of test scores.

When predicting outcomes for individuals with markedly different cultural backgrounds, a better solution is to choose test content on the basis of its predictive validity but investigate the effect of *moderator variables.* Validity coefficients, regression weights, and cutoff scores may vary as a function of certain background conditions of the subjects. For example, the same scholastic aptitude score may be predictive of college failure when obtained by an upper middle class student, but predictive of moderate success when obtained by a lower class student. Follow-up studies must be conducted to establish the predictive meaning of test scores in different subgroups defined by relevant background variables. Several studies comparing the college achievement of public and private school boys in America indicate that when equated in initial IQ, public school boys obtain higher college grades than private school boys (16). Similarly, recent research in Sweden suggests that children from lower social classes profit more than middle-class or upper-class children from transfer to a more favorable academic environment (14).

Finally, in predicting outcome, we should also consider the possible effects of *differential treatments.* It is one of the contributions of decision theory to psychometrics that it provides ways of incorporating differential treatment into the prediction of outcomes from test scores (6). For example, given certain test scores obtained by subgroup A with a particular cultural background, what will be the predicted college achievement if we introduce remedial teaching programs, counseling designed to modify educational attitudes and motivation, or other suitable treatments? The inclusion of moderator variables and differential treatments into the prediction picture provides a more effective way of handling cultural differences than the exclusion of valid content from the tests.

In summary, I have tried to suggest a few of the procedures we can follow to improve the use of tests in intergroup comparisons—first, to describe differences as they exist in the present; second, to investigate their origins in past events; and third, to predict future outcomes.

REFERENCES

1. Anastasi, Anne. The concept of validity in the interpretation of test scores. *Educ. psychol. Measmt.*, 1950, *10*, 67–78.
2. Anastasi, Anne. Heredity, environment, and the question "How?" *Psychol. Rev.*, 1958, *65*, 197–208.
3. Bean, K. L. Negro responses to verbal and non-verbal test material. *J. Psychol.*, 1942, *13*, 253–343.
4. Brown, F. A comparative study of the intelligence of Jewish and Scandinavian kindergarten children. *J. genet. Psychol.*, 1944, *64*, 67–92.
5. Clarke, D. P. Stanford-Binet Scale L response patterns in matched racial groups. *J. Negro Educ.*, 1941, *10*, 230–238.
6. Cronbach, L. J. The two disciplines of scientific psychology. *Amer. Psychologist*, 1957, *12*, 671–684.
7. Davidson, K. S., Gibby, R. G., McNeil, E. B., Segal, S. J., & Silverman, H. Form I of the Wechsler-Bellevue Scale. *J. consult. Psychol.*, 1950, *14*, 489–492.
8. DeStephens, W. P. Are criminals morons? *J. soc. Psychol.*, 1953, *38*, 187–199.
9. Franklin, J. C. Discriminative value and patterns of the Wechsler-Bellevue Scales in the examination of delinquent Negro boys. *Educ. psychol. Measmt.*, 1945, *5*, 71–85.
10. Guilford, J. P. The structure of intellect. *Psychol. Bull.*, 1956, *53*, 267–293.
11. Guilford, J. P. *Personality*. New York: McGraw-Hill, 1959.
12. Hammer, E. F. Comparison of the performances of Negro children and adolescents on two tests of intelligence, one an emergency scale. *J. genet. Psychol.*, 1954, *84*, 85–93.

13. Held, O. C. A comparative study of the performance of Jewish and gentile college students on the American Council Psychological Examination. *J. soc. Psychol.*, 1941, *13*, 407–411.
14. Husén, T., & Svensson, N. Pedagogic milieu and development of intellectual skills. *School Rev.*, 1960, *68*, 31–51.
15. Levinson, B. M. Traditional Jewish cultural values and performance on the Wechsler tests. *J. educ. Psychol.*, 1959, *50*, 177–181.
16. McArthur, C. Subculture and personality during the college years. *J. educ. Sociol.*, 1960, *33*, 260–268.
17. Newland, T. E., & Lawrence, W. C. Chicago Non-Verbal Examination results on an East Tennessee Negro population. *J. clin. Psychol.*, 1953, *9*, 44–46.
18. Straus, M. A. Mental ability and cultural needs: a psychocultural interpretation of the intelligence test performance of Ceylon University entrants. *Amer. sociol. Rev.*, 1951, *16*, 371–375.
19. Straus, M. A. Subcultural variation in Ceylonese mental ability: a study in national character. *J. soc. Psychol.*, 1954, *39*, 129–141.
20. Thurstone, L. L. Primary mental abilities. *Psychometr. Monogr.*, 1938, No. 1.
21. Vernon, P. E. *The structure of human abilities.* London: Methuen, 1950.

Age Changes in Adult Test Performance

Sampling procedures must necessarily vary with the use to which the samples are to be put. Test standardization requires a *normative sample* which shall be as closely representative as possible of a given population. For example, owing to the increasing educational level of the US population during the past decades, older persons living today have had less education, on the average, than younger adults. A normative sample of the contemporary adult population should, of course, reflect this decline in education with age, as is illustrated by the WAIS standardization sample (4, p. 11).

For certain other purposes, however, the type of sampling called for may be described as *controlled sampling.* Thus if we are interested in the effect of age upon test scores, we need groups which vary systematically in age, while being as uniform as possible in all other relevant variables. In such an investigation, successive age groups should have the *same* mean educational level.

To substitute a normative for a controlled sample in this sort of situation can only lead to confusion and misinterpretation. A case in point is provided by Wechsler's discussion of age decrement in intelligence on the basis of the Wechsler-Bellevue standardization sample (3, p. 29). The obtained age decreases in test score could with equal justification be attributed to the lower educational level of the older *S*s. It is interesting to note that, on the more recent WAIS (4), the drop in test score with age is less marked and begins at a later age than on the Wechsler-Bellevue. Since the WAIS standardization *S*s were obtained approximately 15 years after the Wechsler-Bellevue sample, the educational decline with age is also less pronounced and sets in later in the WAIS sample.

Under certain circumstances, controlled samples may be very difficult—or even impossible—to secure. If older persons tend to have less education than younger persons, for example, samples of 20-year-olds and of 50-year-olds matched in education are not comparable, because of differential selection. It would thus seem that, under existing conditions, the question of age changes in adult test per-

Age changes in adult test performance. *Psychological Reports*, 1956, 2, 509. Reprinted by permission of publisher.

33

formance can only be answered by a longitudinal approach (1, 2). By re-using the same individuals, this approach represents one way of achieving controlled sampling.

REFERENCES

1. BAYLEY, N., & ODEN, M. H. The maintenance of intellectual ability in gifted adults. *J. Gerontol.*, 1955, 10, 91–107.
2. OWENS, W. A., JR. Age and mental abilities: a longitudinal study. *Genet. Psychol. Monogr.*, 1953, 48, 3–54.
3. WECHSLER, D. *The measurement of adult intelligence.* (3rd. Ed.) Baltimore: Williams & Wilkins, 1944.
4. WECHSLER, D. *Manual for the Wechsler Adult Intelligence Scale.* N.Y.: Psychol. Corp., 1955.

Establishing Behavioral Norms

One of the chief contributions that psychology can make to psychopathology centers around the establishment of behavioral norms. We need to know the limits of normal behavior in terms of which pathological deviations can be identified. For this purpose, we must have data not only about the average or modal behavior, but also about variability around the mode. For whatever behavior characteristic is under consideration, it is necessary to inquire into the range of variation of, for example, the middle 50%, the middle 80%, ±1 SD, ±2 SD, or some other appropriate limit. These procedures will provide a purely statistical description of existing variability in a representative sample of the population. Such statistical norms represent the very minimum of information required for the interpretation of pathological deviations.

Behavioral norms can be further specified in terms of outcome. How large a deviation in a particular behavioral characteristic is actually compatible with satisfactory life adjustment? Today the concept of adjustment is far more flexible than it once was. It is now widely recognized by psychologists that there are many different patterns for living an effective and happy life or at least for keeping out of trouble. Individuals differ not only in behavioral characteristics but also in adjustment patterns. The same specific behavior that leads to failure or emotional difficulties in the context of one person's life may lead to effective adjustment or superior accomplishment in that of another.

The establishment of both statistical and adjustive norms requires the gathering of extensive empirical data on normal persons, including adults and children in many walks of life and in different cultures and subcultures. Only in this way can we formulate the limits of normal behavior as a frame of reference within which psychopathology can be defined.

As illustrations, let me mention three specific areas in which normative data can be utilized in psychopathology. First, such data help in the interpretation of *case history* material. How does the individual's past history, his reactional biography, compare with that of normal persons from the same cultural milieu? An example

Establishing behavioral norms. Paper presented at the meeting of the International Congress of Psychology, Bonn, August 1960.

of the sort of investigation providing relevant data is the Guidance Study conducted at the Institute of Child Welfare of the University of California (4). Beginning in 1929, 252 infants in the city of Berkeley were examined periodically and extensive data were gathered through interviews with parents. Within the total sample, 126 cases were assigned to the Guidance Group and 126 to the Control Group. The object of the study was to determine the effect of conferences and discussions with parents, which were available to the Guidance but not to the Control Group. An important by-product of the investigation, however, is the normative data collected in the Control Group. One published report gives a detailed account of the nature and frequency of behavior problems encountered among the control cases between the ages of 21 months and 14 years. This type of normative information should prove useful to the clinician who must judge the significance of behavior problems in a particular case history.

A second application of normative data is to be found in the interpretation of *directly observed behavior,* as in an observation ward or institution. In this connection we need to ask to what extent the observed behavior is attributable to the individual's pathological state and to what extent it may have resulted from situational factors. How much aggressive behavior, for example, would be displayed by normal persons subjected to institutional control and routine? Is the exaggerated meticulousness and excessive attention to detail found in some psychotic drawings partly the result of the inactivity and monotony of traditional institutional living? (2). It is admittedly difficult to obtain data on the behavior of normal persons in comparable situations. Some data might be provided by studies of persons with physical disabilities, as well as prisoners. In any event, we should at least consider the possibility of situational factors in interpreting the behavior of institutionalized psychotics.

A third example is provided by the interpretation of *test scores.* Here of course the need for norms is generally recognized and some normative data are usually available. Nevertheless, for many personality tests the given norms are inadequate and unsystematic. The normative samples often differ from the pathological cases in other respects, such as education or socioeconomic level. Responses to personality tests may vary widely among normal persons from different subcultures. To put it differently, the same personality test response may have very different significance in different subcultures. For instance, the over-elaboration of buttons, buckles, belts, and other clothing details in human figure drawings by a civilian man may be signs of emotional immaturity. But when drawn by an

Air Force student pilot, they may indicate strong identification with the Air Force. Drawing a man in military uniform, with appropriate clothing details, may in this setting be a favorable rather than an unfavorable sign (3).

Another example dealing with the interpretation of test scores pertains to the distinction between normative and controlled sampling (1). Test standardization requires a normative sample which shall be as representative as possible of a specified population. For example, owing to the increasing educational level of the population during the past few decades, older persons today have less education, on the average, than do younger adults. A normative sample of contemporary adults should, of course, reflect this decline in education, as is illustrated by the standardization sample of the Wechsler Adult Intelligence Scale (5). For certain other purposes, however, what is needed is not a normative but a controlled sample. Thus if we are interested in the influence of age upon test scores, we must compare groups differing in age but as uniform as possible in all other relevant variables. For such a comparison, different age groups should have the *same* mean educational level (1).

These are just a few scattered examples of the very simple point I have tried to present, namely, that for better understanding and handling of psychopathology, we need more information about *normal behavior.*

REFERENCES

1. Anastasi, Anne. Age changes in adult test performance. *Psychol. Rep.,* 1956, 2, 509.
2. Anastasi, Anne, and Foley, J. P., Jr. A survey of the literature on artistic behavior in the abnormal: III. Spontaneous productions. *Psychol. Monogr.,* 1940, 52, No. 6.
3. Anastasi, Anne, and Foley, J. P., Jr. Psychiatric screening of flying personnel: V. The Human-Figure Drawing Test as an objective psychiatric screening aid for student pilots. *USAF Sch. aviat. Med., Proj. 21-37-002, Rep. No. 5,* 1952.
4. MacFarlane, Jean W., Allen, Lucile, and Honzik, Marjorie P. A developmental study of the behavior problems of normal children between twenty-one months and fourteen years. *Univer. Calif. Publ. Child Develpm.,* 1954, 2, 1-122.
5. Wechsler, D. *Manual for the Wechsler Adult Intelligence Scale.* New York: Psychol. Corp., 1955.

Psychology, Psychologists, and Psychological Testing[1]

It is the main thesis of this paper that psychological testing is becoming dissociated from the mainstream of contemporary psychology. Those psychologists specializing in psychometrics have been devoting more and more of their efforts to refining the techniques of test construction, while losing sight of the behavior they set out to measure. Psychological testing today places too much emphasis on testing and too little on psychology. As a result, outdated interpretations of test performance may remain insulated from the impact of subsequent behavior research. It is my contention that the isolation of psychometrics from other relevant areas of psychology is one of the conditions that have led to the prevalent public hostility toward testing.

THE ANTITEST REVOLT

Without question the antitest revolt has many causes and calls for a diversity of remedies. No one solution could adequately meet its multiplicity of problems. These problems have been repeatedly and thoroughly discussed from several angles.[2] For the present purpose, therefore, a brief overview of the principal objections will suffice.

The one that has undoubtedly received the greatest amount of attention, including Congressional investigations, is the objection that psychological tests may represent an invasion of privacy. Although this problem has generally been considered in reference to personality tests, it can logically apply to any type of test. When elderly illiterates are approached for testing, even with a nonverbal

---

[1] Address of the President, Division of Evaluation and Measurement, American Psychological Association, September 5, 1966.

[2] See, e.g., Carter, Brim, Stalnaker, & Messick (1965), Ebel (1964), Hathaway (1964), Ruebhausen & Brim (1966), Testimony (1966), Testing and Public Policy (1965), Westin (1967), Wolfle (1963). For a survey of the use of tests and the opinions held about them, see the series of questionnaire studies conducted by the Russell Sage Foundation in elementary schools, high schools, and a representative adult sample (Brim, Goslin, Glass, & Goldberg, 1965; Brim, Neulinger, & Glass, 1965; Goslin, Epstein, & Hallock, 1965).

test, it is amazing how many have mislaid or broken their glasses that very morning. This mild little subterfuge is their protection against the risk of being asked to read and the resulting embarrassment of admitting illiteracy. Nor is the problem limited to tests. Any observation of an individual's behavior or any conversation with him may, of course, provide information about him that he would prefer to conceal and that he may reveal unwittingly.

For this problem—as for all other problems pertaining to testing— there is no simple or universal solution. Rather, the solution must be worked out in individual cases in terms of two major considerations. The first is the purpose for which the testing is conducted—whether for individual counseling, institutional decisions regarding selection and classification, or research. In the use of tests for research, preserving the subjects' anonymity substantially reduces but does not eliminate the problem. The second consideration is the relevance of the information sought to the specific testing purpose. For example, the demonstrated validity of a particular type of information as a predictor of performance on the job in question would be an important factor in justifying its ascertainment. The interpretation given to scores on a particular test is also relevant. An individual is less likely to consider his privacy to have been invaded by a test assessing his readiness for a specific course of study than by a test allegedly measuring his "innate intelligence."

A second and somewhat related problem is that of confidentiality. Basically, this problem concerns the communication of test information. It is a two-pronged problem, however, because the implications of transmitting test information to the individual himself and to other persons are recognizably different. With regard to the transmittal of information to other persons—such as parents, teachers, supervisors, or prospective employers—professional ethics requires that this be done only when the individual is told at the outset what use is to be made of his test results. Any subsequent change in the use of such results could then be introduced only with the individual's consent.

There is another difficulty, however, in the communication of test results, which is common to both prongs of the problem. Whether the information is transmitted to the examinee himself or to others, the likelihood of misinterpretation is a serious concern. The questions of how much information is communicated, in what form, and under what circumstances are of basic importance (Berdie, 1960, 1965; Brown, 1961; Goslin, 1963, 1965). Certainly there is no justification for reporting answers to specific questions on a personality inventory, as some laymen apparently fear will be done (see, e.g., Testing and Public Policy, 1965, p. 978). Nevertheless, even total scores, duly referred to appropriate norms and accompanied by a suitable margin of error, can be misleading when perceived in terms of prevalent misconceptions about the nature of certain tests.

There has been considerable concern about the impact that a knowledge of test scores might have upon the individual and his associates; and the need for more research to gauge such impact has been recognized (Berdie, 1965; Goslin, 1963, Ch. 8). Some suggestive evidence is already available, indicating that teachers' knowledge of children's intelligence test scores significantly affects the children's subsequent intellectual development (Rosenthal & Jacobson, 1968). The mechanism of this "self-fulfilling prophecy," as it affects the individual's self-concept and the behavior of his associates toward him, is of course well known. With regard to test scores, however, detrimental effects are most likely to result from misconceptions about tests. Suppose, for example, that an IQ is regarded as a broad indicator of the individual's total intelligence, which is fixed and unchanging and of genetic origin. Under these circumstances, releasing the IQs of individuals to teachers, parents, the individuals themselves, or anyone else is likely to have a deleterious effect on the subsequent development of many children.

A third major category of test criticism has centered on test content. It is a common reaction among laymen, for example, to ask what a specific test item is supposed to show. What does it *mean* if you cross the street to avoid meeting someone you know? If the psychologist falls into the trap of trying to answer the question on the layman's own terms, he will soon find himself in the untenable position of claiming high validity and reliability for a single item. Moreover he may try to defend the item in terms of its factual or veridical content, which can be challenged on many grounds. In this sort of evaluation, the critics not only ignore the objective processes of item selection and test validation, but they also overgeneralize from a relatively small number of selected items.

In the same vein, some critics make much of the fact that multiple-choice items are sometimes misunderstood and that they may occasionally penalize the brilliant and erudite student who perceives unusual implications in the answers (see Dunnette, 1964; Educational Testing Service, 1963). Granted that this is possible, the obvious conclusion is that the tests are not perfect. A realistic evaluation, however, requires that such tests be compared with alternative assessment procedures. How do the tests compare with grades, essay examinations, interviewing procedures, application forms, ratings, and other predictors whose utilization is practicable in specific situations? An even more appropriate question pertains to how much the introduction of a test improves predictions made with other available assessment procedures.

Attention should be called, however, to a few sophisticated critiques of certain item forms, which provide constructive and imaginative suggestions for improvements in test development (e.g., Feifel, 1949; LaFave, 1966; Sigel, 1963). This approach includes thorough logical analyses of the limitations of such existing item forms as analogies, similarities, classification, and vocabulary, together with some ingenious proposals for the analysis of errors, qualitative grading of responses, and the development of items to identify styles of categorization. In contrast to the superficial critiques of the popular writers, these analyses merit serious consideration.

A fourth type of criticism blames the tests for any objectionable features of the criteria they are designed to predict. Thus it has been argued that objective tests of scholastic aptitude tend to select unimaginative college students, or that personality tests tend to select executives who are conformists and lack individuality. Insofar as these criticisms may be true, they are an indictment not of the tests but of the criteria against which selection tests must be validated. If we were to ignore the criteria and choose less valid tests, the persons thus selected would merely fail more often in college, on the job, and in other situations for which they were selected. Predictors cannot be used as instruments of criterion reform. Improvements must begin at the criterion level.

It should be noted, however, that criteria do change over time. The nature and personnel requirements of jobs change in industry, government, and the armed services. Educational objectives and curricula change. It is therefore imperative to conduct periodic job analyses or task analyses in these various contexts. Such analyses may themselves suggest that some of the tests in use as predictors may be outdated in a particular context. Periodic revalidation of instruments against current criteria provides a more definitive safeguard against the retention of instruments that may have become irrelevant.

A fifth type of criticism asserts that psychological tests are unfair to culturally disadvantaged groups (Anastasi, 1961; Deutsch, Fishman, Kogan, North, & Whiteman, 1964). To criticize tests because they reveal cultural influences is to miss the essential nature of tests. Every psychological test measures a sample of behavior. Insofar as culture affects behavior, its influence will and should be reflected in the test. Moreover, if we were to rule out cultural differentials from a test, we might thereby lower its validity against the criterion we are trying to predict. The same cultural differentials that impair an individual's test performance are likely to handicap him in school work, job performance, or whatever other subsequent achievement we are trying to predict.

Tests are designed to show what an individual can do at a given point in time. They cannot tell us *why* he performs as he does. To answer that question we need to investigate his background, motivations, and other pertinent circumstances. No test score can be properly interpreted in a vacuum—whether obtained by a culturally disadvantaged person or by anyone else.

If we want to use test scores to predict outcome in some future situation, such as an applicant's performance in college, we need tests with high predictive validity against the specific criterion. This requirement is commonly overlooked in the development and application of so-called culture-free tests. In the effort to include in such tests only activities and information common to many cultures, we may end up with content having little relevance to any criterion we wish to predict (Anastasi, 1950). A better solution is to choose test content in terms of its criterion relevance and then investigate the effect of moderator variables. Validity coefficients, regression weights, and cutoff scores may vary as a function of certain background conditions of the subjects (Hewer, 1965). For example, the same scholastic aptitude score may be predictive of college failure when obtained by an upper-middle-class student, but predictive of moderate success when obtained by a lower-class student. In addition, we need to consider the interaction of initial test score and available differential treatments (Cronbach, 1957). Given a certain score obtained by Individual A with a particular cultural background, what will be his predicted college achievement following a specified remedial training program?

The inclusion of both moderator variables and differential treatments in the prediction process requires far more empirical data than are now available. Efforts should certainly be made to gather such data. In the meantime, an awareness of the operation of these variables will at least introduce some needed cautions in the interpretation of test scores. Finally, it is apparent that the use of objective selection procedures, such as appropriate tests, should serve to reduce the operation of bias and discrimination against individuals for irrelevant reasons.

A sixth objection to tests is that they foster a rigid, inflexible, and permanent classification of individuals. This objection has been directed particularly against "intelligence tests," and has aroused the greatest concern when such tests are applied to culturally disadvantaged children. It is largely because implications of permanent status have become attached to the IQ that the use of group intelligence tests has been discontinued in New York City public schools (Gilbert, 1966; Loretan, 1966). That it proved necessary to discard the tests in order to eliminate the misconceptions about the fixity of the IQ is a revealing commentary on the tenacity of the misconceptions. Insofar as these misconceptions do prevail, of course, information about a child's IQ would undoubtedly initiate the self-fulfilling prophecy cited ealier. It can be seen that this objection to tests has much in common with questions already discussed in connection with confidentiality and with the testing of culturally disadvantaged groups.

Underlying the popular notion of the fixity of the IQ is the assumption that intelligence tests are designed to measure some mysterious entity known as "innate capacity." In the light of this assumption, the tests are then criticized for their susceptibility to environmental differences. The critics fail to see that it is these very differences in environment that are largely responsible for individual differences in qualifications or readiness for job performance, job training, and educational programs. If these differences in present developed abilities are ignored or obscured by any assessment procedure, the individual will be assigned to a job in which he will fail or be exposed to an educational program from which he will not profit. Under these conditions, he will simply fall farther and farther behind in those abilities in which he is now deficient. A recognition of his present deficiencies, on the other hand, permits the application of suitable and effective training procedures.

A seventh and final type of objection has again been directed chiefly against intelligence tests. It has been argued that, because of their limited coverage of intellectual functions, intelligence tests tend to perpetuate a narrow conception of ability. It is certainly true that the limited sample of cognitive functions included in standard intelligence tests is inconsistent with the global connotations of the test names. This is but one more reason for discarding the label "intelligence test," as some psychologists have been advocating for several decades. To be sure, all test labels are likely to imply more generality than the test possesses. A clerical aptitude test does not cover all the traits required of an office clerk, nor does a mechanical aptitude test cover all aspects of mechanical tasks. A test title that tried to provide a precise operational definition of its content would be unwieldy and impracticable. Hence the layman's tendency to judge a test by its label is always likely to mislead him. Nevertheless, the difficulty is augmented by the use of such a term as "intelligence." Not only is "intelligence" an unusually broad concept, but it has also acquired an impressive array of erroneous connotations.

DISSOCIATION OF PSYCHOLOGICAL TESTING FROM PSYCHOLOGICAL SCIENCE

It is apparent that all seven classes of objections to psychological testing arise at least in part from popular misinformation about current testing practices, about the nature of available tests, and about the meaning of tests scores. Nevertheless, psychologists themselves are to some extent responsible for such misinformation. Nor is inadequate communication with laymen and members of other professions the only reason for such prevalent misinformation. It is my contention that psychologists have contributed directly to the misinformation by actively perpetuating certain misconceptions about tests.

Heretofore, discussions of the current antitest revolt have considered the problems chiefly from a professional point of view. Examining the same problems from the viewpoint of the science of psychology may throw fresh light on them. To be sure, some of the problems—notably invasion of privacy and confidentiality of test results—pertain in large part to questions of professional ethics and responsible professional practice. Even these problems, however, involve substantive considerations stemming from the science of psychology. In the other five types of criticisms outlined, substantive matters are of central importance.

Although the very essence of psychological testing is the measurement of behavior, testing today is not adequately assimilating relevant developments from the science of behavior. The refinements of test construction have far outstripped the tester's understanding of the behavior the tests are designed to measure. I do not mean to belittle the value of these technical advances. Rather I would urge that the understanding of the behavior to be measured keep pace with the development of quantification techniques.

It is noteworthy that the term "test theory" generally refers to the mechanics of test construction, such as the nature of the score scale and the procedures for assessing reliability and validity. The term does not customarily refer to psychological theory about the behavior under consideration. Psychometricians appear to shed much of their psychological knowledge as they concentrate upon the minutiae of elegant statistical techniques. Moreover, when other types of psychologists use standardized tests in their work, they too show a tendency to slip down several notches in psychological sophistication.

A common enough example is encountered when an experimenter sets out to assemble two groups of children to serve as experimental and control subjects. He first decides to equate the groups in such obvious variables as age, sex, parental education, and parental occupational level. As he looks around for other handy variables to hold constant, he thinks, "Ah, of course, the children themselves ought to be equated in IQ." Very likely there are some IQs conveniently available in the children's cumulative school records. They may not all be derived from the same test, but they will provide a good enough approximation for the experimenter's purpose. After all, he wants only a rough estimate of each child's IQ.

What does the experimenter really want to equate the children in? Does his experimental variable utilize verbal material, so that vocabulary should be held constant? Is facility in numerical computation relevant to the experiment? Or perhaps perceptual speed and accuracy or spatial visualization are appropriate. Is overall scholastic aptitude his chief concern? Would a reading achievement test serve his purposes better? What does he believe he is ruling out when he equates the groups in IQ? Perhaps the IQ merely provides a sufficiently obscure label to conceal the fuzziness of his thinking.

We shall probably always have misconceptions with us. But to hold fast to old misconceptions after they have been recognized as such seems to be needlessly conservative. Yet psychometricians themselves have contributed to the perpetuation of the IQ label, with its vast appendage of misleading connotations. Even when the original ratio IQ proved too crude and was generally supplanted by standard scores, the IQ label was retained. The standard score simply became a deviation IQ. Psychologists have even begun to adopt the popular term "IQ test." The IQ is accepted as a property of the organism, and the "IQ test" measures it, of course.

The confusion engendered by this sort of thinking is illustrated by a statement appearing within the past 2 years in a bulletin about testing issued by a government agency. The statement reads:

> Because of the misunderstandings which have arisen over the meaning and use of the IQ, many schools are currently administering scholastic aptitude tests rather than IQ or intelligence tests. Results cannot be reported in terms of an IQ. The report of a scholastic aptitude test is most often in terms of a percentile rank [McLaughlin, 1964, p. 11].

This statement tends to encourage the prevalent confusion between a type of score and a type of test. There is the further and rather startling implication that scholastic aptitude tests do not measure intelligence and intelligence tests do not measure scholastic aptitude. Let me hasten to add that this statement was not chosen as a particularly horrible example, but rather because it appeared in an otherwise sophisticated and carefully written discussion of testing. In the rest of the bulletin, the author reveals considerable familiarity with the technical aspects of test construction.

Some reference should also be made to the strange notion of "innate intelligence." Every psychologist would undoubtedly agree that what the individual inherits is not intelligence in any sense, but certain chemical substances which, after innumerable interactions with each other and with environmental factors, lead eventually to different degrees of intelligent behavior. To identify "intelligence" with any one of the many conditions that contribute to its development appears quite illogical. Nevertheless, one still hears the request for a test of innate intelligence, of potential for intellectual development, of hereditary intellectual capacity. And what is meant is not a biochemical test but a behavioral test. It should be obvious that the relation between the intellectual quality of the individual's behavior at any one time and his heredity is extremely indirect and remote. The traditional multiplicative model of the interaction of heredity and environment is a gross oversimplification of this relationship. The product of each interaction between specific hereditary and environmental factors itself determines subsequent interactions. This cumulative effect leads to a rapid and ever-widening divergence of paths that may have started at the same point with regard to heredity.

All the illustrations cited so far concern intelligence tests. It is about intelligence tests that misconceptions are most prevalent. It is also in reference to intelligence tests that popular objections to testing are most closely bound with substantive matters in which psychologists themselves are involved. But let us take a brief look at personality testing in this light. Because personality testing is a more recent development than intelligence testing, misconceptions are less deeply rooted in this area. Personality testing today is characterized not so much by entrenched misconceptions as by confusion and inconsistencies. For example, there is the inconsistency—I might almost say conflict—between what clinical psychology students learn about personality tests in their psychometrically oriented testing courses and what they often learn to do with the same tests in practicum training. The same discrepancies can be found between the reviews of many personality tests in the *Mental Measurements Yearbooks* and the uses to which the tests are put in professional practice.

The examples mentioned serve to illustrate a growing dissociation between psychological testing and other psychological specialties. One reason for this dissociation is the increasing specialization of psychology itself. The psychometrician is subject to the same isolation that characterizes other specialists. He may become so deeply engrossed in the technical refinements of his specialty that he loses touch with relevant developments in other psychological specialties. Yet these developments may basically alter the meaning of the very tests he is busy elaborating and refining.

A second reason is to be found in the built-in inertia of tests. Because it takes several years to develop a test, gather adequate norms, and obtain a reasonable minimum of validity data, there is an inevitable lag between the original conception of the test and its availability for professional use. Moreover, the effectiveness of a test is likely to increase markedly as more and more data accumulate from long-term longitudinal studies and other research conducted with the test. Consequently, some of our best tests are fairly old tests. Even when they are revised, the original conception of the tests is embedded in the psychology of an earlier period. These long-lived tests are among our most valuable measurement tools. But the test user needs to be aware of intervening changes in the science of behavior and to update his interpretation of test scores.

A third reason for the widening gap between testing and psychological science is an undue willingness on the part of psychologists to accede to the layman's requests. Psychologists feel a strong social obligation to put their findings and techniques to work. In their eagerness to apply their science, they sometimes capitulate to unrealistic and unsound popular demands. The public wants shortcuts and magic. Some test constructors and users have tried to give them just that. It is an important function of the applied psychologist to help laymen reformulate problems in ways that permit a sound solution. It is not their role to provide ready-made solutions for insoluble problems. It might be salutary if testing gave less heed to the pull of practical needs and more to the thrust of behavioral science.

When tests are used by members of other professions, such as educators, sociologists, or psychiatrists, the gap between testing and psychological science is likely to be even wider. In addition to the reasons already mentioned, there is a further lag in communicating substantive advances to persons in other fields. It is a curious fact that members of these related fields tend to find out about new tests sooner than they find out about developments pertaining to interpretive background.

PSYCHOLOGY AND THE INTERPRETATION
OF TEST SCORES

One way to meet the outside pressures that threaten to undermine psychological testing is to make improvements from within. Improvements are needed, not so much in the construction of tests, as in the interpretation of scores and the orientation of test users. Existing tests need not be summarily replaced with new kinds of tests; they sample important behavior and provide an accumulation of normative and validation data that should not be lightly dismissed. It would require many years to gather a comparable amount of information about newly developed instruments.

How, then, can the utilization of available psychological tests be improved in the light of modern psychological knowledge? Let us consider a few examples. First, in the assessment of individual differences, attention should be focused on *change*. Tests do not provide a technique for the rigid and static classification of individuals; on the contrary, they are instruments for facilitating change in desired directions. Not only do they permit the measurement of change as it occurs under different experiential conditions, but they also provide essential information about the individual's initial status, prior to the introduction of any intervention procedures. Any program for effecting behavioral change, whether it be school instruction, job training, or psychotherapy, requires a knowledge of the individual's present condition. Readiness for a particular stage or course of academic instruction, for instance, implies the presence of prerequisite intellectual skills and knowledge. How well the individual has acquired these intellectual prerequisites is what the various ability tests tell us—whether they be called intelligence tests, multiple-aptitude batteries, special aptitude tests, or achievement tests. At different stages and in different testing contexts, one of these types of ability tests may be more appropriate than another; there is a place for all of them in the total testing enterprise. But we should not lose sight of the fact—so often stated and so often forgotten—that all these tests measure current developed abilities and that their scores should be interpreted accordingly.

A second example pertains to the *nature of intelligence,* that human characteristic which so many tests endeavor to measure in one way or another (McNemar, 1964). If we consider intelligence to be the overall effectiveness of the individual's adaptive behavior (Baldwin, 1958), it is evident that the nature and composition of intelligence must vary with time and place. Factor analysis has been employed chiefly to provide detailed descriptions of the composition of intelligence for specific populations and in specific cultural contexts (see, e.g., Guilford, 1959, 1966). Even under these restricted conditions, the resulting factorial picture is not absolute. Whether the description is formulated in terms of a few broad factors or a much larger number of narrower factors depends upon the objectives of the study (Humphreys, 1962; Vernon, 1965). Different levels of fractionation of abilities may fit the data equally well.

Although factor analysis itself is a descriptive technique, it can be employed in experimental designs that help to clarify the nature of intelligence. Factor-analytic research over time or across cultures, for example, can contribute to an understanding of how traits develop and how abilities become organized. There is a growing body of research that utilizes factor analysis in this dynamic fashion. Some investigators have compared the organization of intellectual functions in different cultural milieus, including national cultures, socioeconomic levels, and types of school curricula (Burnett, 1955; Dockrell, 1966; Filella, 1960; Guthrie, 1963; Vernon, 1965). Others have studied changes in factorial composition of intelligence over time. This approach is illustrated by investigations of age changes in the number, nature, and interrelations of factors (Burt, 1954; Garrett, 1946; Hofstaetter, 1954; Lienert & Crott, 1964; Smart, 1965). It should be noted, however, that attempts to subsume all such age changes under the single principle of either differentiation or generalization of ability represent an oversimplification. It would seem more realistic to expect some functions to become more differentiated, others less so, with time, depending upon the nature of intervening experiences in a particular cultural context. Comparative studies of age changes in trait organization among persons in different occupations, for example, would be very informative.

While covering a shorter time span than the age-difference studies, research on the role of learning in trait organization provides more direct information on the conditions that bring about change. These investigations have demonstrated that the factorial composition of the same objective tasks alters systematically in the course of practice or after relevant instruction (Anastasi, 1958, pp. 357–366; Ferguson, 1956; Fleishman & Hempel, 1954, 1955). Another promising application of this approach is illustrated by an ongoing longitudinal study of management performance, which involves repeated factor analyses of various criterion and organizational variables at 6-month intervals (MacKinney, 1967).

Among the possible reasons for observed changes over time as well as population differences in factor patterns is the use of different work methods by different individuals in carrying out a given task. In support of this hypothesis is the finding that the factorial composition of the same test differs between groups of subjects classified according to their typical problem-solving styles (French, 1965).

At the theoretical level, there have been some ingenious attempts to link intelligence with learning, motivation, and other psychological functions. Of particular interest are the discussions of how factors may develop through the establishment of learning sets and transfer of training (Carroll, 1962; Ferguson, 1954, 1956; Hunt, 1961; Whiteman, 1964). The breadth of the transfer effect would determine whether the resulting factor is a broad one, like verbal comprehension, or a narrow one, like a particular motor skill. Traditional "intelligence tests" cover intellectual skills that transfer very widely to tasks in our culture. This may be one of the reasons why they can predict performance in so many contexts. Another reason may be that any given criterion task can be performed by different persons through the use of different work methods which require different patterns of ability. The characteristic heterogeneity of function which contributes to a global intelligence test score may thus fit criterion situations in which a deficiency in one ability can be compensated by superiority in another alternative ability.

From a different point of view, intelligence has been linked with motivation through the strength of certain "experience-producing drives" (Hayes, 1962). Recognizing that intelligence is acquired by learning, this theory maintains that the individual's motivational makeup influences the kind and amount of learning that occurs. Although the theory proposes that the experience-producing drives constitute the hereditary component of intelligence, the basic relationship still holds if the drives themselves are determined or modified by environmental conditions. Regardless of the origin of the experience-producing drives, the individual's emotional and motivational status at any one time in his development influences the extent and direction of his subsequent intellectual development. It might be added that longitudinal studies of intelligence test performance have provided some empirical support for this proposition (Sontag, Baker, & Nelson, 1958; Haan, 1963). It would thus seem that adding a measure of a child's motivational status to tests of developed abilities at any one age should improve the prediction of his subsequent intellectual development.

Personality testing itself provides a third area in which to illustrate the role of psychology in the interpretation of test scores. The hypothesis just discussed suggests one important point to bear in mind, namely, that the separation between abilities and personality traits is artificial and the two domains need to be rejoined in interpreting an individual's test scores. It is now widely recognized that an individual's performance on an aptitude test, in school, on the job, or in any other context is significantly influenced by his achievement drive, his self-concept, his persistence and goal orientation, his value system, his freedom from handicapping emotional problems, and every other aspect of his so-called personality. Even more important, however, is the cumulative effect of these personality characteristics upon the direction and extent of his intellectual development (see, e.g., Combs, 1952). Conversely, the success the individual attains in the development and use of cognitive functions is bound to affect his self-concept, emotional adjustment, interpersonal relations, and other "personality traits." To evaluate either ability or personality traits without reference to the other, because of limited testing or compartmentalized thinking, is likely to prove misleading.

Apart from the need for a comprehensive consideration of the individual's behavior, the user of personality tests must keep abreast of a rapidly growing body of relevant research in personality theory, clinical psychology, and social psychology—to name only the most obvious fields. To continue to use personality tests without keeping in close touch with developments in psychological research is especially unwise, since personality tests represent tentative gropings in promising directions, rather than established techniques. A case in point is the self-report inventory, which began as a canned psychiatric interview, with veridical interpretation of the subject's responses. Gradually these inventories are being metamorphosed into more sophisticated measuring instruments, particularly in the light of research on self-concepts (Loevinger, 1959) and response styles (Jackson & Messick, 1958).

As a fourth and final illustration we may consider the *assessment of environment.* The individual does not behave in a vacuum. He responds in a particular environmental context, which in part determines the nature of his responses. It has been suggested that the prediction of criterion behavior from test scores or from earlier criterion performance could be improved by taking situational factors into account (MacKinney, 1967). Given an individual with a certain level of developed abilities and certain personality characteristics at Time A, how will he react in a specified criterion situation at Time B?

Even more important for prediction purposes is information about the environment to which the individual will be exposed in the interval between Time A and Time B. There is some suggestive evidence that correlations approaching unity can be obtained in predicting intelligence test performance or academic achievement when environmental variables are included along with initial test scores as predictors (Bloom, 1964, Ch. 6).

Despite the general recognition of the importance of environmental variables, little progress has been made in the measurement of such variables. The available scales for evaluating home environment, for example, are crude and the choice of items is usually quite subjective. Moreover, environments cannot be ordered along a single continuum from "favorable" to "unfavorable." An environment that is quite favorable for the development, let us say, of independence and self-reliance may differ in significant details from an environment that is favorable for the development of social conformity or abstract thinking. In this connection, a promising beginning has been made in the empirical development of home environment scales against criteria of intelligence test performance and academic achievement (Wolf, 1965).

SUMMARY

In conclusion, it was the thesis of this paper that psychological testing should be brought into closer contact with other areas of psychology. Increasing specialization has led to a concentration upon the techniques of test construction without sufficient consideration of the implications of psychological research for the interpretation of test scores. Some of the relevant developments within psychology have been illustrated under the headings of behavioral change, the nature of intelligence, personality testing, and the measurement of environment. Strengthening psychological testing from within, by incorporating appropriate findings from other areas of psychology, is proposed as one way to meet the popular criticisms of the current antitest revolt.

REFERENCES

ANASTASI, A. Some implications of cultural factors for test construction. *Proceedings of the 1949 Invitational Conference on Testing Problems, Educational Testing Service,* 1950, 13–17.
ANASTASI, A. *Differential psychology.* (3rd ed.) New York: Macmillan, 1958.
ANASTASI, A. Psychological tests: Uses and abuses. *Teachers College Record,* 1961, 62, 389–393.
BALDWIN, A. L. The role of an "ability" construct in a theory of behavior. In

D. C. McClelland, A. L. Baldwin, U. Bronfenbrenner, & F. L. Strodtbeck, *Talent and society*. Princeton, N.J.: Van Nostrand, 1958. Pp. 195–233.

BERDIE, R. F. Policies regarding the release of information about clients. *Journal of Counseling Psychology*, 1960, 7, 149–150.

BERDIE, R. F. The ad hoc Committee on Social Impact of Psychological Assessment. *American Psychologist*, 1965, 20, 143–146.

BLOOM, B. S. *Stability and change in human characteristics*. New York: Wiley, 1964.

BRIM, O. G., JR., GOSLIN, D. A., GLASS, D. C., & GOLDBERG, I. The use of standardized ability tests in American secondary schools and their impact on students, teachers, and administrators. Technical Report No. 3, 1965, Russell Sage Foundation.

BRIM, O. G., JR., NEULINGER, J., & GLASS, D. C. Experiences and attitudes of American adults concerning standardized intelligence tests. Technical Report No. 1, 1965, Russell Sage Foundation.

BROWN, D. W. Interpreting the college student to prospective employers, government agencies, and graduate schools. *Personnel and Guidance Journal*, 1961, 39, 576–582.

BURNETT, A. Assessment of intelligence in a restricted environment. Unpublished doctoral dissertation, McGill University, 1955.

BURT, C. The differentiation of intellectual ability. *British Journal of Educational Psychology*, 1954, 24, 76–90.

CARROLL, J. B. Factors of verbal achievement. *Proceedings of the 1961 Invitational Conference on Testing Problems, Educational Testing Service*, 1962, 11–18.

CARTER, L. F., BRIM, O. G., STALNAKER, J. M., & MESSICK, S. Psychological tests and public responsibility. *American Psychologist*, 1965, 20, 123–142.

COMBS, A. W. Intelligence from a perceptual point of view. *Journal of Abnormal and Social Psychology*, 1952, 47, 662–673.

CRONBACH, L. J. The two disciplines of scientific psychology. *American Psychologist*, 1957, 12, 671–684.

DEUTSCH, M., FISHMAN, J. A., KOGAN, L., NORTH, R., & WHITEMAN, M. Guidelines for testing minority group children. *Journal of Social Issues*, 1964, 22, 127–145.

DOCKRELL, W. B. Cultural and educational influences on the differentiation of abilities. *Proceedings of the 73rd Annual Convention, American Psychological Association*, 1966, 317–318.

DUNNETTE, M. D. Critics of psychological tests: Basic assumptions: How good? *Psychology in the Schools*, 1964, 1, 63–69.

EBEL, R. L. The social consequences of educational testing. *Proceedings of the 1963 Invitational Conference on Testing Problems, Educational Testing Service*, 1964, 130–143.

EDUCATIONAL TESTING SERVICE. *Multiple-choice questions: A close look*. Princeton, N.J.: ETS, 1963.

FEIFEL, H. Qualitative differences in the vocabulary responses of normals and abnormals. *Genetic Psychology Monographs*, 1949, 39, 151–204.

FERGUSON, G. A. On learning and human ability. *Canadian Journal of Psychology,* 1954, 8, 95–112.

FERGUSON, G. A. On transfer and the abilities of man. *Canadian Journal of Psychology,* 1956, 10, 121–131.

FILELLA, J. F. Educational and sex differences in the organization of abilities in technical and academic students in Colombia, South America. *Genetic Psychology Monographs,* 1960, 61, 115–163.

FLEISHMAN, E. A., & HEMPEL, W. E., JR. Changes in factor structure of a complex psychomotor test as a function of practice. *Psychometrika,* 1954, 19, 239–252.

FLEISHMAN, E. A., & HEMPEL, W. E., JR. The relation between abilities and improvement with practice in a visual discrimination task. *Journal of Experimental Psychology,* 1955, 49, 301–312.

FRENCH, J. W. The relationship of problem-solving styles to the factor composition of tests. *Educational and Psychological Measurement,* 1965, 25, 9–28.

GARRETT, H. E. A developmental theory of intelligence. *American Psychologist,* 1946, 1, 372–378.

GILBERT, H. B. On the IQ ban. *Teachers College Record,* 1966, 67, 282–285.

GOSLIN, D. A. *The search for ability: Standardized testing in social perspective.* New York: Russell Sage Foundation, 1963.

GOSLIN, D. A. The social consequences of predictive testing in education. Paper presented at the Conference on Moral Dilemmas in Schooling, School of Education, University of Wisconsin, May 12–14, 1965.

GOSLIN, D. A., EPSTEIN, R. R., & HALLOCK, B. A. The use of standardized tests in elementary schools. Technical Report No. 2, 1965, Russell Sage Foundation.

GUILFORD, J. P. Three faces of intellect. *American Psychologist,* 1959, 14, 469–479.

GUILFORD, J. P. Intelligence: 1965 model. *American Psychologist,* 1966, 21, 20–26.

GUTHRIE, G. M. Structure of abilities in a nonwestern culture. *Journal of Educational Psychology,* 1963, 54, 94–103.

HAAN, N. Proposed model of ego functioning: Coping and defense mechanisms in relationship to IQ change. *Psychological Monographs,* 1963, 77(8, Whole No. 571).

HATHAWAY, S. R. MMPI: Professional use by professional people. *American Psychologist,* 1964, 19, 204–210.

HAYES, K. J. Genes, drives, and intellect. *Psychological Reports,* 1962, 10, 299–342.

HEWER, V. H. Are tests fair to college students from homes with low socioeconomic status? *Personnel and Guidance Journal,* 1965, 43, 764–769.

HOFSTAETTER, P. R. The changing composition of "intelligence"; A study in T-technique. *Journal of Genetic Psychology,* 1954, 85, 159–164.

HUMPHREYS, L. G. The organization of human abilities. *American Psychologist,* 1962, 17, 475–483.

HUNT, J. McV. *Intelligence and experience.* New York: Ronald Press, 1961.

JACKSON, D. N., & MESSICK, S. Content and style in personality assessment. *Psychological Bulletin,* 1958, 55, 243–252.

LA FAVE, L. Essay vs. multiple-choice: Which test is preferable? *Psychology in the Schools,* 1966, 3, 65–69.

LIENERT, G. A., & CROTT, H. W. Studies on the factor structure of intelligence in children, adolescents, and adults. *Vita Humana,* 1964, 7, 147–163.

LOEVINGER, J. A theory of test response. *Proceedings of the 1958 Invitational Conference on Testing Problems, Educational Testing Service,* 1959, 36–47.

LORETAN, J. O. Alternatives to intelligence testing. *Proceedings of the 1965 Invitational Conference on Testing Problems, Educational Testing Service,* 1966, 19–30.

MACKINNEY, A. C. The assessment of performance change: An inductive example. *Organizational Behavior and Human Performance,* 1967, 2, 56–72.

MCLAUGHLIN, K. F. Interpretation of test results. OE-25038 Bulletin, 1964, No. 7.

MCNEMAR, Q. Lost: Our intelligence? Why? *American Psychologist,* 1964, 19, 871–882.

ROSENTHAL, R., & JACOBSON, L. Self-fulfilling prophecies in the classroom: Teachers' expectations as unintended determinants of pupils' intellectual competence. In M. Deutsch, A. R. Jensen, & I. Katz (Eds.), *Race, social class, and psychological development.* New York: Holt, Rinehart & Winston, 1968.

RUEBHAUSEN, O. M., & BRIM, O. G., JR. Privacy and behavioral research. *American Psychologist,* 1966, 21, 423–437.

SIGEL, I. E. How intelligence tests limit understanding of intelligence. *Merrill-Palmer Quarterly,* 1963, 9, 39–56.

SMART, R. C. The changing composition of "intelligence": A replication of a factor analysis. *Journal of Genetic Psychology,* 1965, 107, 111–116.

SONTAG, L. W., BAKER, C. T., & NELSON, V. L. Mental growth and personality development. *Monographs of the Society for Research in Child Development,* 1958, 23, No. 2.

Testimony before House Special Subcommittee on Invasion of Privacy of the Committee on Government Operations. *American Psychologist,* 1966, 21, 404–422.

Testing and public policy. (Special issue) *American Psychologist,* 1965, 20, 857–992.

VERNON, P. E. Ability factors and environmental influences. *American Psychologist,* 1965, 20, 723–733.

WESTIN, A. F. *Privacy and freedom.* New York: Atheneum, 1967.

WHITEMAN, M. Intelligence and learning. *Merrill-Palmer Quarterly,* 1964, 10, 297–309.

WOLF, R. The measurement of environments. *Proceedings of the 1964 Invitational Conference on Testing Problems, Educational Testing Service,* 1965, 93–106.

WOLFLE, D. Educational tests. *Science,* 1963, 142, 1529.

3
Interpretation of Test Scores: Focus on Modifiability

The papers in Chapter 2 were published between 1950 and 1967. In contrast, the two papers reproduced in this chapter appeared in the 1980s. Over this period, methodological and conceptual sophistication had improved conspicuously. Nevertheless, some of the old confusions and misinterpretations proved to be remarkably viable in the general public, among test users in certain related fields, and even among a few psychologists.

The first paper deals predominantly with some persistent pseudo-distinctions between aptitude and achievement tests. These false distinctions are still encountered all too often in the 1980s, despite the repeated efforts of psychometricians—from T. L. Kelley on—to clarify the relationship between these two categories of tests.

The second paper addresses the concept of academic intelligence and the varied effects of training on tests designed to measure this construct. Although both papers are concerned with some of the same pitfalls covered in Chapter 2, they focus more directly on the modifiability of human abilities. In this regard, they illustrate a sub-theme that runs through all the papers in this volume and is more explicitly examined in the chapters on heredity and environment (Chs. 7 and 8).

Abilities and the
Measurement of Achievement

If a benevolent wizard were to give me the power to eliminate four words from the tester's vocabulary, I would choose "intelligence," "aptitudes," "abilities," and "achievement." Then if a malevolent wizard were suddenly to appear and demand that I take back one word, I would choose to retain "abilities." What are my reasons for wishing thus to tamper with the psychometric vocabulary? Of course, it is not the words themselves that concern me, but rather the excess meanings they have acquired. These excess meanings lead to misuses and misinterpretations of tests. The popular disenchantment with tests, in my opinion, stems in large part from these misuses and misinterpretations. Similarly, the more focused criticisms against specific applications of tests are often directed against either actual or assumed misinterpretations of test scores—and as such they often appear to be justified.

SURPLUS MEANINGS AND
PSEUDODISTINCTIONS

Intelligence and Aptitudes

Within the past decade, there has certainly been an increasing recognition of the hazards of retaining test labels that carry misleading surplus meanings. Authors and publishers of group tests, for example, have largely replaced the term "intelligence" with more neutral terms. That this substitution was more urgently needed in group than in individual tests is understandable. Individual tests are usually administered by examiners with specialized training that should provide some safeguards against unwarranted conclusions. Moreover, in individual testing, the examiner has an opportunity to obtain background information about the examinee, information that is of the utmost importance for the proper understanding of test scores.

Aptitudes are typically defined more precisely than intelligence,

Abilities and the measurement of achievement. In W. B. Schrader (Ed.), *New directions for testing and measurement,* Vol. 5. San Francisco: Jossey-Bass, 1980. Pp. 1–10. Reprinted by permission.

to designate more narrowly limited cognitive domains. Like intelligence, however, aptitudes have traditionally been contrasted with achievement in testing terminology. The contrast dates from the early days of testing, when it was widely assumed that achievement tests measured the effects of learning, while intelligence and aptitude tests measured so-called innate capacity independently of learning. This approach to testing in turn reflected a simplistic conception of the operation of heredity and environment prevalent in the 1920s and early 1930s (Cravens, 1978).

That intelligence (or aptitude) tests are not fundamentally different from achievement tests was illustrated as early as 1927 by Truman L. Kelley. In this connection, Kelley coined the expression "jangle fallacy," to designate the opposite of the jingle fallacy whereby things called by the same name are assumed to be the same. Kelley (1927, p. 64) defined the jangle fallacy as "the use of two separate words or expressions covering in fact the same basic situation, but sounding different, as though they were in truth different." Through an analysis of correlational data, Kelley demonstrated that widely used intelligence tests and achievement batteries overlapped by about 90 percent (Kelley, 1927, pp. 193–209).

Since that time, other investigators have repeatedly found extensive overlap between these two types of tests (Coleman and Cureton, 1954; Cronbach, 1970, pp. 284–285). In fact, in some instances, the correlation between intelligence tests and achievement batteries is about as high as the reliability coefficients of each. Nevertheless, the distinction persists, often with its original implications regarding heredity and environment lurking in the background. For example, in 1973 a four-day conference was organized by CTB/McGraw-Hill on the topic of "The Aptitude-Achievement Distinction." The proceedings of this conference were published the following year in book form (Green, 1974). In a review of this book that I was asked to prepare for the *Review of Education,* my opening paragraph conveyed my general reaction as follows: "One gets the impression that the major purpose of this conference was not to beat a dead horse but to administer massive doses of statistics in the effort to bring the unfortunate animal back to life. Resuscitation did not occur" (Anastasi, 1975, p. 356).

Achievement

To return to our benevolent wizard, I have touched on my reasons for wishing to delete the terms "intelligence" and "aptitudes." What about "achievement?" First, let me admit that I would not be particularly unhappy if all cognitive tests were to be called achievement tests. To be sure, applying the term "achievement" to test performance seems to me a rather odd use of the word. Achievement suggests a deed in the real world, a contribution one makes to a society, such as designing a bridge, composing a symphony, or formulating a theory of learning. So-called achievement tests actually assess what a person has learned in a given area of instruction. The individual's test performance is a sample of what he or she is able to do at the time.

But this imprecise use of the word "achievement" causes me only mild discomfort. My chief objection to the term arises from the fact that, when we speak of achievement tests, there is a strong temptation—and often an implication—that such tests should in some fundamental way be contrasted with aptitude or intelligence tests. This potential contrast, of course, is also the reason why I originally wished for the elimination of the term "abilities." The hazard disappears, however, if the concept of ability tests remains alone, in the absence of anything called achievement tests.

THE CONCEPT OF ABILITY

Developed Abilities

The term "ability" seems to have acquired fewer surplus meanings than has the term "aptitude"—or at least, its excess associations are less widespread, less firmly rooted, and easier to dislodge. People are not so resistant to the idea that abilities can be developed, modified, learned, as they are with regard to aptitudes. In fact, if the malevolent wizard would permit, I should like to attach the adjective "developed" to the term "abilities" whenever it is applied to test performance. Developed ability is a concept that cuts across traditional achievement and aptitude tests and serves to point up the fundamental similarity in what the two types of tests measure. I first heard this term used in the early 1950s by Henry Dyer, in a College Board committee of which I was a member. It was probably an idea ahead of its time and did not have wide impact. I hope we are beginning to catch up with it. Parenthetically, let me explain that I am differentiating here between the concept of developed abilities and an experimental battery, the Tests of Developed Abilities, produced by ETS for the College Board in the late 1950s (Anastasi, 1961, pp. 442–443; Dyer, 1954; Dyer and Coffman, 1957). These tests were eventually abandoned since they proved no more predictive of college success than was a combination of the SAT and existing achievement tests in specific fields, while being more costly to prepare, administer, and score, and less flexible in their use, insofar as all college applicants would have to take the entire six-hour battery. It would nevertheless seem fruitful at this time to re-examine the philosophy underlying this test series in the light of intervening developments in both psychometrics and social policy.

It is also noteworthy that the term "ability" itself is being used increasingly in psychometrics to cover both aptitude and achievement tests; this usage is followed in several current textbooks on testing, including the latest editions of Cronbach (1970, pp. 281–283) and Thorndike and Hagen (1977, pp. 5–7), as well as my own (Anastasi, 1976, pp. 399–400). Although I prefer more specific designations for particular tests, to call an instrument an ability test simply classifies it as a measure of cognitive behavior, as distinguished, for example, from sensory, motor, emotional, motivational, or attitudinal behavior. Any cognitive test, regardless of what it is called, yields a sample of what the individual knows and has learned to do at the time he or she is tested; it measures the level of development attained by the individual in one or more abilities. No test, whatever it is called, reveals how or why the individual reached that level. To answer the latter questions, the examiner needs to delve into other concomitant variables, and especially into the individual's experiential background.

The Formation of Cognitive Traits

From another angle, abilities not only can be *developed* through learning or the cumulative effects of one's reactional biography, but they can also be *formed* by the same process. There is a growing body of evidence suggesting the role of experiential variables in the formation of the factors identified through factor analysis (Anastasi, 1970). It is not only the level of performance in different variables, but also the way in which performance is organized into distinct traits that is influenced by experiential background. Differences in factor patterns have been found to be associated with different cultures or subcultures, socioeconomic levels, and types of school curriculums. Changes in factor pattern over time are also relevant. These include long-term changes—which may reflect the cumulative effects of everyday-life experiences—as well as short-term changes resulting from practice and other experimentally controlled learning experiences (Fleishman, 1972). Research on animals has also yielded suggestive evidence regarding the experimental production of factors through the control of early experience (Whimbey and Denenberg, 1966).

A mechanism for the emergence of factors is provided by the familiar concepts of learning set and transfer of training (Carroll, 1966; Ferguson, 1954, 1956; Whiteman, 1964). The establishment of learning sets enables the individual to learn more efficiently when presented with a new problem of the same kind. Many of the skills developed through formal schooling, such as reading and arithmetic computation, are applicable to a wide variety of subsequent learning situations. Efficient and systematic problem-solving techniques can likewise be applied to the solution of new problems. Individual differences in the extent to which these skills have been acquired will thus be reflected in the performance of a large number of different tasks; and in a factor analysis of these tasks, these widely applicable skills will emerge as broad group factors. The breadth of the transfer effect, or the variety of tasks to which the skill is applicable, would thus determine the breadth of the resulting group factor.

The factors or abilities identified through factor analysis are descriptive categories, reflecting the changing interrelationships of performance in a variety of situations. These factors are not static entities but are themselves the products of the individual's cumulative experiential history. Insofar as the interrelationships of experiences vary among individuals and groups, different factor patterns may be expected among them. As the individual's experiences change—through formal education, occupational functions, or other continuing activities—new traits may become differentiated, or previously existing traits may merge into broader composites.

Some Residual Hazards

If we are to use the concept of ability in the ways I have proposed, we had better take a closer look at it. We need not look very far to discover that, in popular usage, "ability test" often serves as a general name for both intelligence and aptitude tests, and as such it carries all the excess baggage we have been trying to shake loose. If you are confused at this point, it probably indicates that you are facing reality. Trying to understand or clarify the use of terms in discussions about testing is like grasping a giant amoeba-like creature that is constantly putting out pseudopodia in different directions. It is a decidedly squishy experience. Whatever terms we use, we need to remain alert to unintended connotations.

Ability and Knowledge

In the 1969 Invitational Conference, Robert Ebel addressed the concept of ability with special reference to its relation to knowledge. In a characteristically lucid exposition, he concluded that the chief goal of education should be the acquisition of "useful verbal knowledge," and that this goal should accordingly be reflected in the construction of educational tests. In order to be meaningful to the individual learner and retrievable when relevant, each acquisition must be integrated into a coherent structure of knowledge. This process cannot occur independently of the subject matter to which it is applied. We do not think content-free thoughts. In Ebel's words, "If a mental ability can be developed, the best way to develop it is through command of knowledge relevant to the task" (Ebel, 1969, p. 75).

I would certainly agree. The concept of content-free abilities impresses me as both squishy *and* spooky. I see no conflict between any points made in Ebel's paper and the concept of ability as I have used it in my discussion.

SOME DISTINCTIONS ALONG THE TRADITIONAL APTITUDE-ACHIEVEMENT CONTINUUM

Where are we at this point? We have before us a vast collection of measuring instruments that we have designated as tests of abilities, or preferably, tests of developed abilities. We do not recognize sharp contrasts among these instruments. In fact, we are more strongly impressed with the absence of basic, essential, or permanent differences in the sort of information they provide about individuals. This extensive array of instruments can nevertheless be ordered along a continuum with regard to certain significant features. It is important to emphasize the continuous nature of this classification. Although an examination of the endpoints of this continuum can highlight genuine and useful distinctions, these distinctions blur as we approach the center.

If we place the instruments that have traditionally been designated as aptitude and achievement tests into this continuum, and strip them of unwarranted assumptions about their nature, we can discern some meaningful differences. A number of such differences have been identified and discussed with considerable clarity by several psychometricians, including Lee Cronbach (1970, pp. 281–285), Robert Ebel (1974, p. 316), and Lloyd Humphreys (1974, p. 263), among others. Each formulated the distinction somewhat differently and focused on different aspects of the comparison; but their approaches to the question have much in common. I should like to sum up the distinction between instruments at opposite ends of the continuum under two headings: Antecedent Experience and Use of Test Scores. From the standpoint of any particular test, we might say that one distinction concerns its past and the other its future.

Antecedent Experience

The tests traditionally designated as aptitude tests, at one end of the continuum, differ from those designated as achievement tests, at the other end, in the degree of precision with which relevant antecedent experience is defined. This does *not* necessarily mean generality or specificity of test content, nor does it imply breadth of transfer effect or of applicability of the instrument. Intelligence tests and educational achievement batteries can be equally broad in content coverage and in the situational scope of their predictive validity. A spatial aptitude test and a typewriting achievement test can be equally specific and limited in content coverage and in applicability. What I am referring to instead is essentially the *experiential pool* upon which the test constructor draws in formulating test items. This experiential pool is defined with considerable clarity and precision in constructing, let us say, an achievement test in solid geometry, or medieval history, or motor vehicle operation. At the other extreme is a test like the Stanford-Binet, in which the definition specifies little beyond growing up in America in the twentieth century. Broadly oriented educational achievement batteries, which endeavor to dissociate themselves from specific course content, add little to this definition. Their domain of antecedent experience could be defined as growing up and going to school in America in the twentieth century.

I am reminded in this connection of the difference between a learning curve and a growth curve plotted with test scores. The growth curve is a learning curve covering a longer period of time and obtained in the absence of precise knowledge about the independent variables that bring about the observed behavioral changes.

To sum up the first difference: tests of developed ability differ in the degree of precision or vagueness with which the relevant domain of antecedent experience is defined.

Use of Test Scores

The second difference concerns the way in which test scores are utilized. It is generally recognized that traditional achievement tests are designed and used primarily to assess current status, while traditional aptitude tests are designed and used to predict future performance following a specified learning experience. Typical tests of current status, at one end of this continuum, can be illustrated by a licensing examination (as in obtaining a driver's license), a typing test (as in hiring a secretary), a French test (as in selecting an interpreter), a test to assess the effects of self-study or life experience (as in credit by examination), and a competency test in so-called basic skills (presumably chosen because they are prerequisite to a wide variety of roles in our contemporary culture).

At the other end of the continuum, we find typical "intelligence" and "aptitude" tests designed particularly for predictive purposes. What can the individual learn—how much and how fast can he learn—when put through a particular course of study, educational program, industrial apprenticeship, or other systematic learning experience? I am sure that at this point many of you are thinking that traditional achievement tests can often serve as effective predictors of future learning. That is certainly true. An achievement test in arithmetic is a good predictor of students' subsequent performance in an algebra class. Nevertheless, if a test is especially designed to predict performance in a specified area of subsequent learning, it will usually do a more effective predictive job than one designed for another purpose. For one thing, the behavior domain sampled can then be defined in terms of a task analysis of the subsequent performance to be predicted, and the test can concentrate on covering specific prerequisite knowledge and skills. Fundamentally, however, we must bear in mind that all tests assess current status, whether their purpose is terminal assessment or prediction. Hence it is not surprising that some aptitude tests look very much like achievement tests and vice versa.

Let me add one final comment regarding prediction. The concept of prediction has become closely linked with the process of selection: some students are admitted (to college, medical school, or whatever) and others are not; some job applicants are hired and others are not. As a result of several emerging societal changes, selection is beginning to give way to classification. Tests are being used increasingly for such purposes as: assisting individuals to choose among courses of study, careers, or other alternative action plans; placing applicants in different jobs for maximal utilization of their individual qualifications; assessing the prerequisite skills and knowledge of inadequately prepared students and designing programs to overcome specific deficits.

In all these contexts, the concept of *diagnostic testing* is coming to replace that of testing for prediction. But the role of tests in diagnosis and prediction is not fundamentally different. In all these situations, appropriate tests should be chosen or constructed in the light of a task analysis of the desired behavior domain—whether identified through an academic curriculum, a career, a particular job, or whatever. To be effective, a predictive or a diagnostic test should assess the development of those prerequisite skills and knowledge that the individual needs before taking the next step. Although test content may be drawn from a common pool of experiences shared by the examinee population, the selection of relevant items from that pool should be oriented toward the requirements of the subsequent performance pool. Every test has both this backward and forward reference—but the forward reference is especially important for those tests near the predictive-diagnostic end of the continuum.

REFERENCES

Anastasi, A. *Psychological Testing.* (2nd ed.) New York: Macmillan, 1961.

Anastasi, A. "On the Formation of Psychological Traits." *American Psychologist,* 1970, *25,* 899–910.

Anastasi, A. "Harassing a Dead Horse: Review of D. R. Green (Ed.), The Aptitude-Achievement Distinction: Proceedings of the Second CTB/McGraw-Hill Conference on Issues in Educational Measurement." *Review of Education,* 1975, *1,* 356–362.

Anastasi, A. *Psychological Testing.* (4th ed.) New York: Macmillan, 1976.

Carroll, J. B. "Factors of Verbal Achievement." In A. Anastasi (Ed.), *Testing Problems in Perspective.* Washington, D.C.: American Council on Education, 1966.

Coleman, W., and Cureton, E. E. "Intelligence and Achievement: The 'Jangle Fallacy' Again." *Educational and Psychological Measurement,* 1954, *14,* 347–351.

Cravens, H. *The Triumph of Evolution: American Scientists and the Heredity-Environment Controversy, 1900–1941.* Philadelphia: University of Pennsylvania Press, 1978.

Cronbach, L. J. *Essentials of Psychological Testing.* (3rd ed.) New York: Harper & Row, 1970.

Dyer, H. S. *A Common Philosophy for the Tests of Developed Ability.* Unpublished Memorandum, January 5, 1954.

Dyer, H. S., and Coffman, W. E. "The Tests of Developed Abilities." *College Board Review,* 1957, No. 31, 5–10.

Ebel, R. L. "Knowledge vs Ability in Achievement Testing." *Proceedings of the 1969 Invitational Conference on Testing Problems,* 1969, pp. 66–76.

Ebel, R. L. "The Relation of Aptitude for Learning to Achievement in Learning." In D. R. Green (Ed.), *The Aptitude-Achievement Distinction.* New York: McGraw-Hill, 1974.

Ferguson, G. A. "On Learning and Human Ability." *Canadian Journal of Psychology,* 1954, *8,* 95–112.

Ferguson, G. A. "On Transfer and the Abilities of Man." *Canadian Journal of Psychology,* 1956, *10,* 121–131.

Fleishman, E. A. "On the Relation Between Abilities, Learning, and Human Performance." *American Psychologist,* 1972, *27,* 1017–1032.

Green, D. R. (Ed.). *The Aptitude-Achievement Distinction: Proceedings of the Second CTB/McGraw-Hill Conference on Issues in Educational Measurement.* New York: McGraw-Hill, 1974.

Humphreys, L. G. "The Misleading Distinction Between Aptitude and Achievement Tests." In D. R. Green (Ed.), *The Aptitude-Achievement Distinction.* New York: McGraw-Hill, 1974.

Kelley, T. L. *Interpretation of Educational Measurements.* Yonkers, N.Y.: World Book Co., 1927.

Thorndike, R. L., and Hagen, E. *Measurement and Evaluation in Psychology and Education.* (4th ed.) New York: Wiley, 1977.

Whimbey, A. E., and Denenberg, V. H. "Programming Life Histories: Creating Individual Differences by the Experimental Control of Early Experiences." *Multivariate Behavioral Research,* 1966, *1,* 279–286.

Whiteman, M. "Intelligence and Learning." *Merrill-Palmer Quarterly,* 1964, *10,* 297–309.

Diverse Effects of Training on Tests of Academic Intelligence

Popular discussions of the effects of coaching on test performance have been concerned chiefly with tests of "scholastic aptitude" or "general intelligence." Much controversy on this topic arises in part from ambiguity and lack of uniformity in the use of terms. To clear away some of the prevalent confusion, we shall examine first the nature of the tests involved in this controversy. Then we shall consider coaching against the background of diverse types of training that may affect test performance, and we shall inquire into the implications of these various forms of training for the meaning and validity of test scores.

WHAT DO INTELLIGENCE TESTS MEASURE?

The late 1970s witnessed a resurgence of interest in the concept of intelligence. This revival of interest does not imply a return to former views about the nature of intelligence. The concept that is now emerging differs in several important ways from the earlier concept of intelligence that prevailed from the turn of the century to the 1930s, and that still survives in popular discussions of intelligence, intelligence testing, and that particular horror, the IQ. It is well to remember that the IQ was never meant to refer to a trait of the organism, nor to a kind of test. It was only a kind of score—and a poor kind of score at that. In fact, as a score it has been largely replaced by standard scores, as in the so-called deviation IQ of the Wechsler scales and the Stanford-Binet, among others.

This crude, distorted notion of intelligence is *not* what I see revivified in the 1980s. Rather, a new concept of intelligence is emerging among a group of psychometricians who are also knowledgeable in psychology. It is a sophisticated and technically refined concept that reflects the accumulated store of relevant research findings from various disciplines. This concept of intelligence is characterized by explicit definition and by the deletion of excess meanings, vague as-

Diverse effects of training on tests of academic intelligence. In B. F. Green (Ed.), *New directions for testing and measurement: Issues in testing—coaching, disclosure, and ethnic bias*, No. 11. San Francisco: Jossey-Bass, 1981. Pp. 5–19. Reprinted by permission.

sumptions, and fuzzy implications. When freed from these encrustations, intelligence tests are seen as measures of what the individual has learned to do and what he or she knows at the time. Tests can serve a predictive function only insofar as they indicate to what extent the individual has acquired the prerequisite skills and knowledge for a designated criterion performance. What persons can accomplish in the future depends not only on their present intellectual status, as assessed by the test, but also on their subsequent experiences.

Furthermore, intelligence tests are descriptive, not explanatory. No intelligence test can indicate the reason for one's performance. To attribute inadequate performance on a test or in everyday-life activities to "inadequate intelligence" is a tautology and in no way advances our understanding of the individual's handicap. In fact, it may halt efforts to explore the causes of the handicap in the individual's experiential history. Intelligence tests should be used, not to label individuals but to assess their current status. To bring persons to their maximum functioning level we need to start where they are at the time; we need to identify their strengths and weaknesses and plan accordingly.

Having scraped off the excess, implied meanings, we can recognize that intelligence tests measure a limited but important domain of cognitive skills and knowledge. To help us understand more specifically what these tests actually measure, there is available a vast accumulation of data, derived from both clinical observations and hundreds of validity studies against academic and occupational criteria. The findings indicate that the particular combination of cognitive skills and knowledge sampled by these tests plays a significant role in much of what goes on in modern industrialized societies. The concept of a segment of intellectual skills, albeit a broadly applicable and widely demanded segment, is replacing the notion of a general, universal human intelligence.

A particularly relevant series of studies, begun in the 1970s and still in progress, is provided by the research on validity generalization conducted by Frank Schmidt, John Hunter, and their associates (Pearlman and others, 1980; Schmidt and others, 1979; Schmidt and others, 1981). Through sophisticated statistical analyses of data from many samples and from a large number of occupational specialties, these investigators are demonstrating that the validity of tests of verbal, numerical, and reasoning aptitudes can be generalized far more widely across occupations than had heretofore been recognized. The variations in validity coefficients typically found in earlier industrial studies can be ascribed largely to the effects of small sample sizes, restriction of range through preselection, and low reliability of criterion measures. The variance of obtained validity coefficients proved to be no greater than would be expected by chance from these three sources. This was true even when the particular job functions appeared to be quite dissimilar across jobs. Evidently, the successful performance of a wide variety of occupational tasks depends in large part on a common core of cognitive skills.

The tests surveyed in these studies covered chiefly the type of content and skills sampled in traditional intelligence and scholastic aptitude tests. It would seem that this cluster of cognitive skills and knowledge is widely predictive of performance in both academic and occupational activities. Their broadly generalizable predictive validity can probably be understood if we think of the tests operating at three levels. First, they permit a direct assessment of prerequisite intellectual skills demanded by many important tasks in our culture. Second, they assess the availability of a relevant store of knowledge or content also prerequisite for many educational and occupational tasks. Third, they provide an indirect index of the extent to which the individual has developed effective learning strategies, problem-solving techniques, and work habits and utilized them in the past. The effectiveness of this past behavior is reflected in the fullness of the individual's current store of knowledge and the readiness with which relevant knowledge can be retrieved. In at least three ways, therefore, performance on such tests provides clues about the resources available to an individual for subsequent learning, problem solving, and related activities.

CONTRIBUTIONS FROM RELATED FIELDS

In addition to traditional psychometric studies, our understanding of what intelligence tests measure has been enriched in recent years by contributions from other areas of psychology and from related disciplines. Let me cite specifically cross-cultural psychology, developmental psychology, and cognitive psychology.

Cross-Cultural Psychology

Research in cross-cultural psychology demonstrates that there are, not one, but many kinds of intelligence (Berry, 1972; Goodnow, 1976; Neisser, 1976, 1979). For instance, cultures differ in the value they place on generalization and on the search for common features in disparate experiences. In some cultures, behavior is more specifically linked to contexts and situations than is true in the cultures within which most intelligence tests have been developed. Thus, the response may depend on who asks a question and on what type of content is involved. The individual may have learned to apply a particular operation, such as grouping or counting, to one type of content but not to another. Cultural differences in task interpretation may also influence what individuals select from their available response repertoire. For instance, functional classification in terms of use, such as placing a knife with an orange, may be chosen because it is considered more appropriate and sensible than classification into superordinate abstract classes, such as placing a knife with tools and an orange with fruit (Glick, 1975).

Viewing the diverse concepts of intelligence from a different angle, Neisser (1976, 1979) proposes that intelligence is not a quality of a person but a resemblance to a prototype. And he proceeds to show that there are multiple prototypes of the "intelligent person" across cultures. Even within our own culture, he differentiates between what he calls natural, "real-life" intelligence and academic intelligence. The former is quite diversified; it is closely adapted to specific situations; and it is influenced by the individual's own interests and goals. Academic intelligence, in contrast, is essentially what traditional intelligence tests measure. And it is important in school achievement and in many other activities that depend on formal schooling. Some fifty years ago Carl Brigham introduced the term "scholastic aptitude" to designate the test he developed for the College Board, the now well-known Scholastic Aptitude Test (SAT). He preferred this more narrowly descriptive term to the then current designation of intelligence test. The term "academic intelligence" serves the same delimiting function, suggesting that it is only one domain of intellectual functioning that is under consideration.

Some sociologists have coined the term "modern consciousness" to describe the psychological effects of being reared and educated in advanced industrial societies (P. L. Berger and others, 1973). This concept has been applied also to an examination of what intelligence tests measure. When thus viewed, intelligence tests can be said to assess the extent to which the individual has internalized "the cognitive requirements of the modern technological-rationalistic world" (B. Berger, 1978, p. 35). An example of such cognitive requirements is a high level of abstraction, whereby each element of knowledge can be viewed apart from its immediate context.

A similar view has been expressed by Olson (1976), who observes that intelligence tests measure how well the individual has mastered the techniques of abstraction and rationality, which "are to a large extent the necessary but unintended consequences of technological developments" (pp. 200-201). Olson argues that the invention of a particular technology may alter the cognitive activities that constitute intelligence, and he illustrates this point with the invention of phonetic writing systems. He contrasts oral tradition with written language as a means of codifying and preserving the knowledge of a culture. Oral transmission concentrates on persons, events, aphorisms, and commandments; it is not well-adapted to the formulation of principles, laws, and formulas. With the introduction of written language, meaning became less dependent on context or on shared prior knowledge.

If we wish to understand and describe the intelligence of different cultures, we need naturalistic observations to identify the cognitive demands of particular environments. A task analysis of the behavioral requirements of a given culture (or subculture) represents an appropriate first step in constructing an intelligence test to assess how well individuals have acquired the skills and knowledge valued in that culture. If, however, we want an intelligence test to facilitate mobility into another environment, it is the cognitive demands of *that* environment that are relevant. The test should then be constructed from a task analysis of the new environment to which the individual wishes to move—whether it be an educational institution, an academic program, a vocational career, a country to which one is emigrating, or an emerging technology in a developing nation. One approach tells us how individuals arrived where they are in intellectual development; the other tells us what they need in order to go where they want to be.

Developmental Psychology

Within developmental psychology, the recent revival of interest in the work of Jean Piaget is well known. Apart from its specialized methodologies for assessing intelligence, the Piagetian approach has made significant contributions to our understanding of the nature of intelligence across the life span. Essentially, Piaget's observations suggest that intelligence may be qualitatively different at different life periods. This conclusion has found considerable support in the work of other investigators, especially those studying the behavior of infants and young children (Bayley, 1968, 1970; Lewis, 1973; Lewis and McGurk, 1972; McCall and others, 1972).

Such findings are also consistent with the concept of developmental tasks proposed by several psychologists in a variety of contexts (Erikson, 1950; Havighurst, 1953; Super and others, 1957). Educationally and vocationally, as well as in other aspects of daily life, the individual encounters typical behavioral demands and problems at different life stages. For our present purpose, developmental psychology provides evidence, from several sources, that the definition of intelligence may vary across the life span. What intelligence tests measure—and what they ought to measure—may differ qualitatively at different life stages from infancy through adulthood.

Cognitive Psychology

As for cognitive psychology, it is helping to bridge the long-standing gap between psychometrics and experimental psychology. Beginning in the 1950s, cognitive psychologists have been applying the concepts of information processing to describe what occurs in human problem solving. Some have designed computer programs that carry out these processes and thereby simulate human thought. In the late 1960s and 1970s, a few psychologists began to apply these information-processing and computer-simulation techniques to an exploration of what intelligence tests measure (Carroll, 1976; E. Hunt, 1976; E. Hunt and others, 1976; Simon, 1976; Sternberg, 1979). Individual investigators have approached this goal from several different angles, and the research is still in an early exploratory stage. Thus far, information-processing approaches have contributed heuristic concepts to guide further research and have clearly focused attention on processes rather than end-products in problem solving. Analyzing intelligence test performance in terms of basic cognitive processes should certainly strengthen and enrich our understanding of what the tests measure. Moreover, analyzing individuals' performance at the level of elementary component processes may eventually make it possible to pinpoint each person's sources of weakness and strength and thereby enhance the diagnostic use of tests (Estes, 1974; Pellegrino and Glaser, 1979; Sternberg, 1979). This in turn should facilitate the tailoring of training programs to the individual's needs.

TRAINING AND TEST PERFORMANCE

Thus far I have been trying to clarify one aspect of my topic: why focus on intelligence tests, in what sense is the term intelligence being used, and why specify academic intelligence? Now we are ready to turn to the diverse effects of training. The main thrust of this paper is on the word "diverse." It is my contention that different kinds of training interventions have very different effects, consequences, and implications.

In evaluating the effects of training on test scores, a fundamental question is whether the improvement is limited to the particular items included in the test or whether it extends to the broader behavior domain that the test is designed to assess. The answer to this question represents the difference between coaching and education. Obviously, any educational experience the individual undergoes, either formal or informal, in or out of school, should be reflected in his or her performance on tests that sample relevant aspects of behavior. Such broad influences will in no way invalidate the test, since the test score presents an accurate picture of the individual's standing in the abilities under consideration. The difference, of course, is one of degree. Influences cannot be classified as either narrow or broad. They vary widely in scope, from those affecting only a single administration of a single test, through those affecting performance on all items of a certain type, to those influencing the individual's performance in the large majority of his or her activities.

From the standpoint of effective testing, however, a workable distinction can be made. Thus, we can say that a test score is invalidated only when a particular experience raises the score without appreciably affecting the behavior domain that the test samples. With this simple guideline as a starting point, we can examine the implications of three types of training intervention: coaching, test-taking orientation, and instruction in basic intellectual skills.

Coaching

The effects of coaching on test scores have been widely investigated. Several early studies were conducted by British psychologists, with special reference to the effects of practice and coaching on the tests formerly used in assigning eleven-year-old children to different types of secondary schools (Yates and others, 1953–1954). As might be expected, the extent of improvement depended on the ability and earlier educational experiences of the examinees, the nature of the tests, and the amount and type of coaching provided. Individuals with deficient educational backgrounds are more likely to benefit from special coaching than those who have had superior educational opportunities and are already prepared to do well on the tests. It is obvious, too, that the closer the resemblance between test content and coaching material, the greater will be the improvement in test scores. On the other hand, the more closely instruction is restricted to specific test content, the less likely it is that improvement will extend to criterion performance.

Although the term "coaching" was used by the investigators themselves, these early British studies span a wide range of procedures. In view of the age of the subjects and the time period covered (the early 1950s), much of the training may have been simply test-taking orientation. In the case of students with deficient educational backgrounds, some remedial education and training in basic skills may also have been included. Although I maintain that the three types of training can and should be differentiated in practice, I recognize that the term "coaching" is often used loosely to cover all three. We simply have to be alert to what was actually done in each instance, regardless of what it was called.

In the United States, the College Board has for many years been concerned about the spread of ill-advised commercial coaching courses for college applicants. Such courses fit more closely under coaching as I have used the term, in the sense of intensive concentrated drill or "cramming" on sample test questions. To clarify the issues, the College Board has conducted several well-controlled experiments to determine the effects of such coaching on its SAT, and has surveyed the results of similar studies by other investigators (Angoff, 1971; College Entrance Examination Board, 1979a, 1979b). These studies covered a variety of coaching methods and included students in both public and private high schools. Large samples of minority students from both urban and rural areas were also investigated. The general conclusion from such studies was that intensive drill on items similar to those on the SAT is unlikely to produce appreciably greater gains than those that occur when students are retested with the SAT after a year of regular high school instruction.

It should also be noted that in its regular test construction procedures, the College Board investigates the susceptibility of new item types to coaching (Angoff, 1971; Pike and Evans, 1972). Item types on which performance can be appreciably raised by short-term drill or by instruction of a narrowly limited nature are not retained in the operational forms of the tests. Examples of item types excluded for this reason are artificial language and number series completion. Another obvious example is provided by problems that call for an insightful solution which, once attained, can be applied directly to solving similar problems. When encountered in the future, such problems would test recall rather than problem-solving skills. A familiar illustration is the water-jug problem. Once individuals have caught on to the idea of emptying one jug into another one or more times, they can solve all these problems.

From another angle, it should be added that, on the basis of its training studies, the College Board recommends that students who are not enrolled in a mathematics course at the time they take the SAT can benefit from a review of the math concepts they learned in class. This would come under the heading of education rather than coaching. In the verbal domain, such review did not have an appreciable effect, probably because verbal reasoning is such an integral part of the students' daily lives that it has less chance of becoming rusty from disuse.

Test-Taking Orientation

Next we can consider the effects of test sophistication or sheer test-taking practice. In studies with alternate forms of the same test, there is a tendency for the second score to be higher. Significant mean gains have been reported when alternate forms were administered in immediate succession or after intervals ranging from one day to three years (Angoff, 1971; Droege, 1966; Peel, 1951, 1952). Similar results have been obtained with normal and intellectually gifted schoolchildren, high school and college students, and employee samples. Data on the distribution of gains to be expected on a retest with a parallel form should be provided in test manuals, and allowance for such gains should be made when interpreting test scores.

Nor are score gains limited to alternate forms. The individual who has had extensive prior experience in taking standardized tests enjoys a certain advantage in test performance over one who is taking his or her first test (Millman and others, 1965; Rodger, 1936). Part of this advantage stems from having overcome an initial feeling of strangeness as well as from having developed more self-confidence and better test-taking attitudes. Part is the result of a certain amount of overlap in the type of content and functions covered by many tests. Specific familiarity with common item types and practice in the use of objective answer sheets may also improve performance slightly. It is particularly important to take test sophistication into account when comparing the scores obtained by persons whose test-taking experience may have varied widely.

Short orientation and practice sessions can be quite effective in equalizing test sophistication (Wahlstrom and Boersman, 1968). Such familiarization training reduces the effects of prior differences in test-taking experience as such. Since these individual differences are specific to the test situation, their diminution should permit a more valid assessment of the broad behavior domain the test is designed to measure. This approach is illustrated by the College Board publication entitled *Taking the SAT* (College Entrance Examination Board, 1981), a booklet distributed since 1978 to all college applicants who register for this test. The booklet offers suggestions for effective test-taking behavior, illustrates and explains the different types of items included in the test, and reproduces a complete form of the test, which students are advised to take under standard timing conditions and to score with the given key.

More general test-orientation procedures have also been developed. An example is the *Test Orientation Procedure,* designed chiefly for job applicants with little prior testing experience (Bennett and Doppelt, 1967). It comprises a booklet and tape recording on how to take tests, with easy test-like exercises; and a second, twenty-page booklet of sample tests which the prospective applicant can take home for practice. The United States Employment Service also has prepared a booklet on how to take tests, as well as a more extensive pretesting orientation technique for use with educationally disadvantaged applicants who are tested at state employment services (U.S. Department of Labor, 1968, 1970, 1971).

Instruction in Broad Intellectual Skills

Some researchers have been exploring the opposite approach to the improvement of test performance. The goal is the development of widely applicable intellectual skills, work habits, and problem-solving strategies. The effect of such interventions should be manifested in *both* test scores and criterion performance, such as college courses. This type of program is designed to provide education rather than coaching. And it is concerned with the modifiability of intelligence itself.

Contrary to the still prevalent popular notion regarding the fixity of the IQ, there is a growing body of evidence that the behavior domain sampled by intelligence tests is responsive to training. It is interesting to note that, despite subsequent misinterpretations of the Binet scales, Binet himself rejected the view that intelligence is unchangeable. He and his associates developed procedures, which they called "mental orthopedics," for raising the intellectual level of mental retardates. As early as 1911, Binet wrote that for "children who did not know how to listen, to pay attention, to keep quiet, we pictured our first duty as being . . . to teach them how to learn" (Binet, 1911, p. 150).

The decades of the 1960s and 1970s witnessed a strong upsurge of interest in programs for improving academic intelligence. These programs were developed largely in the United States and in Israel, where there were large minority populations that were having difficulty in adapting to the majority culture. By far the largest number of these programs was directed at the infant and preschool levels (B.

Brown, 1978; Consortium for Longitudinal Studies, 1978; Day and Parker, 1977; J. McV. Hunt, 1975; Peleg and Adler, 1977). These educational programs ranged widely in content and quality. A few were well designed and are relevant to the present topic insofar as they endeavored to develop cognitive skills judged to be prerequisite for subsequent schooling. It is these programs that yielded the most promising results. The more successful also included parental involvement as a means of supplementing the preschool experiences and ensuring their continuation after the program terminates.

Other programs, on a smaller scale, have been designed for school-age children (Bloom, 1976; Jacobs and Vandeventer, 1971; Olton and Crutchfield, 1969; Resnick and Glaser, 1976). Although these programs are still at a research stage, their preliminary findings are encouraging. Some investigators have focused on still older age levels, working with college and professional school students (Bloom and Broder, 1950; Whimbey, 1975, 1977). It is noteworthy that they, too, report significant improvement in academic achievement and in performance on scholastic aptitude tests. Still other investigators have concentrated on educable mentally retarded children and adolescents, with results that have both theoretical and practical implications (Babad and Budoff, 1974; Belmont and Butterfield, 1977; A. L. Brown, 1974; Budoff and Corman, 1974; Campione and Brown, 1979; Feuerstein, 1979). Some investigators have even been conducting exploratory research on such training effects with profoundly retarded children, and they too report promising results (Tryon and Jacobs, 1980).

At all age levels, these programs have been directed primarily to persons from educationally disadvantaged backgrounds. In connection with his work with mental retardates in Israel, Feuerstein (1979) offers a provocative definition of cultural deprivation. He identifies the culturally deprived as persons who have become alienated from their own culture through a disruption of intergenerational transmission and mediational processes. As a result, they have failed to acquire certain learning skills and habits that are required for high-level cognitive functioning. Culturally different persons, on the other hand, having learned to adapt to their own culture, have developed the prerequisite skills and habits for continued modifiability and can adapt to the demands of the new culture after a relatively brief transition period. The same concept underlies Whimbey's work with college students. Designating his approach as "cognitive therapy," Whimbey observed that it resembles "the type of parent-child verbal dialogue in problem solving that researchers believe constitutes the academic advantage middle-class children have over lower-class children" (Whimbey, 1975, p. 68).

Another important concept that emerges from this training research is that of self-monitoring. This is reminiscent of Binet's inclusion of self-criticism as a component of intelligent behavior (Binet, 1911, p. 122). Whimbey (1975, pp. 137–138) also emphasizes the need for training in this process in view of the high frequency of shoddy, careless, and impulsive responses among poor test performers. Flavell (1979) has devoted special attention to cognitive monitoring under the broader heading of metacognition, or the individual's knowledge about himself or herself and other persons as cognitive processors.

The training research on intelligence has yielded some provocative concepts and some promising procedures for developing the academic intelligence measured by traditional tests. Improvement can occur at considerably later ages than heretofore anticipated. But the later the training is begun, the more limited will be its effectiveness. Through special training programs, one can learn widely applicable cognitive skills, problem-solving strategies, efficient study habits, and other useful behavioral processes. It takes a long time, however, to accumulate the relevant content store in long-term memory, which is also a part of intelligence and which contributes to the person's readiness to learn more advanced material. Although the older person, armed with efficient learning techniques, can build up this content store more quickly than he or she would have as a child, it is nevertheless unrealistic to expect this to occur after short training periods distributed over a few months. There are no shortcuts to intellectual development—at least not *that* short! It is well to bear this limitation in mind. Otherwise, if unrealistic expectations remain unfulfilled, there is danger that disillusionment will weaken confidence in the entire training approach. Intelligence *can* be improved at any age, but the earlier one begins, the greater will be the returns from one's efforts.

Implications for Test Validity

We have considered three approaches to the improvement of test performance, whose objectives are clearly differentiable. How do these types of training affect the validity of a test and its practical usefulness as an assessment instrument? The first was coaching, in the sense of intensive, massed drill on items similar to those on the test. Insofar as such coaching might improve test performance, it would do so without a corresponding improvement in criterion behavior. Hence it would thereby reduce the test's predictive validity. Test-orientation procedures, on the other hand, are designed to rule out or minimize differences in prior test-taking experience. These differences represent conditions that affect test scores as such, without necessarily being reflected in the broader behavior domain to be assessed. Hence the test-orientation procedures should make the test a more valid instrument by reducing the influence of test-specific factors. Finally, trianing in broadly applicable intellectual skills, if effective, should improve the trainee's ability to cope with subsequent intellectual tasks. This improvement will and should be reflected in test performance. Insofar as both test scores and criterion performance are improved, such training leaves test validity unchanged.

REFERENCES

Angoff, W. H. (Ed.). *The College Board Admissions Testing Program: A Technical Report on Research and Development Activities Relating to the Scholastic Aptitude Test and Achievement Tests.* New York: College Entrance Examination Board, 1971.

Babad, E. Y., and Budoff, M. "Sensitivity and Validity of Learning-Potential Measurement in Three Levels of Ability." *Journal of Educational Psychology,* 1974, *66,* 439–447.

Bayley, N. "Behavioral Correlates of Mental Growth: Birth to Thirty-Six Years." *American Psychologist,* 1968, *23,* 1–17.

Bayley, N. "Development of Mental Abilities." In P. H. Mussen (Eds.), *Carmichael's Manual of Child Psychology.* Vol. 1. New York: Wiley, 1970.

Belmont, J. M., and Butterfield, E. C. "The Instructional Approach to Developmental Cognitive Research." In R. V. Kail, Jr. and J. Hagen (Eds.), *Perspectives on the Development of Memory and Cognition.* Hillsdale, N.J.: Erlbaum, 1977.

Bennett, G. K., and Doppelt, J. E. *Test Orientation Procedure.* New York: Psychological Corporation, 1967.

Berger, B. "A New Interpretation of the IQ Controversy." *The Public Interest,* 1978, No. 50, 29–44.

Berger, P. L., Berger, B., and Kellner, H. *The Homeless Mind: Modernization and Consciousness.* New York: Random House, 1973.

Berry, J. W. "Radical Cultural Relativism and the Concept of Intelligence." In L. J. Cronbach and P. J. D. Drenth (Eds.), *Mental Tests and Cultural Adaptations.* The Hague: Mouton, 1972.

Binet, A. *Les Idées Modernes sur les Enfants.* Paris: Flammarion, 1911.

Bloom, B. S. *Human Characteristics and School Learning.* New York: McGraw-Hill, 1976.

Bloom, B. S., and Broder, L. *Problem-Solving Processes of College Students.* Chicago: University of Chicago Press, 1950.

Brown, A. L. "The Role of Strategic Behavior in Retardate Memory." In N. R. Ellis (Ed.), *International Review of Research in Mental Retardation.* Vol. 7. New York: Academic Press, 1974.

Brown, B. (Ed.). *Found: Long-Term Gains from Early Intervention.* Boulder, Colo.: Westview Press, 1978.

Budoff, M., and Corman, L. "Demographic and Psychometric Factors Related to Improved Performance on the Kohs Learning Potential Procedure." *American Journal of Mental Deficiency*, 1974, *78*, 578-585.

Campione, J. C., and Brown, A. L. "Toward a Theory of Intelligence: Contributions from Research with Retarded Children." In R. J. Sternberg and D. K. Detterman (Eds.), *Human Intelligence: Perspectives on Its Theory and Measurement.* Norwood, N.J.: Ablex, 1979.

Carroll, J. B. "Psychometric Tests as Cognitive Tasks: A New 'Structure of Intellect.'" In L. B. Resnick (Ed.), *The Nature of Intelligence.* Hillsdale, N.J.: Erlbaum, 1976.

College Entrance Examination Board. *Taking the SAT: A Guide to the Scholastic Aptitude Test and the Test of Standard Written English.* New York: College Entrance Examination Board, 1981. (1st ed., 1978).

College Entrance Examination Board. *The Admissions Testing Program Guide for High Schools and Colleges, 1979-81.* New York: College Entrance Examination Board, 1979a.

College Entrance Examination Board. "The Effect of Special Preparation Programs on Score Results of the Scholastic Aptitude Test." *Research and Development Update*, January 1979b. (Also reprinted in *The College Board News*, February 1979, p. 7.)

Consortium for Longitudinal Studies. *Lasting Effects after Preschool.* Washington, D.C.: U.S. Government Printing Office, 1978.

Day, M. C., and Parker, R. K. (Eds.). *The Preschool in Action: Exploring Early Childhood Programs.* Boston: Allyn & Bacon, 1977.

Droege, R. C. "Effects of Practice on Aptitude Scores." *Journal of Applied Psychology*, 1966, *50*, 306-310.

Erikson, E. H. *Childhood and Society.* New York: Norton, 1950.

Estes, W. K. "Learning Theory and Intelligence." *American Psychologist*, 1974, *29*, 740-749.

Feuerstein, R. *The Dynamic Assessment of Retarded Performers.* Baltimore, Md.: University Park Press, 1979.

Flavell, J. H. "Metacognition and Cognitive Monitoring: A New Area of Cognitive-Developmental Inquiry." *American Psychologist*, 1979, *34*, 906-911.

Glick, J. "Cognitive Development in Cross-Cultural Perspective." In F. D. Horowitz (Ed.), *Review of Child Development Research.* Vol. 4. Chicago: University of Chicago Press, 1975.

Goodnow, J. J. "The Nature of Intelligent Behavior: Questions Raised by Cross-Cultural Studies." In L. B. Resnick (Ed.), *The Nature of Intelligence.* Hillsdale, N.J.: Erlbaum, 1976.

Havighurst, R. J. *Human Development and Education.* New York: Longmans, Greens, 1953.

Hunt, E. "Varieties of Cognitive Power." In L. B. Resnick (Ed.), *The Nature of Intelligence.* Hillsdale, N.J.: Erlbaum, 1976.

Hunt, E., Frost, N., and Lunneborg, C. "Individual Differences in Cognition." In G. Bower (Ed.), *The Psychology of Learning and Motivation: Advances in Research and Theory.* Vol. 7. New York: Academic Press, 1973.

Hunt, J. McV. "Reflections on a Decade of Early Education." *Journal of Abnormal Child Psychology*, 1975, *3*, 275-330.

Jacobs, P. I., and Vandeventer, M. "The Learning and Transfer of Double-Classification Skills: A Replication and Extension." *Journal of Experimental Child Psychology*, 1971, *12*, 140–157.

Lewis, M. "Infant Intelligence Tests: Their Use and Misuse." *Human Development*, 1973, *16*, 108–118.

Lewis, M., and McGurk, H. "Evaluation of Infant Intelligence: Infant Intelligence Scores—True or False?" *Science*, 1972, *178* (4066), 1174–1177.

McCall, R. G., Hogarty, P. S., and Hurlburt, N. "Transitions in Infant Sensorimotor Development and the Prediction of Childhood IQ." *American Psychologist*, 1972, *27*, 728–748.

Millman, J., Bishop, C. H., and Ebel, R. "An Analysis of Test-Wiseness." *Educational and Psychological Measurement*, 1965, *25*, 707–726.

Neisser, U. "General, Academic, and Artificial Intelligence." In L. B. Resnick (Ed.), *The Nature of Intelligence*. Hillsdale, N.J.: Erlbaum, 1976.

Neisser, U. "The Concept of Intelligence." *Intelligence*, 1979, *3*, 217–227.

Olson, D. R. "Culture, Technology, and Intellect." In L. B. Resnick (Ed.), *The Nature of Intelligence*. Hillsdale, N.J.: Erlbaum, 1976.

Olton, R. M., and Crutchfield, R. S. "Developing the Skills of Productive Thinking." In P. H. Mussen, J. Langer, and M. Covington (Eds.), *Trends and Issues in Developmental Psychology*. New York: Holt, Rinehart & Winston, 1969.

Pearlman, K., Schmidt, F. L., and Hunter, J. E. "Test of a New Model of Validity Generalization: Results for Job Proficiency and Training Criteria in Clerical Occupations." *Journal of Applied Psychology*, 1980, *65*, 373–406.

Peel, E. A. "A Note on Practice Effects in Intelligence Tests." *British Journal of Educational Psychology*, 1951, *21*, 122–125.

Peel, E. A. "Practice Effects Between Three Consecutive Tests of Intelligence." *British Journal of Educational Psychology*, 1952, *22*, 196–199.

Peleg, R., and Adler, C. "Compensatory Education in Israel: Conceptions, Attitudes, and Trends." *American Psychologist*, 1977, *32*, 945–958.

Pellegrino, J. W., and Glaser, R. "Cognitive Correlates and Components in the Analysis of Individual Differences." *Intelligence*, 1979, *3*, 187–214.

Pike, L. W., and Evans, F. R. "Effects of Special Instruction for Three Kinds of Mathematics Aptitude Items." *College Entrance Examination Board Research Report* 1, 1972.

Resnick, L. B. (Ed.). *The Nature of Intelligence*. Hillsdale, N.J.: Erlbaum, 1976.

Resnick, L. B., and Glaser, R. "Problem Solving and Intelligence." In L. B. Resnick (Ed.), *The Nature of Intelligence*. Hillsdale, N.J.: Erlbaum, 1976.

Rodger, A. G. "The Application of Six Group Intelligence Tests to the Same Children, and the Effects of Practice." *British Journal of Educational Psychology*, 1936, *6*, 291–305.

Schmidt, F. L., Hunter, J. E., Pearlman, K., and Shane, G. S. "Further Tests of the Schmidt-Hunter Bayesian Validity Generalization Procedure." *Personnel Psychology*, 1979, *32*, 257–281.

Schmidt, F. L., Hunter, J. E., and Pearlman, K. "Task Differences as Moderators of Aptitude Test Validity in Selection: A Red Herring." *Journal of Applied Psychology*, 1981, *66*, 161–185.

Simon, H. A. "Identifying Basic Abilities Underlying Intelligent Performance of

Complex Tasks." In L. B. Resnick (Ed.), *The Nature of Intelligence*, Hillsdale, N.J.: Erlbaum, 1976.

Sternberg, R. J. "The Nature of Mental Abilities." *American Psychologist*, 1979, *34*, 214–230.

Super, D. E., and others. *Vocational Development: A Framework for Research.* New York: Teachers College Press, 1957.

Tryon, W. W., and Jacobs, R. S. *"Effects of Basic Learning Skill Training on Peabody Picture Vocabulary Test Scores of Severely Disruptive, Low-Functioning Children."* Paper presented at the meeting of the Eastern Psychological Association, Hartford, Conn., April 1980.

U.S. Department of Labor, Employment and Training Administration. *Pretesting Orientation Exercises (Manual; Test Booklet)*. Washington, D.C.: U.S. Government Printing Office, 1968.

U.S. Department of Labor, Employment and Training Administration. *Pretesting Orientation on the Purposes of Testing (Manual; Illustrations)*. Washington, D.C.: U.S. Government Printing Office, 1970.

U.S. Department of Labor, Employment and Training Administration. *Doing Your Best on Aptitude Tests*. Washington, D.C.: U.S. Government Printing Office, 1971.

Wahlstrom, M., and Boersman, F. J. "The Influence of Test-Wiseness upon Achievement." *Educational and Psychological Measurement*, 1968, *28*, 413–420.

Whimbey, A. *Intelligence Can Be Taught*. New York: Dutton, 1975.

Whimbey, A. "Teaching Sequential Thought: The Cognitive-Skills Approach." *Phi Delta Kappan*, 1977, *59*, 255–259.

Yates, A. J., and others. "Symposium on the Effects of Coaching and Practice in Intelligence Tests." *British Journal of Educational Psychology*, 1953, *23*, 147–162; 1954, *24*, 57–63.

4

Factor Analysis and Traits: Studies on the Organization of Memory

The setting for the two studies excerpted in this chapter, as part of the Columbia studies on the identification of group factors, has already been described in Chapter 1. Using T. L. Kelley's adaptation of the tetrad criterion, the first study was designed to test Kelley's proposed memory factor in a different population and with a more extensive and systematically developed battery of memory tests. From the original, 61-page, five-chapter report, excerpts have been selected to provide a brief overview of the rationale, procedures, and results of the study.

While corroborating the presence of a differentiable group factor through tests of immediate memory, I did not believe that this factor represented the *memory factor; this concern was reflected in my insistence that the title of the study carry the indefinite article "a" rather than "the." It was my hypothesis that there are several, more or less independent memory factors, varying with such conditions as test content, initial memorizing procedures, delay, and method of recall.*

The second study, designed in part to test this hypothesis, supported the hypothesis, as did later factor-analytic research on memory by other investigators.[1] The factor I had identified in my first study corresponds closely to a factor subsequently identified by Thurstone, which he called "associative memory." This factor is

---

[1] E.g., Christal, R. E. Factor analytic study of visual memory. *Psychological Monographs,* 1958, 72(13, Whole No. 466).

found principally in tests demanding immediate rote memory for paired associates.

The second study also suggested that this factor may depend largely on the respondent's ability to devise and utilize memory "crutches," "tricks of the trade," "special devices," or what would now be designated as effective information-processing strategies. This point is discussed in both the introduction and the summary of the study, which are reproduced in this chapter. It might also be noted that the last sentence of the summary foreshadows the object of my later research on the effect of special training on the organization of abilities, as well as my enduring interest in the general process of trait formation.

A Group Factor in Immediate Memory

THE PROBLEM*

I. Purpose of the Present Investigation

The present study is an experimental attack upon a specific problem in the organization of mental traits. Recent discussions regarding the presence of a number of independent "group factors" in mental organization make experimental identification and isolation of such factors timely and desirable. It is with one of these proposed "group factors," namely memory, that the present investigation is concerned. This study undertakes to find an experimental answer to the question of the existence of a common factor through a number of memory tests and its relation to other factors. If such a memory factor is discovered, a battery of tests for measuring it will then be constructed and the efficiency with which this battery estimates the central factor determined.

II Principles Underlying the Choice of Tests

One of two principles could logically be followed in the selection of memory tests to be used in such a study. On the one hand, we could select a random sampling of as many different types of memory tests as possible, including variations in modality, materials, method, and duration of delay. On the other hand, we could restrict the scope of the tests, and proceed to an intensive investigation of some one phase of memory ability. The method of selection finally adopted is intermediate between these two principles. Obviously, the first method only could lead to a conclusive answer to the question of a general memory factor. However, if there should be no factor as general as this, but only more restricted memory group factors, it would be impossible to identify such smaller factors unless a sufficiently large

*This study is one of a series of researches (under the general direction of Professor H. E. Garrett) supported by a grant from the Council for Research in the Social Sciences, Columbia University.

A group factor in immediate memory. *Archives of Psychology,* 1930, No. 120. (Pp. 5-9, 24-25, 28-29, 58, and corresponding references.)

number of tests of each type had been used. If this were done, however, the number of necessary tests would be too large to use in a
single study on a single group of subjects. On the other hand, if the
study is restricted too narrowly, then whatever group factors are
found will be too restricted to be of much significance. It was finally
decided to limit the study to immediate memory for visually presented material. Within this field, variations of method and material
were introduced. If the existence of a group factor of immediate
memory is established in the present study, it will then be feasible to
combine tests of immediate and delayed memory in a more comprehensive search for a group factor through all memory tests.

In the construction of the memory tests, the attempt was made
to eliminate as far as possible the presence of variables other than
memory, in order not to complicate the relationships found. Any
procedure involving fine discriminations or very close or sustained
attention was carefully excluded. The use of "logical" material was
also considered undesirable, since its recall depends on too many
variables other than memory, such as interest in and understanding
of the passage used, information, past experience, etc.

In order to establish the independence of the memory factor, it
is essential to include in the study a number of non-memory tests.
For this purpose, three tests were selected which were as nearly as
possible measures of three other group factors, *viz.,* verbal and
numerical ability and a possible spatial ability. Although the presence
of the last-named factor has not yet been established, the most carefully constructed "spatial" test available was used. The factors of
verbal and numerical ability having already been investigated (34), it
was possible in these cases to use tests whose efficiency in measuring
the central factor was definitely known.

III. Principles Underlying the Choice of Subjects

A special attempt has been made in the present study to obtain a
high degree of homogeneity within the group of subjects used, in
order to avoid spurious correlations resulting from extreme variations
within the group. Heterogeneity may arise from differences in maturity, sex, racial or national descent, educational or social status,
and similar influences of heredity or environment; such heterogeneity may either raise or lower a correlation coefficient, depending
upon whether the two variables correlated vary in the same or opposite direction, respectively, as the third variable. A group heterogeneous with respect to maturity usually yields correlations higher
than the true value, since most capacities increase with age. The two

variables correlated, in this case, would always vary in the same direction with the third variable, age, both increasing as age increases. It is also possible, however, for heterogeneity to lower a correlation coefficient. Let us suppose that a sampling is made up of two groups, of, for example, different racial extraction. Now, if one of the two races excels the other markedly in trait A, but is decidedly inferior to it in trait B, then lumping the two groups would tend to produce a negative correlation between traits A and B, and would therefore yield a value lower than the relationship existing within either of the two groups.

Having shown that heterogeneity does affect a correlation co-efficient, it may be well to discuss just how far homogeneity in a sampling yields results which are the best approximation to the "true" relationships sought. If it were possible to obtain a group of subjects perfectly identical with respect to all influences of heredity and environment, there would be zero variability in all traits within the group and no correlation between any of the variables could be obtained. Obviously, we should not want to eliminate all hetero-geneity, even if such a thing were possible. What we actually want to find in any study of trait organization are the relationships existing within the total population about which we draw conclusions, in most studies this population being the total human race. Now, if we select extreme groups and lump them together in treating the data, obviously the relationships found will not be those which we would find if we tested the entire human race. Since most abilities have been found to be distributed according to the normal Gaussian curve, extreme cases will be very few in the total population. Furthermore, the effect of a few extreme deviations on a correlation coefficient will be less, the larger the number of cases. It is obvious that, since

$$r = \frac{\Sigma xy}{N \sigma_x \sigma_y},$$

the effect of any one product-deviation on r increases inversely as the size of N. Therefore, if we wish to obtain the relationships exist-ing in the total population, we must have fewer extreme deviations, *i.e.,* our group must be more homogeneous, the smaller the N. It is, of course, impossible to determine the exact degree of homogeneity required in the sampling to make the results representative. The safer policy therefore seems to be to err in the direction of excess rather than insufficient homogeneity, obtaining as a result correlations lower, rather than higher than the "true" relation. This may obscure a "true" relationship which is very small; however, the discovery of such a relationship, so small in the first place, would hardly be very valuable. This result certainly seems less seriously misleading than the spurious appearance of correlation where there is no "true" relationship.

The maturity factor was controlled in the present study by the use of adult subjects, all of whom were either past or very close to their growth limit in mental capacities. This was considered preferable to the use of children of the same chronological age. Until more definite information is available on growth curves, we cannot justifiably assume that all children of the same chronological age have attained the same proportion of their ultimate adult capacity. Hence, we cannot be certain that we have controlled the maturity factor by holding chronological age constant, unless all our subjects have reached or passed their mental growth limit.

THE LITERATURE

A survey of the experimental literature on memory in search of data bearing on the interrelationships of memory tests yields a number of miscellaneous correlation coefficients, frequently computed only incidentally to the solution of some other problem. In most studies, only a few of all the possible intercorrelations of the variables used have been computed; systematic correlation studies on memory are very rare; only two or three go beyond correlation and apply some more conclusive criterion in the attempt to arrive at a general memory factor. These latter studies will be discussed in greater detail further in the present chapter. In addition, an attempt has been made to present a systematic analysis of correlations which have been reported in the literature on memory. These include correlations among different tests of memory, as well as a few correlations between memory tests and tests or estimates of other capacities. The data have been analyzed and tabulated on the basis of the criteria considered most significant in the present approach to the problem. These criteria include: number and description of subjects, in an attempt to get at the statistical reliability of the results with regard to size of N and homogeneity of the sampling; a brief description of the tests used, with special reference to materials, modality, number of repetitions, duration of delay, and method of testing retention; finally, the reliability coefficients of the tests used whenever reported, and the intercorrelations computed are given. It is hoped that whatever value the present or similar investigations may derive from these past studies on memory, will be brought out more fully by this analysis of the data. This analysis is presented in Table I.[a] The studies reported have been arranged in chronological order. . . .

Critique of Previous Studies

An examination of Table I and of the accompanying discussion suggests a number of inadequacies or defects in previous studies which make any conclusive evaluation of the results extremely dubious. Perhaps the most fruitful and suggestive conclusion that can be drawn from such a survey of the literature is an enumeration of just those defects in methodology and technique which make any conclusions regarding the presence of a memory factor impossible. One or more of the following criticisms could be offered against any of the studies reported.

1. The use of small samplings: The size of N affects $P.E._r$ and $P.E._t$ very markedly. If a P.E. is extremely large, it merely shows that our determination of the correlation coefficient, or tetrad difference, as the case may be, *may differ very widely* from the true value; but it hardly justifies a conclusive evaluation of the obtained value in terms of such a P.E.
2. The use of samplings heterogeneous with respect to age, sex, racial or national background, educational and social status, etc.: Column III of Table I gives adequate evidence that this criticism applies to a large number of studies. The effect of heterogeneity on the correlations obtained has been discussed in Chapter I.
3. No reliability coefficients are reported in a number of studies. Since many of the memory tests used are very short, the reliabilities are probably quite low, thus lowering the intercorrelations obtained. In several cases, the reliability coefficients are reported, but are fairly low, and hence the resulting corrections for attenuation very large. In such cases it seems rather dangerous to work with results which *might* have been obtained had the reliabilities of the tests been perfect, and which nevertheless have been *estimated* from results obtained with highly unreliable tests. The only safe procedure in such cases seems to be the construction of new tests which are more reliable in the first place.
4. The large majority of studies which report only correlation coefficients can at best be only suggestive, not conclusive. Some further criterion is necessary in establishing the presence or absence of group factors.
5. Studies using only tests of memory can at best only show the presence of a central memory factor, but cannot show its independence from other variables, or from "general capacity." Non-memory tests must be included to test the independence of a possible memory factor.
6. The tests used are frequently complex with respect to the capacities involved.

---

[a]A 13-page table, not herein reproduced.—Ed.

The situation obviously complicates the relationships and makes evaluation of results more difficult and indirect. The tests should be as far as possible measures of sheer retentivity.

7. The selection of tests and treatment of results in several studies is such that, although the presence or absence of a general factor through all the tests may be established, no light can be thrown on the presence of narrower group factors. The latter would be especially useful when negative results are obtained regarding the presence of the more inclusive factor. This point has been discussed more fully in Chapter I.

8. The use of the formula for obtaining the P.E. of an entire distribution of tetrad differences has been criticized by Kelley (26), on the grounds that it assumes a normal distribution of the tetrad differences. The actual form of the distribution, as Kelley points out, is probably not normal, due to the correlation of the chance errors in the correlation coefficients, causing the chance errors in the tetrads also to be correlated. This shorter technique has nevertheless been used in most studies as the final criterion in evaluating the obtained tetrad differences.

9. Spearman's formula for the correlation of a test with what is common to it and a number of other tests (r_{ag}) has been used in detecting group factors. This is hardly justifiable, since the formula assumes the absence of any such group factors in its derivation. . . .

THE TESTS

The following eight memory tests were used. All were tests of immediate memory for visually presented material.

1. Paired Associates: word–word.
   All the words were simple four-letter English words.

2. Paired Associates: picture–number.[b]
   Pictures of common objects, approximately 3 × 3 inches, in black and white were paired with two-place numbers. The pictures were cut from newspapers and magazines. In constructing the two-place numbers, all digits except zero were used. Especially familiar combinations, such as 25 and 75 were omitted.

3. Paired Associates: form–number.
   Geometrical forms, approximately 3 × 3 inches were drawn in India ink on white cards, and paired with two-place numbers as in test 2. In constructing the geometrical forms, care was taken to make the forms sufficiently different from each other in order not to necessitate fine discriminations.

4. Paired Associates: color–word.
   Triangles, circles, squares, and lozenges, in red, green, blue, yellow, orange, and purple or combinations of any two of these colors were paired with

---

[b]An adaptation of this test is included in the ETS kit of factor-referenced tests (Ekstrom, R. B., French, J. W., Harman, H. H., & Dermen, D. *Manual for kit of factor-referenced cognitive tests,* 3rd ed. Princeton, N.J.: Educational Testing Service, 1976, p. 94.)—Ed.

four-letter English words. The colored forms were cut out of Dennison's gummed papers, dull finish (numbers 122, 124, 125, 126A, 120, and 140).

5. Digit span: four parallel forms of this test were used, each ranging from four to thirteen digits.
6. Retained members: four-letter English words.
7. Recognition of geometrical forms, similar to the forms used in test No. 3.
8. Recognition of three-letter nonsense syllables:
   The nonsense syllables were taken from a list published by Glaze (18). The particular syllables used were selected from a list of 101 syllables found by Glaze to have zero associative value for his group of subjects.

All the test materials were glued on rectangular white cardboard cards. Black two-inch letters and numbers were used throughout. Each of the recall tests contained a total of forty items, divided into shorter sub-tests, as described further. Each of the two recognition tests contained forty "old" and forty "new" items.

In addition to the eight memory tests described above, the following three tests of other traits were used, making a total of eleven tests.

1. Multiple Choice Vocabulary Test:
   The test used was the vocabulary test used by Schneck (34) and found by him to correlate .90 with the central "verbal" factor.
2. Arithmetic Reasoning Test:
   This was also one of the tests used by Schneck and found to correlate .75 with the central "number" factor.
3. Minnesota Paper Form Board Test, forms A and B.
   This test is described by Anderson (3), and was used in the attempt to get at a measure of a possible "spatial ability." . . .

SUMMARY

1. A group of 225 subjects,[c] chosen because of their homogeneity with respect to age, racial descent, educational and social status, etc., were given 8 tests of immediate memory for visually presented material and 3 non-memory tests.

2. Evidence of the presence of a central factor through the memory tests was found in (1) the size of the average intercorrelation of the memory tests; (2) the results of the application of the tetrad criterion; and (3) the correlations of each test with the central

---

[c]All male upperclassmen at the College of the City of New York, drawn from the same population as that employed by Schneck (34) on the verbal and number factors.—Ed.

factor. The last criterion (r_{ag}) is shown to be the most crucial on theoretical grounds.

3. The independence of the central factor in our memory tests was shown by the correlations of the non-memory tests with the central memory factor, all of which were smaller than 4 P.E.$_r$.

4. A multiple regression equation for estimating scores in the central memory factor from our battery of memory tests is given.

5. Coefficients of total and net determination showing the per cent of the variance of our central memory factor attributable to the entire battery and to each of our tests, are given. The per cent of the variance of each of our tests due to the central memory factor is also given.

6. A comparison of our data with those of Schneck (34) on the verbal and number factors shows considerable uniformity in the results of the two studies.

REFERENCES CITED IN EXCERPT
(as originally numbered)

3. Anderson, D. L. The Minnesota Mechanical Ability Tests. Pers. J., 6, 1928, 473–478.
18. Glaze, J. A. The Association Value of Nonsense Syllables. J. Gen. Psychol., 35, 1928, 255–269.
26. Kelley, T. L. Crossroads in the Mind of Man. Stanford, Calif.: Stanford University Press, 1928.
34. Schneck, M. M. R. The Measurement of Verbal and Numerical Abilities. Arch. Psychol., No. 107, 1929, Pp. 49.

Further Studies
on the Memory Factor

INTRODUCTION*

I. Setting of the Problem

The present series of studies center about the problem of whether memory may be considered a unitary and differentiable mental trait. The investigations reported in this monograph were undertaken as a continuation and an elaboration of a preliminary study on the memory factor published in 1930 (2). The procedure and results of the present study should be considered throughout in the light of the earlier study. The reader is referred to the 1930 study for an analysis and critique of the literature bearing on the general problem. It was pointed out in that study that it is very difficult to draw any definite conclusions from the literature on the memory factor because of various limitations in the techniques employed by other investigators. The results obtained in the 1930 study yielded several lines of evidence suggesting the presence of a single common factor through tests of immediate rote memory for visually presented material. Furthermore, this memory factor varied quite independently of performance in three other tests used, which were taken as measures of verbal,[1] numerical,[2] and spatial[3] ability, respectively. The data in that study were secured exclusively on a group of male college students, nearly all of whom were in the junior year. These results were therefore limited, first, from the standpoint of the tests used, and secondly, from the standpoint of the type of subjects on whom they were established. Insofar as the tests and the subjects constituted random samplings of certain populations, in the statistical sense, we can generalize our conclusions to cover the entire populations. Since

*The writer wishes to express her appreciation to Prof. H. E. Garrett of Columbia University for helpful suggestions and criticisms, as well as for having allotted a portion of a grant from the Columbia University Council for Research in the Social Sciences to cover the larger portion of the statistical and clerical expenses of this study.

[1] Vocabulary Test used by Schneck (26).
[2] Arithmetic Reasoning Test used by Schneck (26).
[3] The Minnesota Paper Form Board Test (3).

Further studies on the memory factor. *Archives of Psychology,* 1932, No. 142. (Pp. 5–8, 55–58, and corresponding references.)

95

our tests represented a fairly wide and random selection of immediate rote memory tests for visual material, we may conclude that our results indicated the presence of a common factor through *such tests* in general, but not necessarily through any other varieties of memory tests not sampled in our study. Likewise, our subjects were fairly representative of male college students of a certain specified social and racial status (cf. 2, p. 26–27). We cannot assume, however, that the same trait relationships would hold for a group differing in sex, age, race, social or educational status from our experimental group. It is quite justifiable—in fact, fundamental in most statistical work— to generalize from the experimental sampling to the population from which it is drawn, but that population should itself be clearly defined and delimited, and the conclusions should not be extended indiscriminately to other populations, without experimental verification.

A further limitation inherent in any single statistical study of trait organization is that the results throw little or no light upon the *nature* of the common factor discovered. This is especially true when the range of functions tested is fairly narrow and the tests used are similar in more than one respect. Although the presence of a common factor may be established mathematically, it is usually difficult to determine just what it is that is common to all the tests concerned. For example, the common factor might result from special skills and techniques acquired during the course of general training and education. All the tests in which one of these special techniques or "tricks of the trade" could be applied would show a common factor. One such technique is the well-known device of forcing meaningful associations in rote memory tests. Subjects probably differ considerably in the readiness and appropriateness of such associations, a fact which *might* account to a large extent for the differences in performance on such tests. Common devices such as this could easily produce a common factor by themselves. A second explanation that suggests itself is in terms of community of *material*, or content, of the tests used. Some subjects may display greater proficiency than others in dealing with a given type of material, irrespective of what is to be done with that material. Thus, an individual especially adept in mechanics might excel in mechanical construction, perceiving mechanical relations, and recalling mechanical facts and concepts. Such special proficiencies in dealing with a certain type of material might in turn have resulted from any number of factors, such as innate capacity, training, interest. A third explanation which may be offered to account for a mathematically established common factor is that the tests involved are all based on a common mental *process*, a unitary trait, which is manifested to a greater or lesser degree whatever the material may be. Other explanations could no doubt be suggested. All too often the third explanation is assumed to be the correct one, although there may be no direct evidence for it in the data. By repeating an investigation on different types of subjects, and using different combinations of tests covering a wide range of material, it should be possible to arrive at a somewhat clearer understanding of the nature of the common bond.

II. Plan of the Present Study

The present study is divided into three parts, each part representing a separate investigation. In Part I, the results of the 1930 study were checked on a different population. The subjects were college women, one year younger on the average than the college men used in the earlier study, and the majority were sophomores rather than juniors. In addition, it was possible in the present study to analyze more fully the relation between memory and the verbal and numerical factors, since *two* verbal and *two* numerical tests were used, rather than one of each as in the earlier study. Tetrads could therefore be computed with two memory tests combined with two tests of one of the other abilities, and the independence of the group factors involved could be demonstrated. In the 1930 study, it was not possible to demonstrate the independence of the memory factor by means of the tetrad criterion, but only by the size of the correlations themselves. Finally, the data in Part I of our study offer a means of checking on a different population some of the results on the verbal and numerical factors, secured by Schneck (26), since some of the original tests used by Schneck were repeated on our subjects. Part I may, therefore, be characterized in general as a checking over of results formerly obtained, by varying the type of subjects. No new tests were used, and the procedure was purposely kept identical to that previously followed.

In Part II, the *tests* themselves were varied. Our main purpose now was to find the extent of the memory factor and to throw some light, if possible, on its nature. Can the memory factor previously found be regarded as sheer retentivity, so that it will be manifested in any test involving retention, or is some of the overlapping found due to similarity of material, special techniques, etc.? The tests used in this part of the study differed as much as possible from each other and from the earlier tests, the only common feature through all of them being the fact that the subjects were required to *retain* certain impressions, in each test.

Part III is a special analysis of logical recall and recognition. In any analysis of the memory factor, the relation of these two processes should be considered. They have frequently been discussed as two separate processes, and statements have been made as to their relationship, their relative difficulty and the differences in their susceptibility to various factors.[4] In this study, our aim was to make the tests of recall and recognition as comparable as possible, so as to eliminate the effect of any extraneous factors.

The implications for the memory factor of all the three studies are brought together and analyzed in Chapter VII. Hypotheses regarding the extent and nature of the memory factor are offered, in the light of the results secured through the various attacks on the problem in Parts I, II, and III. . . .

SUMMARY AND EVALUATION

In Part I of the present investigation, 140 college women were tested with four memory tests, two verbal tests, and two numerical tests. All of the tests had been used before, in the same form. The four memory tests dealt with a particular type of memory which may be described as immediate rote memory for visually presented material. In Part II, 170 subjects drawn from the same population as those in Part I, were given ten tests, most of which were new. Eight of the tests were memory tests, varying widely in all aspects save the common feature of retentivity. In Part III, an analysis of logical recall and recognition was undertaken, based upon some of the data from Study II, in conjunction with certain specially obtained control data. For the specific findings in each part, the reader is referred to the conclusions at the end of each section. In the present chapter, we shall bring together the various suggestions gleaned from each section, and endeavor to work out certain general implications of the results.

The chief conclusion that can be drawn from the present study is, clearly, that we cannot speak of a single common factor running through *all* forms of memory. The evidence from Part II is especially conclusive on this point. The very fact that in Part I, as well as in the 1930 study, the multiple correlation between our battery of memory tests and the factor common to those tests was so high, may be regarded as a precursor of our later findings. It seems to us that a factor which is measured so completely by a group of simple tests of a relatively narrow phase of memory, is not very likely to extend

---

[4] Cf., for example, Strong (30, 31) and Hollingworth (11).

through a wide range of performance, not as likely at least, as if the multiple correlation had been lower, indicating that certain aspects of the common factor had not been touched upon by the tests used. The common factor previously found may have consisted almost entirely of certain special devices[5] which could be applied generally to rote memory for verbal material. A concrete example may make this point clearer. When confronted with a series of disconnected words, many individuals, some more readily than others, will tend to group the words into a sentence or other more or less meaningful unit. This device is an undoubted advantage in any test involving memory of disconnected words. Differences in the speed, frequency, and skill with which different individuals group the words may produce variability in test scores through this factor alone. When changes in material, or in any other aspect of the tests, are introduced, as in Part II of our study, the same devices can no longer be of assistance in the tests, and the common factor disappears. Of course, all that our data can show directly is the *extent* of the common factor. Any statements regarding its *nature* are offered only as very tentative hypotheses. Reference has been made throughout this study to two probable interpretations of common factors: i.e., community of material and special techniques. These two interpretations are not mutually exclusive, but, on the contrary, the one *may* be explained in terms of the other. The evidence for either interpretation is admittedly meagre, as it was not our main purpose in this study to analyze the *nature* of the memory factor. It may be of some value nevertheless, to summarize at this point the facts that suggested each hypothesis.

First, let us consider the interpretation in terms of community of test *material*. The data of Achilles (1), Lee (15), and Bolton (4) on this question have been cited as inconclusive. The data in our 1930 study suggest that community of material is more significant in producing correlation than community of method, since the two pairs of tests which had to be pooled on account of exceptionally high correlations were both characterized by community of material. One of these test pools consisted of the word–word test and the retained members words tests; the other contained the picture–number and form–number tests. In Part I of the present study, likewise, the correlation between word–word and retained members was much higher than that between word–word and picture–number; in the former combination, material is similar and method differs, in the latter,

---

[5] We are using the terms "special device" and "technique" in a very similar sense to that in which Gates (10) uses these terms in his discussion of the nature of improvement due to training.

method is identical but material differs. The very high correlation found in Part II between logical recall and recognition furnishes further evidence of the effect of material. Using the two methods of testing memory which have usually been regarded as the most diverse, but applying them to materials which had been closely equated, we obtained with these two tests the highest correlation of any in the table. Finally, we may find some rather indirect evidence for our hypothesis in a comparison of Schneck's results on the verbal and numerical factors, both of which are *content* factors, with our results on the memory factor, a factor of *process,* or method. The tetrad equations in Schneck's study gave very clear-cut evidence of the presence of a single common factor through each of the two types of material, with no disturbing group factors through overlapping of method. In our 1930 study on the memory factor, on the other hand, we found many disturbing group factors from similarity of material, necessitating the pooling of tests and leaving a suggestion of minor group factors even in the final tetrad with the pooled tests. Throughout this discussion, we have purposely used the terms method and material, rather than form and content, because we wish to make the distinction in terms of the actual test situation, not in terms of the mental activity of the subject in dealing with that situation. The latter obviously cannot be discussed in a statistical study.

The second interpretation of group factors is based upon the common applicability to several test situations of certain special techniques which facilitate the subject's performance. If such devices account in large measure for inter-test correlations, we should expect large changes in such correlations when the procedure of the test is changed even slightly, as by introducing a delay. This is exactly what we do find, when we compare the correlations of the retained members test with the corresponding correlations of the delayed memory test, the correlations differing very markedly in the two cases. It will be remembered that these two tests were very similar except for the factor of delay. Certain devices which might facilitate the recall of a series of words immediately after their presentation might be of little or no value when recall is tested after 48 hours. For example, a preliminary survey of the subjects' responses in these two tests shows that in immediate recall, a large number of subjects tend to reproduce the words in the reverse order from the order of presentation, whereas in the delayed reproductions the original presentation order is found more commonly. This fact suggests a possible difference in the nature of the two tests brought about by the delay alone. The effect of specific aids and devices is again suggested by the relatively high correlation found between tonal memory and memory for movement. Both tests involve a very immediate sort of memory for short series of discrete impressions, making possible the use of various common devices. Finally, all the evidence cited above as indicative of the greater potency of material than method, or process, in determining inter-test correlations, *might* be explained in terms of the use of common facilitating devices. It would seem that such devices could be applied more effectively and more widely within a given type of *material,* than within a given *process.* If the explanation of common factors in terms of such more or less widely applicable devices be correct, it suggests interesting possibilities regarding environmental influences and training in relation to problems of mental organization. Especially fruitful in this connection would be the experimental study of the effect of special training on inter-test correlations, as well as the comparison of correlation results in groups of widely diverse training and background.

REFERENCES CITED IN EXCERPT
(as originally numbered)

1. Achilles, E. M. Experimental Studies in Recall and Recognition. Arch. Psychol., No. 44, 1920. Pp. 80.
2. Anastasi, A. A Group Factor in Immediate Memory. Arch. Psychol., No. 120, 1930. Pp. 61.
3. Anderson, D. L. The Minnesota Mechanical Ability Tests. Pers. J., 6, 1928, 473–478.
4. Bolton, E. B. The Relation of Memory to Intelligence. J. Exper. Psychol., 14, 1931, 37–67.
10. Gates, A. I. The Nature and Limit of Improvement Due to Training. 27th Year-Book Natl. Soc. Stud. Educ., Ch. 23, 441–460.
11. Hollingworth, H. L. Characteristic Differences between Recall and Recognition. Amer. J. Psychol., 24, 1913, 532–544.
15. Lee, A. L. An Experimental Study of Retention and Its Relation to Intelligence. Psychol. Rev. Monogr., 34, 1925. Pp. 45.
26. Schneck, M. M. R. The Measurement of Verbal and Numerical Abilities. Arch. Psychol., 107, 1929. Pp. 49.
30. Strong, E. K., Jr. The Effect of Length of Series upon Recognition Memory. Psychol. Rev., 19, 1912, 447–462.
31. Strong, E. K., Jr. The Effect of Time Interval upon Recognition Memory. Psychol. Rev., 20, 1913, 339–372.

5

Factor Analysis and Traits: Nature and Origin of Traits

*The ferment and controversy that characterized factor-analytic litera-
ture of the 1930s are reflected in this chapter. The opening article
was stimulated by the confusions and disagreements arising from the
use of ambiguous terminology and fuzzy concepts. It represents an
attempt to provide operational definitions of factors and to call
attention to group differences in factorial organization that may be
associated with differences in experiential background. The recommendations offered in my "Further Studies on the Memory Factor"
(Ch. 4) and reiterated in this article were implemented in a research
project, which undertook to demonstrate that trait organization can
be modified through brief but sharply focused training interventions.
The report of this study is excerpted in the second selection.*

*The object of this study was to illustrate, on a small scale, the
role of experience in trait formation. The procedure reproduced in
miniature the sort of process that may lead to trait formation over
several years of formal schooling and other gradually accumulating
experiences of daily life. An incidental aspect of the study was its
attempt to improve children's performance of certain intellectual
tasks by providing instruction in relevant problem-solving strategies—
a goal that underlies much of the cognitive training developed in the
1970s and 1980s (see, e.g., Anastasi, 1982, Ch. 12; Lidz, 1981, Ch.
3; Whimbey, 1977; Whiteley & Dawis, 1974).*

*With regard to the nature of the traits identified through factor
analysis, it is clear from the papers in this chapter that I resisted the
notion of traits as underlying, unchanging, causal entities. Trait constructs could nevertheless provide useful descriptive categories if they
were stripped of these excess meanings and defined operationally.*

The expression of these views, together with my rudimentary ex-
perimental demonstration of the modifiability of trait organization,
led Thurstone to publish a 14-page critique of my monograph (Thur-
stone, 1938). My reply to this critique is reproduced in the last
selection of this chapter.

REFERENCES

Anastasi, A. *Psychological testing* (5th ed.). New York: Macmillan, 1982.

Lidz, C. S. *Improving assessment of schoolchildren.* San Francisco: Jossey-Bass, 1981.

Thurstone, L. L. Shifty and mathematical components: A critique of Anastasi's monograph on the influence of specific experience upon mental organization. *Psychological Bulletin,* 1938, *35,* 223–236.

Whimbey, A. Teaching sequential thought: The cognitive-skills approach. *Phi Delta Kappan,* 1977, *59,* 255–259.

Whiteley, S. E., & Dawis, R. V. Effects of cognitive intervention on latent ability measured from analogy items. *Journal of Educational Psychology,* 1974, *66,* 710–717.

Some Ambiguous Concepts in the Field of "Mental Organization"

Investigations of trait relationship, or "mental organization," beginning with the pioneer work of Spearman,[1] have at present attained very considerable proportions both in the extent and variety of subjects and test material employed, and in the development and refinement of mathematical techniques for the treatment of the data. The problem of trait relationship is coming to the attention of an increasingly large body of psychologists, and its implications for a variety of other problems are being rapidly recognized. It seems timely, therefore, to clarify certain concepts and points of terminology which have caused some confusion. Among workers in the field of mental organization, there is gradually developing a tendency towards mutual agreement and consistency of interpretation as more inclusive theories and viewpoints are beginning to replace the necessarily limited earlier theories. Recent studies[2] suggest more and more, for example, the influence upon the relationship obtained of such conditions as age, developmental status, and educational background of the subjects, relative homogeneity of the group, and specific materials employed in the tests. It would indeed seem unwarranted to expect any one rigid formula to fit all results, or to insist that the above conditions be "ruled out" by arbitrarily selecting any one age, educational level, degree of heterogeneity, or type of material in order to find "true" mental organization. The very differences in the findings of various investigators are illuminating when considered in relation to the factors which brought them about, since these factors are thereby shown to be of fundamental significance in determining and modifying mental organization.

With differences among current theories of mental organization, the present paper has no concern. These differences are gradually working themselves out with the accumulation of more data and the

---

[1] Carl Spearman, "General intelligence" objectively determined and measured, this JOURNAL, 15, 1904, 201–293.

[2] Cf. Anne Anastasi, Further studies on the memory factor, *Arch. Psychol.*, 1932, (no. 142), 1–60; H. E. Garrett, R. Bryan and R. E. Perl, The age factor in mental organization, *ibid.*, 1935, (no. 176), 1–31.

Some ambiguous concepts in the field of "mental organization." *American Journal of Psychology*, 1935, 47, 509–511.

more comprehensive interpretation of such data. There still remain, however, a number of common criticisms repeatedly brought to the fore by that larger body of psychologists who, although not immediately concerned with statistical techniques in their own research, nevertheless exhibit various degrees of interest, concern, or skepticism over the psychological implications of studies which do employ such techniques.

The use of the term "mental organization" to denote the field of investigation creates a rather unfortunate impression because of its historical connotations. The term is, it seems, strongly suggestive of a reversion to early scholasticism and faculty psychology. It is the belief of the writer, however, that such a reversion is by no means implied. The major differences between faculty psychology and the current theories of mental organization will be summarized briefly. Maher, representing the scholastic viewpoint, writes, "By a faculty is meant the mind's capability of undergoing a particular kind of activity; thus our sensations of colour are due to the faculty of vision, our judgments to the faculty of intellect, and our volitions to the faculty of will."[3] The recent statistical studies are concerned not with vague, mystical, psychical entities, but with *concrete behavior manifestations.* The data of such studies are the varied responses of individuals to standardized test situations or stimuli, and it is only with the relationships among groups of such concrete behavior manifestations that the current theories are concerned. By relationship is meant nothing more than the tendency for a given response to vary concurrently with some responses and independently of other responses. This tendency for concomitant variation among a group of responses, or behavior manifestations, is all that a *group factor* can mean statistically. If some investigators have gone further and posited entities underlying the group factors, such entities are quite independent of the statistically established group factors and are not implied by them. This suggests a second difference between scholastic faculties and statistical factors; namely, that the latter are not in any sense *causal.* Since the group factor is nothing more than a condensed statement of the fact that certain responses do vary concomitantly among themselves and independently of other responses, it certainly cannot be offered as an explanation or cause of such a relationship. Finally, as recent experiments have especially demonstrated, statistical factors are not fixed, permanent, immutable, or innate.[4] They are statements of relationships found under given con-

---

[3] Michael Maher, *Psychology: Empirical and Rational,* 1929, 29.

[4] Cf. Garrett et al., *op. cit.*

ditions at a given time. The study of the conditions which bring about changes in such relationships are an even more fruitful approach to the problem than the identification of the factors themselves.

Even if the purely statistical definition of "factor" is accepted, however, there are still heard dissenting voices which object that it is not clear whether the factors are in the tests, in the group, or in the individuals. There can be only one answer to this: the factor is a mathematical statement of relationships within the *individual's responses to the test stimuli.* If the tests are altered in any way, then naturally the factor will be altered, since the individual is responding to different stimuli. The rôle played by the group needs further clarification. We are essentially concerned with the relationship of behavior within the individual, so that we shall ultimately be enabled to say that if the individual is 'proficient' in response *A*, he will also be 'proficient' in response *B*, but not necessarily so in response *C*. Thus we have a statement of what a group factor means in terms of the individual. The difficulty arises in defining the term "proficient," or differently put, in finding a standard, a point of reference, or measuring rod whereby the individual's reaction may be unambiguously described. The group is required in order to furnish such a point of reference. We can now restate our hypothetical group factor. The individual who is more 'proficient' than the average of a given group in response *A* will be more 'proficient' than the average of the same group in response *B*, but not necessarily so in response *C*.

Objections will immediately be raised to such an oversimplified statement. It will be argued that the relationship of *A, B,* and *C* as described above does not hold for *every* individual in the group, but only for the majority. This, of course, is only another way of saying that the correlation between *A* and *B* is not perfect. This correlation is lowered by the fact that any response made by the individual—especially by such a complex organism as the human—is complex, however physically simple the stimulus may be. Since more than one elementary type of response is occurring simultaneously, any one individual's standing in *A* or *B* in the group may be displaced because of the influence of other simultaneous responses, *x, y, z*. The latter are "specific factors" in the terminology of mental organization.

A second objection may be raised that the individual's 'factors' do not remain constant when he is tested in different groups. It will be seen that this must necessarily follow from the above arguments. If the individual's behavior is described in terms of the group as a point of reference, it will be differently described depending upon the group. It is a fact of common observation that an individual who is above average in elementary school, becomes average in high school, and may fall behind and be distinctly inferior if he goes to college, not because of any deterioration in the individual, but because he is evaluating his performance in terms of an ever-rising standard. Similarly, we should expect the relationships among various types of behavior to differ when the behavior is measured in terms of the standards of different groups. The individual may be above the average of one group in responses A, B, C, and D, whereas in another more select group, he may be above the average in only A and B. It follows from this discussion that findings on mental organization should always be described with reference to the particular type of group in which they are to be applied.

The attempt has been made in the present paper to give the most natural, objective, and simple interpretation to some widely misunderstood and variously interpreted terms. It has been assumed that these interpretations are essentially those implied whenever such terms are employed in statistical studies on mental organization. Should these be at variance with the interpretations intended by any workers in the field, this difference should certainly be brought to light. The discovery of such differences, if there be any, may well be considered an incidental purpose of the present paper.

The Influence of Specific Experience upon Mental Organization

GENERAL PROBLEM AND LITERATURE[1]

The Problem under Investigation

That field of psychology which has come to be known as "mental organization" is rapidly attaining very extensive proportions and attracting interest in all branches of the science. The theories, methods, or findings on mental organization have made their way into such diverse fields as test construction (11, 85, 121, 132, 161, 257), the interpretation of group differences (18), the analysis of personality (29, 69, 135, 137, 142, 202, 243, 259), abnormal psychology (206, 245), the measurement of interests (38, 242, 245, 247), and the study of animal behavior (12, 56, 122, 238), to name only the most outstanding examples. At the same time, however, students of mental organization have been engaged in controversies of long standing on fundamental differences in method or interpretation. It seems to the writer that much of this controversy has arisen from the attempt to generalize too broadly from the results of single investigations, with the resulting expectation that studies employing subjects who differ in age, environmental background, occupation, etc., should yield similar results. In 1932, the writer (8, p. 58) called attention to the "possibilities regarding environmental influences and training in relation to problems of mental organization" and added, "Especially fruitful in this connection would be the experimental study of the effect of special training on intertest correlations, as well as the comparison of correlation results in groups of widely diverse training and background." It would indeed seem that the nature of trait relationship can most profitably be investigated through the comparison of just such discrepancies from group to group, when these are considered in relation to the factors producing them. A crucial test of this hypothesis would be the *experimental*

[1] The present study was conducted under the auspices of the Columbia University Council for Research in the Social Sciences.

The influence of specific experience upon mental organization. *Genetic Psychology Monographs*, 1936, *18*(4), 245–355. (Pp. 251–252, 275–281, 336–338, and corresponding references.)

production of such changes in mental organization as are found in the studies on different groups. This has been the purpose of the present study. But before proceeding, it may be well to review briefly and formulate more clearly, the present status of the problem of mental organization. . . .

It would seem that recent, better-controlled studies have demonstrated more and more the importance of a fact only casually noted at the outset, namely, that mental organization is very largely a function of the particular population under consideration. Nor can this fact be evaded by lumping all populations and seeking a sort of "universal" mental organization in a random and highly heterogeneous sampling, even if such a procedure were feasible and desirable from a practical standpoint. If definite differences in mental organization are demonstrated between groups differing in specific known characteristics, such as age, educational, occupational, or cultural status, these differences should not be ignored nor ruled out, but should themselves be investigated for the light they may throw on the nature of mental organization. The time seems ripe to turn from the investigation of the existence of relationships to the experimental study of the causes of relationship.

DESCRIPTION OF THE PRESENT STUDY

General Plan of the Experiment

The specific object of the present study was to investigate the possibility of "producing" experimentally a factor pattern other than that originally found in a given group of subjects. This problem may be approached from various angles. Mental organization may become altered in the course of the individual's everyday experiences, and particularly in the course of school instruction. Hence one approach to the problem might be the retesting of a group of children at different ages and academic levels. The interpolated experimental factor in such a set-up would be the sum total of the subject's intervening experiences. A disadvantage of this method is that the experimenter has no control over the intervening experience of the subject and little knowledge of it. A further and probably more serious disadvantage, from the standpoint of theoretical implications, lies in the fact that such a procedure can throw no light upon the relative significance of maturational and experiential factors in bringing about the change.

A second approach would be through a study of the influence of practice upon the interrelations of the functions tested. The relevant data on this problem suggest that the relative weights and location of the various factors will, indeed, change in the course of practice. In this case, however, the situation is complicated by the marked increase in variability as well as the rise in reliability coefficients during practice.[2] The influence of these changes in variability and reliability upon the intercorrelations is so pronounced as to obscure any other independent modifications in factor pattern which might result directly from the practice.

A third approach is to be found in the study of transfer of training. The subjects could be trained in one function related more or less closely to some or all of the other functions tested; the intercorrelations among the untrained functions before and after the related training could then be compared. Group factors of varying extent could be produced, depending upon the number of functions affected by the transfer and upon the subjects' differential susceptibility to such transfer. With this technique, however, it is impossible definitely to establish a priori, and difficult to determine even a posteriori, just which functions are affected by the interpolated training. The function to be trained may have been selected because of its community of material with certain of the other functions tested. But it may also exhibit a certain community, in other respects, with any number of the other tests employed. Furthermore, such community, which determines the extent and direction of transfer, may vary with the individual. The experimenter cannot ascertain what is occurring to his individual subjects during the training period. One individual may develop a technique as a result of the training, which will carry over and improve his performance on one particular test X; another individual, exposed to the same training, may develop a different technique which may hinder his performance on test X, or may leave his performance on test X unchanged and affect his performance on another test Y. A certain gross effect can be established by means of this technique, but the exact nature of the influence or influences operative in bringing about the changes in interrelation among the tests would remain obscure.

The fourth method to be considered brings us a step closer to the understanding and direct control of the influence producing the change. This method depends not upon a prolonged period of training but upon some specific experience in which the subjects are given definite information or techniques that will be of assistance in some

---

[2] For a fuller discussion of this problem, cf.: Anastasi, A. Practice and variability. *Psychol. Monog.*, 1934, **45**. Pp. 55. Cf. also: The influence of practice upon test reliability. *J. Educ. Psychol.*, 1934, **25**, 321-335.

of the tests but not in others. The techniques presented can be made sufficiently specific so as to be definitely limited in the extent of their application. Rather than depend upon the various techniques haphazardly developed by the subjects in the course of the successive repetitions of a test, the experimenter himself furnishes the techniques. Thus, by this method, a more direct control is exerted over what occurs in the course of the experiment than by any of the other methods. At the same time, this set-up is more similar to what actually occurs in everyday life than either the practice or transfer methods, since the subjects are given instruction, which to most individuals is a more natural situation than repetition without comment. Finally, it will be noted that, with the method of "specific techniques," the effect of maturational factors is reduced to a minimum. The initial and final tests can be administered within a very short interval, thus reducing growth changes to a negligible quantity. In each of the other methods, on the other hand, the interpolated influences must operate over a much longer period in order to produce appreciable effects.

It should be pointed out that the differences among the four methods described above are not fundamental. The difference between practice and transfer is obviously one of degree only. Likewise, school instruction is essentially a means of improving performance along given lines, and in this respect its fundamental similarity to practice, transfer, and the "specific techniques" set-ups is apparent. The differentiation made above is based simply on the relative degree of control which can be exerted over the intervening influences, as well as the degree to which the nature and extent of these influences are known to the experimenter.

A question which enters into any investigation of this sort concerns changes in the nature of the tests in the course of the experiment. These changes must occur, regardless of the method employed. It is obvious that any intervening experience which is sufficiently relevant to alter the relationships of a test with other tests must also alter the specific nature of that test for the particular individual. This problem can easily become a *reductio ad absurdum.* It is well known that the nature of a test usually changes in the course of successive repetitions, as in a practice experiment. To a slighter degree, a single repetition will alter the stimulus value of a test for the subject. Similarly, a code learning test administered for the first time to a third-grade child and to a college student will not call into play the same processes. Thus no test can remain unaltered for the same individual on any two occasions.

It may be objected that, if the nature of the test is altered, then we should hardly expect the correlations of this test with others to remain unchanged, since different processes are being measured. This question is closely tied up with the essential meaning of mental organization. If mental organization refers only to the observed relationships among particular groups of behavior manifestations, then it must change as the nature of the tests changes. It would indeed be futile to attempt to prevent or "rule out" such changes in the tests, since similar changes must and do occur in everyday life as the subject's experiences accumulate. The problem with which we are concerned might be reworded as follows: What effect do the changes in the nature of tests or of the stimulus value of objects, which must of necessity occur in the course of the subject's life, have upon mental organization? Our contention is that if a change in factor pattern is revealed by the set-up of the present experiment, then similar changes will be found to occur in the course of the subject's life. In all cases, the specific nature of the test will change; if this causes a change in factor pattern in our set-up, it will likewise cause such a change in other situations. . . .

SUMMARY

The literature on the rapidly developing field of mental organization was surveyed with respect to theories, methodology, and findings. The present-day *theories*, although exhibiting a more fundamental agreement than they did at their inception, still present major differences in emphasis and interpretation. All of the theories are, however, converging towards a universal acceptance of group factors of varying extent. An examination of the mathematical *methods* of treating the data of mental organization, from the original "hierarchal" test of Spearman to current techniques of factor pattern analysis, reveals the dependence of all methods upon certain initial assumptions or limiting conditions. In selecting a particular method for use, one should be cognizant of the limiting conditions imposed by that method and should take them into consideration in interpreting the final results. A comparison of the specific *findings* of studies on different populations reveals a lack of constancy in the obtained patterns of relationship. Chief among such differences is that between different age groups. Several investigators have reported a tendency for the "general" factor to decrease and for "group" factors to increase with age. This finding, together with other minor differences, suggests that mental organization may be altered or determined by environmental influences.

The essential problem of the present study was the experimental alteration of a factor pattern by a brief, relevant, interpolated experience. Five tests, including vocabulary, digit span, pattern analysis, verbal reasoning, and code multiplication, were administered on two successive days to 200 sixth-grade school children of both sexes. The subjects were then given instruction in the use of special devices which would facilitate performance on the last three tests only. After a lapse of 13 days, parallel forms of all of the five tests were administered under exactly the same conditions as in the initial testing.

An analysis of the separate variables in the initial and final testing shows a reliable increase in mean score in all five tests, although the gain was much larger in the three "instruction" tests. The variability and the reliability coefficients of the tests did not, however, exhibit any marked or consistent change, and could not adequately account for any significant change in the relationships of the variables. A comparison of the intercorrelations among the five variables in the initial and final testing shows practically no change in the correlation between the two "non-instruction" tests, a slight change in the correlations between "instruction" and "non-instruction" tests, and a marked change in the correlations among the three "instruction" tests. Factor pattern analyses, found by Hotelling's method of principal components, show a wide variation from the initial to the final testing. A tentative identification of the factors isolated in the two patterns is offered, and the analysis is interpreted in terms of the specific influence of the interpolated instruction.

Two mutually related conclusions are suggested for the theory of mental organization: (1) factor patterns may be experientially determined; (2) factor patterns will differ in the same subjects at different times, as well as from one population to another. "Factors" should be empirically defined in terms of the concrete relationships from which they are found, and should be regarded as "shifting mathematical components" rather than as fixed, underlying psychological entities.

REFERENCES CITED IN EXCERPT
(as originally numbered)

8. ANASTASI, A. Further studies on the memory factor. *Arch. Psychol.*, 1932, No. 142. Pp. 60.

11. ASHER, E. J. The predictive value of mental tests that satisfy Spearman's tetrad criterion. *J. Appl. Psychol.*, 1929, 13, 152–158.

12. BAGG, H. J. Individual differences and family resemblances in animal behavior. A study of habit formation in various strains of mice. *Arch. Psychol.*, 1920, No. 43. Pp. 58.

18. BRIGHAM, C. C. Validity of tests in examination of immigrants. *Indus. Psychol.*, 1926, 1, 413–417.

29. BURT, C. General and specific factors underlying the primary emotions. *Rep. Brit. Asso. Adv. Sci.*, 1915, 85, 694–696.

38. CARTER, H. D., PYLES, M. K., & BRETNALL, E. P. A comparative study of factors in vocational interest of high school boys. *J. Educ. Psychol.*, 1935, 26, 81–98.

56. DUNLAP, J. W. The organization of learning and other traits in chickens. *Comp. Psychol. Monog.*, 1933, No. 9. Pp. 55.

69. FLANAGAN, J. C. Factor analysis in the study of personality. Stanford University, Calif.: Stanford Univ. Press, 1935. Pp. 103.

83. GERMAIN, J., & RODRIGO, M. Primeros resultados de un test de inteligencia general. *Arch. de neurobiol.*, 1933, 13, 1189–1221.

121. MARSHALL, A. J. The standardization of Spearman's "measure of intelligence" for Perth, Western Australia. *Aust. Council Educ. Res. Ser.*, 1934, No. 22, 23–50.

122. McCULLOCH, T. L. A study of the cognitive abilities of the white rat with special reference to Spearman's theory of two factors. *Duke Univ. Contrib. Psychol. Theory*, 1935, No. 2. Pp. 66.

132. N. Y. COLLEGE ENTRANCE EXAMINATION BOARD. Reports of the Commission on Scholastic Aptitude Tests, 1926–1935.

135. OATES, D. W. Group factors in temperament qualities. *Brit. J. Psychol.*, 1929, 20, 118–136.

137. PALLISTER, H. The negative or withdrawal attitude: a study in personality organization. *Arch. Psychol.*, 1933, No. 151. Pp. 56.

142. PERRY, R. C. A group factor analysis of the adjustment questionnaire. *So. Calif. Educ. Monog.*, 1934, No. 5. Pp. 93.

161. SMITH, C. E. The construction and validation of a group test of intelligence using the Spearman technique. *Bull. Dept. Educ. Res., Ontario Coll. Educ.*, 1935, No. 5. Pp. 55.

202. STEPHENSON, W. An introduction to so-called motor perseveration tests. *Brit. J. Educ. Psychol.*, 1934, 4, 186–208.

206. STEPHENSON, W., MACKENZIE, M., SIMMONS, C. A., KAPP, D. M., STUDMAN, G. L., & HUBERT, W. H. de B. Spearman factors and psychiatry. *Brit. J. Med. Psychol.*, 1934, 14, 101–135.

238. THORNDIKE, R. L. Organization of behavior in the albino rat. *Genet. Psychol. Monog.*, 1935, 17. Pp. 70.

242. THURSTONE, L. L. A multiple factor study of vocational interests. *Person. J.*, 1931, 10, 198–205.

243. ——. The theory of multiple factors. Chicago: Author, 1933. Pp. 65.

245. ——. The vectors of mind. *Psychol. Rev.*, 1934, 41, 1–32.

247. ——. A vocational interest schedule. *Psychol. Bull.*, 1935, 32, 719.

257. WALTERS, E. H., & THOMAS, F. C. Some notes on the standardization of Professor Spearman's "measure of 'intelligence' for use in schools." *Forum Educ.*, 1929, 7, 35–42.

259. WEBB, E. Character and intelligence. *Brit. J. Psychol., Monog. Suppl.*, 1915, No. 3. Pp. 99.

Faculties *Versus* Factors: A Reply to Professor Thurstone

In a critique of the writer's monograph on "The Influence of Specific Experience upon Mental Organization,"[1] which appeared in the April issue of this journal, Thurstone argues for a conception of factors as "psychological entities." The writer is in complete agreement with Thurstone's premise that investigations of mental organization should become more, rather than less, psychological. But she disagrees with the methods proposed by Thurstone for achieving this purpose, viz., mathematical analysis plus intuition. The problems of mental organization cannot be clarified by hypostatizing psychological entities. Such contemporary psychological mysticism is all the more misleading and confusing because it appears in a quasi-objective, statistical guise.

The concept of factors described by Thurstone represents a return to faculty psychology. The factors identified by mathematical analysis are regarded as underlying psychological entities or abilities which the subject *uses* when he performs a test problem or behaves in response to any stimulus. Thus a sharp dichotomy is introduced between *ability* and *behavior.* These abilities—or faculties, as Thurstone himself calls them—seem to be enjoying an independent existence in a relatively sheltered realm of their own and may remain quite unaffected even when the subject's behavior changes. Thus, for example, Thurstone scoffs at the idea that "the mental organizations of a whole class of children" could possibly be altered in the course of a brief experimental period during which the subjects undergo certain relevant experiences that change their test performance (p. 231).[2] Apparently it would require a much more strenuous and drastic procedure to penetrate into the carefully guarded recesses of the mind where faculties hide!

The writer maintains that to speak in terms of such inferential constructs is not the best way to arrive at psychologically meaningful results. Psychology as an experimental science demands that we remain as close as possible to the objectively observable facts and that we define our concepts operationally.

[1] *Genet. Psychol. Monog.*, 1936, **18**, No. 4, 245-355.
[2] Page references are to Thurstone's critique, *Psychol. Bull.*, 1938, 35, 223-236.

Faculties *versus* factors: A reply to Professor Thurstone. *Psychological Bulletin*, 1938, *35*, 391-395.

From a purely objective and empirical viewpoint, what is factor analysis? It is, in the first place, a descriptive and not an experimental technique. Like all statistical methods, it is a device for concise expression of the relationships existing among observed facts. A "factor" isolated by such analyses is simply a statement of the tendency for certain groups of behavior manifestations to vary concomitantly. It does not indicate the presence of any other characteristic or phenomenon beyond or beneath the concrete behavior. Nor can we penetrate beyond behavior by any amount of rotation of axes. The latter is simply a technique for arriving at the most clearly intelligible description of the obtained relationships; it cannot in any way suggest an *interpretation* of such relationships.

It should be apparent that no method of factor analysis—however refined or wisely chosen—can transform behavior phenomena into independently existing psychological entities, or transcend time and space, or reveal causal relationships. Thus we could not discover primary human abilities by factorizing the test scores obtained by a sampling of twentieth century American college students. Such a procedure can, to be sure, reveal the mental organization of the particular population under consideration and this information would be very valuable in such practical problems as the construction of tests for use with the same population. This information could not, however, be employed in constructing a test for ten-year-old children or for Australian aborigines—the latter groups may have quite a different set of "primary" abilities, owing to their differing experiential backgrounds.

It is doubtful whether anyone who has worked with factor analysis would regard factors as causal. When, however, factors are described in the terminology of faculty psychology and set up as psychological entities and underlying abilities, the layman may easily be misled into thinking of them in terms of cause and effect. From the statement that the individual uses a certain primary ability in performing a given activity to the assertion that the quality of his performance is caused by the amount of the given primary ability which he possesses, is but a short step.

Thurstone objects to certain specific procedures followed by the writer in the investigation under consideration. These points can be considered directly, and independently of the general theoretical questions. Thurstone states that the writer "tried to give a psychological interpretation to her findings, but the experimental arrangement was weak and the factor analysis faulty so that none of the conclusions of the monograph can be justified" (pp. 223–224). Apparently Thurstone believes that the writer's discussion of the factor patterns found in this study did not make "psychological sense" because it did not reveal the presence of certain commonly found group factors such as verbal aptitude, numerical aptitude, etc. This indicates a misunderstanding of the purpose of the study. The writer was not interested in arriving at a descriptive account of the mental organization of sixth grade public school children. Had this been her object, she would have proceeded quite differently. When Thurstone exclaims that "the whole study was lost at the start" and was "ruined by inadequate methods of analysis" (*i.e.* Hotelling's method of principal components), he is referring to a study which the writer never set out to do.

All of these criticisms are based upon the unwarranted assumption that the writer was trying to explore "the" mental organization of her subjects. Had the tests been selected so as to bring out the already existing group factors as clearly as possible, they would have been quite unsuited to the nature of the experiment. Briefly, the writer's essential aim was to determine whether group factors might be *experimentally produced* among tests which initially showed no such common factors. If the original set-up had included several tests to measure each factor or "primary ability," the relationships already existing among such tests would have obscured any additional linkages introduced by the experiment.

Insofar, then, as the nature of this experiment necessitated the choice of tests which were as nearly unrelated as possible at the outset rather than clusters of similar tests, it is apparent that the centroid method would have been of little use. Thurstone himself reports that after trying to apply the centroid method to the writer's data, he had to abandon the attempt because "the number of factors is too large for a psychologically unique solution" (p. 227). This should have been apparent from the nature of the set-up, without the necessity of resorting to "trial and error."

In brief, the writer set out to discover whether the interrelationships among a set of test scores could be altered experimentally, in this case by a brief series of relevant experiences. The result clearly showed that such a change was produced. The factorial analysis by the method of principal components served merely to corroborate further the conclusion which had already been indicated in the correlation coefficients themselves. Rotation of axes would not have been of assistance, insofar as only the *changes* from initial to final testing were of interest. The changes obtained, furthermore, proved to be in the expected direction, when examined in the light of the specific influence of the interpolated experiences. Nor could the change possibly be a mathematical artifact. Since the same test batteries were employed in the initial and final testing, the shifts in factor loadings cannot be attributed to the factorization of tests in differing contexts. The only possible cause for the obtained shift in factor pattern is to be found in the experimentally interpolated experiences.

In summing up the empirical and objective nature of factors as well as their susceptibility to experiential influences, the writer uses the expression "shifting mathematical components." This seems to be particularly annoying to Thurstone. The writer's use of these terms should probably be clarified at this point. The term "shifting" (*not* shifty) refers to the fact that the components or factors are not rigid, fixed, and innate. Thurstone himself admits this (cf. p. 233). In several parts of his critique of the writer's monograph, however, he creates the erroneous impression that the term "shifting" has been used to denote chance or haphazard variations in factor pattern. This was not the case. "Shifting" referred to the changes in factor pattern with the varying experiential background or reactional biography of the subject, as well as to the differences in factor pattern which have been found by several investigators among different age levels and other populations.

The term "mathematical" was used advisedly in order to adhere as closely as possible to an operational definition of factor. It should be noted in this connection that to say a component is mathematical does not imply that it is a mathematical *artifact.* Anyone would admit that the standard deviation of the heights of a group of men is not a physical entity, and yet it is not an artifact. Similarly, a factor can be a mathematical expression rather than a psychological entity, without necessarily being an artifact. To insist that we call a mathematically derived factor a psychological entity does not thereby make it more psychological. Such wishful thinking merely confuses the real issue. The writer would insist, on the contrary, that a better way to introduce "psychological sense" into factor analysis is to employ experimental approaches as she did in the investigation under discussion, and to investigate mental organization in populations with widely varying experiential backgrounds.

And this brings us to our last point. Thurstone makes frequent reference to "psychological sense" as a standard. Although the intention to make sense is indisputably good, one wonders how stable, or valid, or applicable such a criterion may be. Instances are not unknown in which one psychologist's sense is another's nonsense. As a concrete illustration of the difficulty of applying such a subjective criterion, we might mention some of the concepts embodied in the present discussion. Thus when Thurstone states: "We assume that the subjects are using their abilities in producing test performances" (p. 228); or "there may be a biologically more basic faculty that happens to be well represented in numerical work" (p. 235); or "some of the mental faculties may be in the nature of parameters in the dynamics of the physiological system" (p. 235), to the writer these statements do not make psychological sense.

6

Factor Analysis and Traits: Cumulative Evidence on Trait Formation

*The "modifiability" subtheme was discernible in the selections repro-
duced in Chapter 5. It is even more clearly evident in the two papers
reprinted in this chapter. The basic question addressed in these
papers is: "Whence do traits arise?" The first paper, published in
1948, critically analyzed trait concepts and discussed available research on the effect of group differences in prior experience upon
the emergence and interrelationships of intellectual traits, together
with a few more direct studies of experimentally interpolated
experiences.*

*The relevant literature was again surveyed in the 1970 paper. By
that time, a considerable body of research had accumulated, both
from comparative analyses of groups with differing educational,
socioeconomic, occupational, or cultural backgrounds and from experimental investigations utilizing a variety of procedures. The results
generally supported the hypothesis that, not only does the nature of
one's antecedent experiences affect the degree of differentiation of
"intelligence" into distinct abilities, but it also affects the particular
traits that emerge, such as verbal, numerical, or spatial abilities. Thus,
experiential variables may influence not only the level of a person's
intellectual development, but also the trait categories into which his
or her abilities become organized.*

The Nature of Psychological 'Traits'[1]

I do not propose to add another to the many definitions and classifications of traits which have appeared within the past decade. Rather is it my object to inquire into the sources of diversity among trait theories, in the belief that such an analysis will itself help to clarify the problem of traits and to point the way toward significant investigations.

SIMILARITIES AND DIFFERENCES AMONG EXISTING TRAIT THEORIES

First we may ask whether *any* common ground can be found in a survey of existing trait concepts. Reduced to its most elementary terms, a trait may be regarded as a category for the orderly description of the behavior of individuals. Even this simple statement, however, will undoubtedly meet with difficulties. Some may argue over the term 'category'; others will object to 'description'; a few may be alarmed by such a word as 'behavior'; some will resent the *s* in 'individuals'; while a number will give descriptions that are the reverse of orderly!

But if for the moment we keep our eyes firmly fixed upon similarities, even though these similarities may not be universal, we find that most trait theories are concerned with the *organization and interrelationships* of behavior, and are therefore derived from the observation of varied behavior manifestations of the individual. Trait concepts also refer, as a rule, to relatively *enduring* characteristics which thus have some predictive value. In general, they cover those characteristics which appreciably *differentiate* the individual from others. Thus if the observable similarities in a particular mode of response far exceed any individual differences therein, such a characteristic is not likely to be incorporated in current trait schemas. Finally, a *cultural frame of reference* is also evident, although not always explicit, in most trait classifications. It is those aspects of be-

[1] Presidential address delivered at the annual meeting of the Eastern Psychological Association in Atlantic City, New Jersey, April 25, 1947.
The nature of psychological 'traits.' *Psychological Review*, 1948, 55, 127–138. (Pp. 127–131, 136–137, and corresponding references.)

havior which are significant within a particular culture or environmental setting that are usually identified and described as traits.[2]

From this brief overview of the possible points of agreement among trait theories, we may turn to the less taxing search for their disagreements. The *number* of traits proposed varies from a single general factor to innumerable highly specific elements, with the majority of those psychologists who approach traits through the medium of factor analysis favoring a relatively small number of 'group factors' of an intermediate degree of generality. As to *stability,* traits are regarded by some as fixed and immutable throughout life, by others as undergoing a uniform and predetermined course of development with age, by still others as the constantly evolving resultant of the myriad influences which play upon the individual. Similarly, in the degree of *universality* of the proposed traits, theories vary from an implicit belief in a universal pattern of primary human traits, at one extreme, to the insistence that truly significant traits are unique to each individual, at the other. Attempts have also been made, at a highly speculative level, to identify traits with various *anatomical mechanisms,* such as neural patterns or genes. On the other hand, some writers have argued that such identifications are precluded by the very concept of traits as they envisage it. Similarly, traits have been endowed with *causal* properties by some psychologists, while others regard them as theoretical constructs or as points of reference in the classification of behavior.

DESCRIPTIVE APPROACH VERSUS
A SEARCH FOR PRINCIPLES

It is our thesis that this diversity of trait concepts is the result of an underlying methodological limitation which has characterized not only trait studies but many other types of psychological investigations as well. The trait investigator has usually asked: *"What* is the organization of behavior?" or *"What* are the traits into which the individual's behavior repertory groups itself?" rather than asking, *"How* does behavior become organized?" and *"How* do psychological traits develop?" Much of the content of psychology—including trait theories—still consists of generalized factual descriptions rather

---

[2] For typical discussions of the concepts of 'trait,' 'ability,' and 'factor,' as well as proposed schemas of classification, *cf.* Allport (1), Burt (11, 12), Carr and Kingsbury (13, 14), R. B. Cattell (15), Guilford (23, 24), Thurstone (38), and Tryon (39). For a recent survey of methods and results of factor analysis, *cf.* Wolfle (46).

than principles of behavior.[3] It represents a cataloguing of responses within a specific (although not usually specified) setting, without reference to the conditions which bring about such responses. Within the typical textbook, for example, one finds an account of how the individual looks and acts—and possibly how he feels—when angry or afraid or elated; or a discussion of the stages through which the child passes in learning to climb stairs, pick up objects, or talk English; or a compilation of the drives which motivate behavior; or a listing of primary mental abilities.

Such content has been criticized by students of comparative culture as being 'community-centric' (34). It has been argued that textbooks of so-called general psychology are in large part textbooks of the 'psychology' of people in western Europe and America. A good portion of their content might in fact be characterized as the psychology of "American college students and urban school children." When emotional expressions, or stages of child development, for example, are checked in different cultures, the results are quite dissimilar to those reported in the typical text which purports to cover human behavior. The writings of many anthropologists and social psychologists furnish a rich source of illustrations of such behavior divergencies in different cultures (cf., e.g., 26, 34).

The factuo-descriptive approach is at once too narrow and too broad. From the viewpoint of comparative culture, its findings have proved to be too narrow. The clinical psychologist, on the other hand, often complains that it is too broad for his purposes. This is the basis for the aversion to what has been inappropriately labeled the 'nomothetic' approach. By definition, a nomothetic approach is one which seeks fundamental laws and principles. The clinician objects to so-called nomothetic generalizations because they yield only crude approximations of the individual cases with which he must deal. But it is not against the *principles* of behavior that he is actually arguing. It is against the generalized—or perhaps unduly overgeneralized—factual descriptions that his criticism is in effect directed.[4] The truly nomothetic principles of behavior apply equally to all individuals and will in fact explain the very uniqueness of each individual's behavior in terms of the unique combination of antecedent conditions.

It is no real solution to revert to the solitary contemplation of one individual. To do so is simply to substitute an individuo-centrism

---

[3] *Cf., e.g.,* the discussion of this point by Foley (18, 19).

[4] Essentially the same point has been made by Chein (16), who discusses the confusion between 'law' and 'statistical generalization' with special reference to Allport's *Psychology of Personality* (1).

for the community-centrism of many current psychological general-izations.[5] At best this would only yield information known to be applicable to a single subject, information whose usefulness would quietly expire with the demise of that privileged individual. But actually, if followed seriously and faithfully, such an individuo-centric method would not even furnish that much information. It is doubtful whether any understanding of such an individual could be achieved without previous familiarity with at least a few behavior principles which had been discovered under controlled conditions. It is as if a physician attempted to diagnose a case of cancer or appendi-citis through a prolonged and sympathetic observation of his patient, but without benefit of any of the experimental findings of physi-ology, histology, chemistry, and other nomothetic disciplines.

To repeat, the factuo-descriptive approach yields approximate knowledge of relatively restricted groups of individuals. Such knowl-edge is neither sufficiently extensive—*i.e.,* applicable outside the cultural setting in which it was obtained, nor sufficiently intensive—*i.e.,* completely and precisely applicable to any one individual. Principles of behavior, on the other hand, are at once universal and precisely applicable to each individual.[6] It is only through a search for principles, therefore, and not through anti-scientific revolts and individuo-centric procedures, that we can transcend the limitations of the factuo-descriptive approach.[7]

THE THEORETICAL IMPLICATIONS OF FACTUAL INCONSISTENCIES IN TRAIT RESEARCH

A survey of recent trait studies reveals various superficial incon-sistencies, which we would expect to find because of the predomi-nantly factuo-descriptive approach of such investigations. The diversity of trait concepts which have been proposed is closely paralleled by a diversity of factual material collected in descriptively oriented research.

---

[5] For further critical discussions of this point, see Bills (9) and Guilford (23).

[6] Hull (25) has suggested, for example, that innate individual and species differences may be represented by 'empirical constants' in the equations expressing the laws of behavior.

[7] Most trait concepts, whether derived from clinical observations or factor analysis, provide at best only statements of response-response relationships, which have no tie-up with the stimulus variables and are therefore of dubious value in prediction and control of behavior. *Cf.,* in this connection, the comprehensive analysis of theory construction in psy-chology by Spence (35).

'Intellectual' and 'Emotional' Traits

In the search for the *conditions* associated with this diversity of results, we first come upon a differentiation between studies concerned with 'abilities,' or *intellectual traits,* and those concerned with *emotional traits* or 'personality characteristics' in the popular sense. In studies on intellectual characteristics, the emphasis has generally been on 'common traits,' such as those discovered by factor analysis—traits which are common to large groups of people. Verbal, numerical, and spatial factors are among the now familiar 'traits' which have been identified in various factor pattern analyses. On the other hand, students of 'personality,'[8] concerned primarily with the emotional and motivational aspects of behavior, have more often argued for 'individual traits,' rejecting common traits as unrealistic, artificial, and abstract. Some have maintained that they find it more useful to describe each individual in terms of his own peculiar behavior relationships, rather than to look for common patterns of relationship shared by many individuals. Factor pattern analyses of emotional and motivational characteristics have also yielded results which are less consistent and more difficult to interpret than in the case of intellectual characteristics.[9]

Whether found by factor analysis, type studies, or genetic and biographical observation of a single individual, a trait is always essentially a pattern of relationship within the individual's behavior. The so-called 'common trait,' located by studying a group of persons rather than a single individual, is simply a generalized description of a pattern of behavior relationship which is shared by a group of individuals. Why, then, have such common traits found more support in studies of the intellectual aspects of behavior than in those dealing with its emotional and motivational aspects?

The reason is not difficult to find when we consider the greater

---

[8] *Cf., e.g.,* Allport (1).

[9] *Type theories* may be regarded as an attempted compromise between the two extremes of common and individual traits. Such theories imply essentially a pattern of behavior relationships shared by a relatively limited group, narrower than the groups to which the common traits of factor analysis are ascribed. It might be added parenthetically that the use of so-called inverted factor analysis, in which the rôle of persons and tests is reversed in computing correlation coefficients, is not fundamentally different from the more usual procedure of locating traits. Type theorists have enthusiastically claimed inverted factor analysis as their own special method, adapted to the discovery of types rather than common traits. As Cyril Burt (11) has clearly demonstrated, however, the same group factors will emerge whether we begin by correlating tests or persons. Ultimately, both procedures deal with the relationships among the responses of persons to test stimuli. Whether we begin our analysis with tests or with persons will make no difference in the relationships which we find in the end.

uniformity and standardization of experience in the intellectual than in the emotional and motivational sphere. An obvious illustration of this fact is furnished by our system of formal education in which the standardized content of instruction is directed towards intellectual rather than emotional development. Furthermore, even if the schools were to institute a rigidly standardized curriculum of 'personality development' (a rather depressing thought!), we still would not find the uniformities of organization characteristic of intellectual development, since much of the individual's emotional development occurs through domestic or recreational activities. Not only educational courses, but also occupations and other traditional areas of activity within any one cultural setting tend to crystallize the individual's intellectual development into relatively uniform patterns. Such patterns become more clearly evident the longer the individual has been exposed to these common experiences.[10] Those aspects of behavior in which the individual's activities are less standardized in our culture will exhibit a correspondingly more idiosyncratic organization into traits. A further reason for the greater standardization of intellectual responses is the relative degree to which these responses have been verbalized, as contrasted to emotional responses which are more largely unverbalized.[11] It is also relevant to point out that the very distinction between intellectual and emotional aspects of behavior is itself culturally determined.

Nature of Subjects

A second major source of diversity in trait research is associated with the type of subject under investigation. We may consider in this connection the categories of age, educational level, occupation, sex, cultural grouping, and species. *Age differences* in the pattern of trait organization have now been quite clearly established. Correlation studies on preschool children show a large general factor, frequently identified with 'intelligence,' with little or no specialization into group factors. Among school children, the weight of the general factor decreases with increasing age, and group factors of memory, verbal, numerical, spatial, and other aptitudes appear. The independence of these factors from each other tends to increase with age. Studies on college students have consistently shown prominent and relatively independent group factors, with only a negligible general

---

[10] A similar point has been made by John E. Anderson (5) in reference to the feasibility of *measurement* within different areas of behavior as well as at different ages.

[11] A point made as early as 1924, by John B. Watson (44, pp. 130–131).

factor. The latter, furthermore, is more closely identified with verbal ability among the older subjects. The increasing differentiation of ability and clearer emergence of specialized traits with age has been demonstrated both by the comparison of subjects of different age levels and by the more direct approach of re-testing the same children at successive ages.[12]

Such a developmental approach to trait organization is a step toward the reconciliation of factual divergencies. No longer need we be disturbed by the fact that an investigator who obtains his data from fifth grade school children seems to support a general factor theory, such as Spearman's 'g,' whereas another investigator, testing college sophomores, 'proves' the presence of verbal, numerical, spatial, or other aptitudes which are almost completely uncorrelated with each other. Both are demonstrating the differentiation of traits with increasing age.

In discussions of age changes, however, there is often a tacit implication that maturational processes are involved, that the changes would occur regardless of what the individuals had been doing during those years. This is not a matter for assumption, but rather for investigation. Other group comparisons need to be made in the effort to clarify the source of the obtained age differences. Some of these comparisons have been made, but the available data are not so extensive as in the case of age differences. In fact, the information is often so meager as to do no more than point the way for a type of comparative investigation which should be pursued as thoroughly as has been done with age. . . .[a]

In summary, it has been the object of this paper to demonstrate that the diversity of trait concepts as well as the apparent factual inconsistencies in trait research result in large part from a predominantly factuo-descriptive approach. It is suggested that the greater consistency and ease of identification of traits in the intellectual as contrasted to the emotional aspects of behavior illustrate the greater cultural standardization of activities in the former category. The comparison of factor patterns among subjects differing in age, education, occupation, sex, cultural grouping, and species contributes towards an understanding of the conditions under which traits develop and presents a fruitful field for future research. A more direct approach is the experimental manipulation of behavior organization through the interpolation of relevant controlled activities. The problem of 'traits' is seen as but one illustration of the need for a more

---

[12] For a comprehensive summary of the data on age differentiation of intellectual traits, *cf.* Garrett (20).

[a] The deleted portions report the scattered research findings then available, which have been incorporated in the fuller coverage provided in the following paper.—Ed.

active search for the underlying behavior principles which unify the superficial divergencies of the descriptive approach.

REFERENCES CITED IN EXCERPT
(as originally numbered)

1. Allport, G. W. *Personality: A psychological interpretation.* New York: Holt, 1937. Pp. 588.
5. Anderson, J. E. Freedom and constraint or potentiality and environment. *Psychol. Bull.,* 1944, 41, 1–29.
9. Bills, A. G. Changing views of psychology as a science. PSYCHOL. REV., 1938, 45, 377–394.
11. Burt, C. *The factors of the mind: An introduction to factor-analysis in psychology.* New York: Macmillan, 1941. Pp. 509.
12. ——. Mental abilities and mental factors. *Brit. J. Educ. Psychol.,* 1944, 14, 85–89.
13. Carr, H., & Kingsbury, F. A. The concept of ability. PSYCHOL. REV., 1938, 45, 354–376.
14. ——. The concept of traits. PSYCHOL. REV., 1938, 45, 497–524.
15. Cattell, R. B. *Description and measurement of personality.* Yonkers: World Book Co., 1946. Pp. 602.
16. Chein, I. Personality and typology. In Harriman, P. (Ed.), *Twentieth century psychology.* New York: Philos. Library, 1946. Pp. 94–115.
18. Foley, J. P., Jr. Psychological "ultimates": A note on psychological "fact" versus psychological "law." *J. gen. Psychol.,* 1936, 15, 455–458.
19. ——. The scientific psychology of individual and group differences. *J. soc. Psychol.,* 1938, 9, 375–377.
20. Garrett, H. E. A developmental theory of intelligence. *Amer. Psychol.,* 1946, 1, 372–378.
23. Guilford, J. P. Unitary traits of personality and factor theory. *Amer. J. Psychol.,* 1936, 48, 673–680.
24. ——. Human abilities. PSYCHOL. REV., 1940, 47, 367–394.
25. Hull, C. L. The place of innate individual and species differences in a natural-science theory of behavior. PSYCHOL. REV., 1945, 52, 55–60.
26. Klineberg, O. *Race differences.* New York: Harper, 1935. Pp. 367.
34. Sherif, M. *The psychology of social norms.* New York: Harper, 1936. Pp. 209.
35. Spence, K. W. The nature of theory construction in contemporary psychology. PSYCHOL. REV., 1944, 51, 47–68.
38. Thurstone, L. L. Current issues in factor analysis. *Psychol. Bull.,* 1940, 37, 189–236.
39. Tryon, R. C. A theory of *psychological* components—an alternative to "mathematical factors." PSYCHOL. REV., 1935, 42, 425–454.
44. Watson, J. B. *Behaviorism.* New York: Norton, 1924. Pp. 251.
46. Wolfle, D. L. Factor analysis in 1940. *Psychometr. Monogr.,* 1940, No. 3. Pp. 69.

On the Formation of Psychological Traits[1]

It is a special privilege to give this first lecture of the Robert Choate Tryon Memorial Lectureship. I welcome the opportunity to honor an outstanding psychologist and a valued friend. In choosing a topic related to one of Dr. Tryon's own contributions, I had a wide field available to me. There was, of course, his pioneer research on behavior genetics (Tryon, 1940) and the subsequent methodological and theoretical developments that continued to engage his efforts over the years (Hirsch & Tryon, 1956; Tryon, 1963). There were his many contributions to statistical method, especially within the area of factor analysis (Tryon, 1939, 1967). That the work of a single psychologist should span the genetics of animal behavior and the techniques of factor analysis is itself a striking indication of the unusual breadth of Dr. Tryon's activities. His applications of factor-analytic methodology to substantive problems gave further evidence of the varied and innovative nature of his research. To cite only one example, his cluster analysis of census data for different neighborhoods (Tryon, 1955, 1968) represents one of the early uses of factor-analytic techniques with variables other than test scores—and it highlighted the need for analyzing the variables of man's cultural environment with the same thoroughness traditionally followed with organismic variables.

What I finally chose as the point of departure for my talk was a 1935 article in the *Psychological Review* that illustrates still another facet of Dr. Tryon's contributions, namely, his theoretical insight into the nature and origins of psychological traits (Tryon, 1935).

Let me first clarify some terms. When psychologists speak of the development of traits, they usually refer to the level or amount of a given trait that the individual manifests at different times, as when plotting growth curves or learning curves. The term "trait pattern" is employed in more than one sense but usually signifies the relative amounts of different traits displayed by an individual or group. Thus, cultural differences in trait patterns characteristically pertain to the

[1] First Annual Robert Choate Tryon Memorial Lecture presented at the University of California at Berkeley, February 26, 1970.

On the formation of psychological traits. *American Psychologist*, 1970, *25*, 899–910.

relative performance of different cultural groups in, for example, verbal, numerical, and spatial tests (e.g., Lesser, Fifer, & Clark, 1965). If Group A scores highest in verbal and lowest in spatial tests, while Group B scores lowest in verbal and highest in spatial tests, these findings are reported as a group difference in trait patterns.

In the factor-analytic literature, on the other hand, trait pattern traditionally connotes the very dimensions or traits identified by factor analysis and in terms of which the performance of individuals or groups may then be described. It is with trait patterns in this sense that the present discussion is concerned. How does behavior become organized into traits? What do we know about the origin or emergence of behavioral traits? It is apparent that these questions do concern the development of traits or trait patterns, but because of the alternative connotations of these terms I have chosen the less familiar expression, "formation of psychological traits."

Insofar as the traits under consideration are those identified by factor-analytic techniques, the question of trait formation becomes essentially an inquiry into the causes of correlation among different behavioral samples, as represented, for example, by test scores. It should be added that for simplicity the discussion will be limited to abilities. The same mechanisms, however, would undoubtedly apply to the formation of personality traits, albeit the specific substantive details might differ.

THEORETICAL ANALYSES OF TRAIT FORMATION

From the earliest discussions of trait organization, one can find explicit recognition of the fact that factor-analytic techniques yield only descriptive categories and that different schemas of classification are applicable to the same data. This approach to factors has been more fully presented in the writings of British investigators, such as Burt (1941, 1954), Thomson (1916, 1948), and Vernon 1961, 1969). These writers, moreover, have gone on to explain the empirically identified group or general factors in terms of the overlap or association of innumerable intrinsically unrelated determiners. To be sure, other factor analysts have occasionally expressed agreement with these interpretations of factors. Thus, even Thurstone (1940) observed in one of his articles that factors should not be regarded as ultimate psychological entities but rather as "functional unities" or aggregates of more elementary components. His treatment of factors in other publications and especially his continued use of the term "primary mental abilities," however, strongly suggest the concept of factors as relatively permanent, underlying, causal entities.

In his 1935 article, Tryon explored the process of trait formation fully and systematically, proposing a psychological interpretation of factors and outlining three mechanisms whereby correlations among specific behavioral determinants may develop. First, he suggested that the elementary psychological components of behavior are concepts and conceptual relations, which themselves evolve when the appropriate environmental stimuli occur in conjunction with an adequate conceptual background in the behaving organism. This process thus recognizes the need for a suitable set of stimuli or external environmental field, as might be provided by an educational program, as well as the prerequisite antecedent conceptual development of the organism.

To account for correlation among different psychological measures, such as test scores, Tryon proposed three mechanisms: overlap of psychological components, correlation between independent environmental fields, and correlation between independent gene blocks. The major source of correlation he attributed to overlap among the many conceptual components brought into play by different tasks. The magnitude of correlation between two tests, he argued, depends on the extent to which they "sample similar universes of conceptual components." The correlations among different intelligence tests, for example, are generally high, "not because some mystic general factor saturates them all heavily, but because all these tests sample to a marked extent the same complex welter of concepts determining vocabulary, reading, and arithmetic abilities [Tryon, 1935, p. 450]." Intercorrelations among tests or test items also depend in part on the breadth of application or generality of the individual concepts themselves. For instance, the concept expressed by the verb "to sing" has much more limited applicability than does the concept corresponding to the verb "to be."

A second source of correlation among test scores is to be found in the correlation between the environmental fields in which the different psychological components originated. This can be illustrated by the fact that a child reared in a cultural milieu that provides environmental fields eliciting superior verbal concepts tends also to be exposed to environmental fields eliciting superior numerical concepts. The third source of test correlation, arising from the correlation of independent gene blocks, is attributed to assortative mating. Since individuals tend to marry within their own general socioeconomic and educational level, persons superior in quite different respects are likely to interbreed. Their offspring would thus tend to receive genes for superior development in a number of initially unrelated characteristics; and the same type of selection would occur in the interbreeding of persons of diverse inferiority.

It should be noted that cultural factors may operate in all three of the mechanisms described by Tryon. The nature and breadth of concepts available to an individual in solving a problem or performing an intellectual task obviously vary not only with the language he has been taught but also with many other aspects of his cultural background. Culture also determines which environmental fields covary in quality in the individual's experiences. From another angle, it determines which environmental fields are encountered in the same temporal or spatial context, as when different academic subjects are included in an organized educational curriculum, or when different topics are covered within a single course. Similarly, cultural factors provide the opportunities and social pressures that encourage inbreeding within subcultures or social classes having certain common characteristics. From these considerations it follows that different traits may be formed in different cultures.

Approaching the question from a somewhat different angle, Ferguson (1954, 1956) proposed an explanation of the formation of factors in terms of transfer of training. Regarding abilities as prior overlearned acquisitions, he attributed correlation among abilities to the result of positive transfer. According to Ferguson, abilities emerge through a process of differential transfer. Because cultural factors influence what the child shall learn at each age, moreover, different cultural environments lead to the development of different ability patterns. The breadth of the transfer effect determines whether the resulting factor is a broad one, like verbal comprehension, or a narrow one, like a specialized perceptual skill. Traditional intelligence tests measure intellectual skills that transfer widely to tasks in our culture. Similarly, many of the skills acquired through formal schooling, as in reading or arithmetic computation, are applicable to a wide variety of subsequent learning situations. Individual differences in the extent to which these skills have been developed will thus be reflected in the performance of many different tasks. In a factor analysis of such tasks, these widely applicable skills would emerge as broad group factors.

From still another angle, Whiteman (1964) pointed to a relation between the formation of learning sets, as illustrated in Harlow's classic experiments with monkeys (Harlow, 1949, 1960), and the development of factors. Establishing a learning set to differentiate between certain shapes, such as triangle and circle, enabled the animal to learn more rapidly when presented with a new problem requiring the differentiation of *other* shapes. The animal had established a learning set for differentiating shapes: he knew what to look for when faced with a new problem. Differences in the amount of such prior shape-discrimination experience or in the degree to which the individual had profited from this experience would be reflected in individual differences in the strength of the learning set. These individual differences would in turn increase the correlation among all tasks to which such a learning set was applicable. Whiteman (1964) also relates trait formation to Piaget's concept of operations, as does Hunt (1961). For the present purpose, the most relevant features of Piaget's operations are their intersituational or intertask consistency, their development through the organism's interaction with his environment, and their progressive organization into a hierarchy of increasing complexity.

The similarities among these explanations of the origin of factors in terms of generality of concepts, extent of transfer effects, and the intersituational applicability of learning sets and operations should now be evident. Still other writers have focused on other mechanisms of factor formation. While recognizing the importance of transfer and learning sets, Vernon (1961, 1969) repeatedly cites examples of the emergence of factors through contiguous educational experiences. Thus, what he designates as the broad verbal-educational factor (v:ed) is commonly found across intellectual functions taught in school, and its nature and breadth may vary in different cultures as a function of varying content coverage in formal schooling. Narrower group factors are likewise seen to be associated with the organization of course content in different types of schools or training programs.

In a discussion of the factors of verbal achievement, Carroll (1966) refers to several possible mechanisms for the emergence of factors, among which he lists prerequisite learning, transfer, and contiguous occurrence in experience. Commenting on these mechanisms, he writes: "Note, now, that this last possibility makes no appeal to any psychological considerations about the two responses; it merely refers to the actuarial fact of their co-occurrence, beyond chance, in the particular sample under study [p. 408]." Much of Carroll's further discussion centers around the operation of this mechanism of co-occurrence through the clustering of experiences in the school, the home, and the community.

AGE CHANGES

Now we may turn from these theoretical analyses of trait formation to some illustrative empirical investigations. Such studies may be grouped under three principal approaches: developmental, comparative, and experimental.

Since the mid-1930s, a fairly large number of factor-analytic studies followed a developmental approach, at least in the sense that trait patterns were investigated in different age groups. Few utilized longitudinal procedures. After surveying the results of research conducted prior to 1946 on groups ranging from preschool children to college students, Garrett (1946) concluded that "intelligence" is relatively undifferentiated in early childhood and becomes increasingly specialized with age. Later investigations raised doubts regarding this simple differentiation hypothesis. As a group, they yielded highly inconsistent results regarding age trends in factor patterns (see Anastasi, 1958, p. 358, for references). A careful analysis of these studies, however, led Burt (1954) to the conclusion that their contradictory findings resulted from methodological deficiencies. Having himself proposed an age differentiation hypothesis as early as 1919, Burt reaffirmed his position after this survey of intervening research.

When one considers the remarkable potpourri of tests, subject characteristics, and factor-analytic techniques represented by studies purporting to test the differentiation hypothesis, it is not surprising that every possible trend (or lack of trend) can be found in their results. Many of the studies failed to provide an adequate test of the hypothesis because unsuitable instruments or statistical techniques were employed; some failed to maintain comparability in test content, reliability, or variability at different age levels; in still others, the subjects employed at different age levels were not comparable in other important respects, or the age range covered was too narrow to permit the detection of age trends.

Another notable limitation of many of these studies stems from their failure to consider what experiences the subjects were undergoing during the time spans covered. To be sure, both Burt and Garrett explained age differentiation chiefly in terms of maturation rather than experiential factors. But the data become more intelligible when examined in the light of the previously considered hypotheses of trait formation. What are the implications of such hypotheses? On the one hand, exposure to a more or less standardized educational curriculum in our culture should lead to the emergence of a very broad factor, variously designated as Spearman's *g*, intelligence, or Vernon's verbal-educational factor. Those children who receive better schooling, or who for motivational or any other reasons profit more from their schooling, will tend to excel in all the abilities fostered by the school curriculum; those exposed to poorer schooling or who respond less favorably to the school experience will tend to fall behind in the same combination of academic abilities. The resulting broad factor can be more clearly identified in educationally heterogeneous groups and may appear of negligible magnitude when factor analyses are carried out in fairly homogeneous samples.

On the other hand, as the child advances through school, the academic curriculum becomes increasingly structured and differentiated into traditional subject matter areas. Thus, his instruction in verbal and numerical areas comes gradually to be separated into different class periods and eventually is even given by different teachers and possibly in different classrooms. Similar separations occur with regard to instructional areas involving predominantly perceptual or spatial abilities, as in art, mechanical drawing, shop work, and other "practical" subjects. This differentiation of academic experiences is accompanied by the increasing prominence of somewhat narrower group factors, such as those represented by Thurstone's primary mental abilities or Guilford's Structure of Intellect model. It is with this type of change over time that the proponents of the differentiation hypothesis have been concerned.

When we examine relevant research conducted since 1960 with appropriate procedures and more carefully controlled conditions, the results do in fact indicate an increasing differentiation of group factors from early childhood to late adolescence (Dye & Very, 1968; Lienert & Crott, 1964; Mukherjee, 1962; Osborne & Lindsey, 1967; Quereshi, 1967). By way of illustration, we may consider a study by Quereshi (1967), in which 14 test scores were separately factor analyzed in seven groups of 100 children each, ranging in age from 3 to 9 years. The factor-analytic techniques employed ensured that the same general and group factors would be identified in each age group. Increasing differentiation of performance with age was demonstrated in three ways. First, the percentage of variance attributable to the general factor decreased consistently with age from 41.3% to 22.8%. Second, with only minor exceptions, the percentage of variance attributable to each group factor increased with age. Third, the mean intercorrelation among the factors decreased with age from .68 at age 3 to .38 at age 9.

A word should be added about age changes in factor patterns among adults. Although several investigators have reported such adult data as evidence for or against the differentiation hypothesis, it should be noted that this hypothesis as originally formulated was restricted to developmental changes in childhood and adolescence. Moreover, the interpretation of such differentiation in terms of school experience cannot be extrapolated to adults who have completed their education. Beyond maturity, subsequent individual experiences vary too widely to suggest any clear hypothesis applicable throughout a culture. Different factor patterns might be expected to develop, for example, in persons pursuing different occupations.

It is nevertheless interesting to observe that when the older subgroups in an adult sample have had less education than the younger, or when their level of performance is significantly lower than that of the younger, the older groups usually show *less* differentiation of abilities than do the younger (Balinsky, 1941; Green & Berkowitz, 1964; Lienert & Crott, 1964; Weiner, 1964). Greater educational heterogeneity in the older groups would also have the effect of increasing the relative weight of the general factor and decreasing the contribution of the narrower group factors (Balinsky, 1941; Weiner, 1964).

GROUP DIFFERENCES

A second major type of investigation is characterized by a comparative approach to the understanding of trait formation. Trait patterns have been compared among groups differing in type of educational program, socioeconomic level, sex, and national or other broad cultural categories. In order to test hypotheses arising from the previously cited theoretical analyses of the origin of factors, several conditions need to be met. The investigator must administer a fairly large number of suitable tests to sufficiently large groups; he must employ appropriate factor-analytic techniques; and he must have access to at least some data regarding relevant cultural and other experiential variables. These conditions are admittedly difficult to meet in any one study. Consequently, few if any available studies provide definitive or clearly interpretable data on trait formation. What we find instead is a number of interesting leads and provocative results, frequently gathered incidentally in connection with the investigation of other problems.

Both *educational* and *socioeconomic* differences in factor patterns were found by Filella (1960) in a study of high school students in Colombia, South America. In all groups, two factors were identified in a battery of six tests, representing an adaptation of the Differential Aptitude Tests for use in Colombia. The nature of these factors, however, varied among the groups, as indicated by the tests yielding high loadings in each factor. Among boys enrolled in technical high schools, the two factors could best be described as quantitative reasoning and spatial-mechanical reasoning. In this group, the two verbal tests in the battery had marginally low loadings in one or the other of these factors. Among academic high school boys, on the other hand, the same tests revealed a verbal and a nonverbal factor.

Socioeconomic differences were explored by comparing factor patterns in public and private high schools, in which an identical curriculum was followed but the students differed in socioeconomic level. A major difference between these two groups was to be found in the sharper differentiation between verbal and nonverbal factors in the private school group. One indication of this difference was the lower correlation between the oblique axes in the private than in the public high school group (.42 versus .77). In addition, a number of differences were observed in the relative weights of the two factors in specific tests, suggesting certain differences in the nature of these factors. Thus, in the public high school group, the verbal factor appears to be a broad academic factor (akin to Vernon's v:ed), while the nonverbal factor is more nearly a spatial factor. In the private high school group, on the other hand, the nonverbal factor appears to be primarily an abstract reasoning factor; and the verbal factor emerges in the strictly verbal tests, with some additional loading in mechanical reasoning problems, which these students may solve largely in verbal terms.

A similar study was conducted in England by Dockrell (1966). Taking as his point of departure the theoretical orientation provided by Ferguson (1954) and Vernon (1961), Dockrell hypothesized certain differences in the degree of differentiation as well as in the nature of group factors as a function of both social class and secondary school curriculum. A battery of 10 tests covering verbal and nonverbal aptitudes, linguistic and numerical skills, and practical or spatial ability was administered to 10-, 12-, and 14-year-old school children classified according to father's occupation into middle and lower social groups. The 12- and 14-year groups, who were attending secondary schools, were also subdivided with reference to type of school attended, including academic, technical, and general. With regard to social class, the results confirmed the hypothesis that the middle class would show more differentiation of ability than the lower class. This finding agrees with those reported by Filella (1960) for Colombian students and by Mitchell (1956) in a study of American school children. In Dockrell's study, differentiation also occurred at an earlier age in the middle than in the lower class.

Comparisons among types of secondary schools in Dockrell's study revealed more differentiation of abilities in the academic and technical schools than in the general schools. The general factor accounted for the largest proportion of battery variance in the general school group, less in the academic school group, and least in the technical school group. Moreover, these differences among schools increased from the 12-year-old to the 14-year-old group. As in Filella's study, verbal skills tended to be more clearly differentiated in the academic schools, while spatial and numerical skills tended to be more highly differentiated in the technical schools. In this connection, mention may also be made of similar variations in the organization of abilities reported by Vernon (1961, pp. 116–120) from factor-analytic studies of several groups of technicians in the British military services.

Relevant data are also reported by Sutherland (1960) who compared the performance of students exposed to departmentalized and nondepartmentalized school instruction. The SRA Primary Mental Abilities Tests were administered to students enrolled in Grades 6–10 in four school systems in Kentucky. Departmentalized instruction, whereby each subject is taught by a different teacher, was introduced at different grade levels in the different school systems. Separate analyses by age and type of instruction suggested a possible effect of departmentalization on trait organization. The correlations between verbal and numerical subtests revealed a significant decrease approximately two to three years following the introduction of departmentalization. The spatial subtests, which are less closely related to school instruction, showed no consistent changes in their correlations with other subtests.

There is a considerable body of scattered data regarding *sex differences* in factor patterns. A number of early studies conducted in the United States and Great Britain at the elementary, high school, and college levels indicated greater differentiation of those abilities in which each sex excels (see Anastasi, 1948, pp. 133–134). For example, girls excelled in verbal tests and also yielded higher intercorrelations among verbal tests and lower correlations between verbal and other types of tests than did boys. Thus, among girls, verbal aptitude showed more evidence of having become differentiated into an identifiable trait. The same was true of memory tests, in which girls likewise excelled. In numerical and spatial tests, the reverse was true, boys excelling in mean scores and also providing more evidence of trait differentiation.

Several more recent studies report sex differences in the number, nature, or distinctness of factors identified in male and female groups (Avakian, 1961; Dye & Very, 1968; Filella, 1960; Irvine, 1969; Lindsey, 1966; Tyler, 1951; Very, 1967). In a few instances, interesting parallelisms are noted between sex differences in educational curricula or other cultural experiences and the particular differences in factor patterns found between the sexes (Filella, 1960; Irvine, 1969). Some investigations provide further evidence for the association of ability level with degree of differentiation in particular areas. Thus, in a study on primary school children, two verbal factors were required to account for the test performance of girls, while a single verbal factor was sufficient for the boys (Lindsey, 1966). An investigation on high school students identified two spatial-visualization factors among boys in addition to a spatial factor found for both sexes (Very, 1967).

Some investigators have approached the relation between *ability level* and trait differentiation more directly. In an early study, Segel (1948) compared the intercorrelations among some of the primary mental abilities tests and other linguistic and mathematical tests in two contrasted groups of ninth-grade boys selected on the basis of total scores on the battery. There was a clear tendency for the correlations to be lower in the high-scoring group, suggesting greater differentiation in the more able individuals. Similarly, in a factor-analytic investigation of normal six-year-old children and institutionalized retardates of the same mental age, Myers and his associates (Myers et al., 1962) found more clearly differentiated abilities in the normal children. Lienert and Crott (1964) report a number of German studies which corroborate these findings with subjects at several intellectual and age levels. Differences were found with regard to magnitude of mean intercorrelations among tests, number of factors isolated, and weights of the first centroid in individual variables. The same authors even cite supporting data from psychopharmacology. In a study by Lienert (1964), the experimental lowering of performance by pharmacological stress (LSD or alcohol) was accompanied by a dedifferentiation of the factor structure. From still another angle, Manley (1965) found different factor loadings in concept attainment tasks when comparing "solvers" with "nonsolvers."

The correspondence between all these findings and the previously reported results on age and educational differences in both children and adults is clearly evident. It is also interesting to note that Ferguson (1954) deduced the relationship between ability level and trait differentiation from his transfer theory, concluding that "as the learning of a particular task continues, the ability to perform it becomes gradually differentiated from . . . other abilities [p. 110]."

The decade of the 1960s has seen an increasing number of *cross-cultural studies* of trait organization (Das, 1963; Guthrie, 1963; Guttman & Guttman, 1963; Irvine, 1969; Vandenberg, 1959; 1966; Vernon, 1965, 1969). Factor analysis has been applied to the results of test batteries administered in Israel, India, the Scottish Hebrides, the Philippines, the West Indies, and several African nations; to Indian and Eskimo boys in Canada; and to Chinese and Latin American students in the United States.

In one of the most far-flung of these projects, Vernon (1965, 1969) administered an extensive and highly diversified battery of individual and group tests to school boys in southeastern England, the Hebrides, Jamaica, and Uganda, and to Indian and Eskimo boys in Canada. The number tested in each group varied from 40 to 50, except that the English sample used for normative purposes numbered 100. Testing was followed by individual interviews to elicit background information.

Although Vernon's factor patterns exhibited many cross-cultural similarities, some noteworthy differences were found which appeared to have a basis in cultural characteristics. For example, in the Hebrides and in Jamaica, the verbal-educational factor was actually a general factor, having substantial loadings not only in educational tests but also in many tests of a noneducational nature. In other words, verbal, reasoning, perceptual, and spatial abilities were less clearly differentiated in these groups. In the light of its correlation with certain background factors, this broad verbal-educational factor was interpreted as reflecting the extent of assimilation of the culture represented by the schools. In Uganda, on the other hand, no general factor was found, but only a verbal-educational factor that was quite distinct from other aspects of cognitive functioning. It had negligible loadings, for example, in the Progressive Matrices and Draw-a-Man tests. These tests would thus have little or no predictive value for school work in this culture, where educational achievement depends so heavily on the specific ability to acquire the English language. Vernon (1969) identified another broad factor in the Uganda data, with loadings in many of the performance and nonverbal tests, which he described as "an ability to cope with perceptual analysis, concrete operations, and the world of objects, quite distinct from educational attainments [p. 187]."

Another extensive investigation was that conducted by Irvine (1969) on several thousand elementary and high school students in Kenya, Zambia, and Rhodesia. The batteries consisted of group tests covering verbal, numerical, spatial, mechanical, and perceptual content. Cross-cultural uniformities in the loadings of certain broad factors were attributed by Irvine to uniformity of education in the British-style schools attended by his samples. The greatest uniformities of factorial composition were found in overlearned drill skills, such as language usage and the mechanics of arithmetic. On the other hand, perceptual and reasoning skills requiring manipulation of nonverbal stimuli showed much less factorial consistency, being more dependent on culturally diverse learning outside of school.

It should be added that cross-cultural studies usually employ selected samples, because the individuals who attend school are generally more highly assimilated to the Western culture than are those not in school. Moreover, the test batteries administered in such studies are frequently overloaded with tests requiring the intellectual skills taught in these Western-style schools. Such a choice of tests is understandable in cultures that are in the process of adopting at least to a limited degree the skills and values of the Western culture. Most of the tests employed in these studies were undergoing development or evaluation as instruments for use in this assimilation process. Had the investigations been designed primarily to study cultural differences in trait development, a quite different selection of subjects and tests would have been appropriate.

EXPERIMENTAL STUDIES

The third major approach to the investigation of trait formation represents the experimental alteration of trait relationships. Such studies provide a condensed and relatively controlled version of what probably occurs more gradually, over a longer time period, in the individual's daily experience. The investigator thus tries to reproduce the process of trait formation that can be inferred from the observation of age changes, educational differences, and variations among other experientially dissimilar groups.

One type of study following this approach is concerned with the effects of *practice* upon factor patterns. Early studies by Woodrow (1938, 1939) and by Greene (1943) found many changes in the factorial composition of tests in the course of practice. Some of these changes showed interesting correspondences to changes in observed performance or in subjects' reports. More recently, Fleishman and his co-workers have investigated the factorial composition of several complex perceptual-motor tasks at different stages of learning (see Fleishman & Bartlett, 1969; Fleishman & Hempel, 1954; Fleishman & Rich, 1963). Their results revealed progressive and systematic changes in factor loadings with practice. In the course of learning, there was a decrease in the contribution of such "nonmotor" factors as verbal and spatial aptitudes relative to motor factors, as well as an increase in the contribution of a factor specific to each task. These general findings were confirmed in a subsequent independent investigation (Kohfeld, 1966) and were extended in still other studies to conceptual (Bunderson, 1964; Dunham, Guilford, & Hoepfner, 1966), memory (Frederiksen, 1969; Games, 1962), and perceptual (Fleishman & Fruchter, 1960) tasks. The nature of the observed changes in factor patterns with practice suggests an increasing differentiation of functions as learning proceeds. This finding is consistent with the previously cited results of studies on age, educational differences, and ability level.

A somewhat related procedure follows directly from Ferguson's hypothesis regarding the role of *transfer* in the emergence of factors. Subjects are given practice in one test, which may be supplemented by verbal explanations and other instructional procedures. The effect of such learning on the factorial structure of a battery of related tests is then investigated. This approach is illustrated by two Swedish studies, one using motor tests (Heinonen, 1962), the other using a variety of verbal, numerical, and spatial tests (Melametsa, 1965). Both found evidence of increasing differentiation of factor patterns following training.

Still another procedural variant is represented by an early exploratory study by Anastasi (1936). Five tests, including vocabulary, memory span for digits, verbal reasoning, code multiplication, and pattern analysis, were administered to 200 sixth-grade school children. All subjects were then given one session of *instruction* in the use of special techniques that would facilitate performance on the last three tests only. In its general nature, this instruction resembled that received in the course of schooling, as, for example, in the teaching of arithmetic operations, shortcuts, and the like. After a lapse of 13 days, parallel forms of all five tests were administered under the same conditions as in the initial testing.

The rationale of this study was derived from the mechanism of contiguous experience, or Tryon's correlation of independent environmental fields. Essentially, it was hypothesized that the more an individual profited from the interpolated experience, the greater gain he would show on the three "instructed" tests. Consequently, the interrelations of the three "instructed" tests should alter, while the relations of the "noninstructed" tests to each other and to the "instructed" tests should remain virtually unchanged. A comparison of the correlations among initial and final tests supported this hypothesis. The factor patterns showed a number of changes, several of which could be understood in terms of the interpolated experience. For example, the factor accounting for the largest proportion of battery variance in the initial tests had the highest loading in tests most closely related to school work; in the final tests, on the other hand, this factor had the highest loadings in the three "instructed" tests.

An ongoing *longitudinal study of job performance* by MacKinney (1967),[2] although not strictly experimental in approach, bears some resemblance to these learning studies. Beginning with the premise that the job performance of individual workers changes over time, not only in level but also in nature, MacKinney has been investigating the factorial composition of criterion job performance at annual intervals. The specific job chosen was that of second-echelon managers, although its choice was fortuitous. Department heads in several plants of a large manufacturing company were given the Minnesota Scholastic Aptitude Test, the California Psychological Inventory, and the Strong Vocational Interest Blank, together with an extensive series of questionnaires covering biographical data, leadership style, job satisfaction, and the subject's perception of his working environment and his job activities. In addition, ratings of the subject's job performance and personal traits were obtained from his supervisors and subordinates. The hypothesized time changes are expected to occur not only as a function of worker variables—as illustrated by the effects of practice in job skills—but also as a function of changing situational variables to which the same individuals may be exposed over time. In terms of both duration and experimental design, MacKinney's research appears to fall about midway between the age studies and the learning experiments.

From a different angle, French (1965) investigated the relationship of individual differences in *problem-solving styles* to the factorial composition of tests. Fifteen cognitive tests were administered to 177 male high school and college students. Individual problem-solving styles were explored through questionnaires, interviews, and oral solution of typical test items. Factor analysis of the stylistic variables thus identified, together with the 15 test scores, yielded 17 psychologically meaningful stylistic factors. Many of these factors fell loosely into a category that could be described as a tendency toward "systematizing" or toward "analyzing versus scanning." The entire sample was divided successively into two subsamples differentiated on the basis of these stylistic factors, and the test scores were separately factor analyzed in the two subsamples. The resulting factor patterns exhibited a number of differences that were related to the problem-solving styles. Not only did the factorial composition of individual tests differ as a function of response style, but the factor patterns also differed in number and nature of factors that emerged and in the magnitude of correlation between oblique factors.

---

[2] Supplemented by personal communication and unpublished reports received from Arthur C. MacKinney, January 1970.

The problem-solving styles studied by French bear some resemblance to the "cognitive strategies" posited by Frederiksen (1969). In the course of learning, an individual may change his choice of strategy and thereby alter the factorial composition of the task as performed by him. Moreover, the applicability of a given cognitive strategy to several tasks may account for transfer of improvement from practice as well as for the clustering of these tasks into an identifiable trait.

For our final example of the experimental approach to trait formation, we may ask what research on infrahuman organisms has to offer. The answer is: very little thus far, although potentially it should be a rich field for testing the hypotheses that have been proposed. Most factor-analytic studies on animals are purely descriptive and cross-sectional (see Anastasi, 1958, pp. 362–364). The large majority have used the familiar laboratory white rat, although a few other species have occasionally been investigated. As in the human studies, there is evidence that the factor structure of the same task may change in the course of training (see, e.g., Anastasi, Fuller, Scott, & Schmitt, 1955). On the whole, however, the animal studies have yielded factors that proved more difficult to interpret than the factors obtained with humans. Rarely do we find broad aptitude factors such as have been identified in human studies. What factors are found are usually quite limited in scope. Some have been defined in terms of specific techniques applicable to the solution of more than one problem, such as the principle of turning alternately right and left, or the utilization of visual cues. To be sure, this type of finding now appears to be of considerable interest in connection with the role of transfer, learning sets, problem-solving styles, and cognitive strategies in the development of factors.

It is also characteristic of the animal data that cognitive and emotional aspects of behavior are not sharply differentiated. Thus, even when the variables analyzed are derived from performance on typical learning tasks, such as mazes, discrimination apparatus, and problem-solving situations, one finds such factors as docility, wildness–timidity, and impulsiveness or activity. This intertwining of aptitude and emotional factors may have an experiential origin. Unlike the school children or college students of the typical human factor-analytic studies, animals have not been exposed to that classic dichotomy between curricular and extracurricular experiences, between standardized intellectual development and unstandardized emotional development.

Probably the most significant contribution that animal research can make to our understanding of traits is to be found in experimental studies of the development of factors under controlled conditions. This approach is exemplified in a well-designed study by Whimbey and Denenberg (1966), in which the investigators quite literally created group factors through the experimental control of early experiences in a homogeneous group of rats. Within a total sample of 96 rats, three males and three females were randomly assigned to each of 16 experimental treatment groups. Each of these 16 groups was exposed to a different combination of the following four treatment variables: (*a*) whether or not the mother had herself been handled in infancy; (*b*) whether or not the subject was handled in infancy; (*c*) whether the mother and litter were housed in a maternity cage or in a free environment between birth and weaning; (*d*) whether the subject was housed in a laboratory cage or in a free environment between weaning and the age of 42 days.

Between the ages of 42 days and 220 days, all animals lived under identical conditions. Beginning at 220 days, they were put through a test battery that yielded 23 score variables. The mean scores of each of the 16 groups on each of these 23 variables were intercorrelated and factor analyzed. Because of the random assignment of animals to each group, these intergroup score differences, which proved to be significant, could be attributed to the experimental treatments. Hence, the obtained correlations were a function of known experimental inputs. Six factors were found, of which four could be clearly identified as emotional reactivity, avoidance learning, consumption-elimination, and field exploration. Whimbey and Denenberg's own concluding remarks are noteworthy. They write:

> The factor structure obtained in this experiment is surprisingly similar to ones obtained when heterogeneous groups of rats or mice were employed in factor analytical studies. . . . This could mean that one can generate as great and complex a range of individual differences by means of experimental manipulation as one can by capitalizing on random genetic variations; or it may mean that the uncontrolled ("random") life experiences of the animals played a much more important role in shaping and establishing the behavioral patterns (individual differences) of the animals than has been realized heretofore [p. 285].

REFERENCES

ANASTASI, A. The influence of specific experience upon mental organization. *Genetic Psychology Monographs,* 1936, **18,** 245–355.

ANASTASI, A. The nature of psychological "traits." *Psychological Review,* 1948, **55,** 127–138.

ANASTASI, A. *Differential psychology.* (3rd ed.) New York: Macmillan, 1958.

ANASTASI, A., FULLER, J. L., SCOTT, J. P., & SCHMITT, J. R. A factor analysis of the performance of dogs on certain learning tests. *Zoologica,* 1955, 40, 33–46.

AVAKIAN, S. A. An investigation of trait relationships among six-year-old children. *Genetic Psychology Monographs,* 1961, 63, 339–394.

BALINSKY, B. An analysis of the mental factors of various age groups from nine to sixty. *Genetic Psychology Monographs,* 1941, 23, 191–234.

BUNDERSON, C. V. Transfer functions and learning curves: The use of ability constructs in the study of human learning. *Educational Testing Service Research Bulletin,* RB-64-62, 1964.

BURT, C. *The factors of the mind: An introduction to factor-analysis in psychology.* New York: Macmillan, 1941.

BURT, C. The differentiation of intellectual ability. *British Journal of Educational Psychology,* 1954, 24, 76–90.

CARROLL, J. B. Factors of verbal achievement. In A. Anastasi (Ed.), *Testing problems in perspective.* Washington, D.C.: American Council on Education, 1966.

DAS, R. S. Analysis of the components of reasoning in nonverbal tests and the structure of reasoning in a bilingual population. *Archiv für die gesamte Psychologie,* 1963, 115, 217–229.

DOCKRELL, W. B. Cultural and educational influences on the differentiation of ability. In, *Proceedings of the 73rd Annual Convention of the American Psychological Association.* Washington, D.C.: APA, 1965. (Summary)

DUNHAM, J. L., GUILFORD, J. P., & HOEPFNER, R. Abilities pertaining to classes and the learning of concepts. *Reports from the Psychological Laboratory, University of Southern California,* No. 39, 1966.

DYE, N. W., & VERY, P. S. Growth changes in factorial structure by age and sex. *Genetic Psychology Monographs,* 1968, 78, 55–58.

FERGUSON, G. A. On learning and human ability. *Canadian Journal of Psychology,* 1954, 8, 95–112.

FERGUSON, G. A. On transfer and the abilities of man. *Canadian Journal of Psychology,* 1956, 10, 121–131.

FILELLA, J. F. Educational and sex differences in the organization of abilities in technical and academic students in Colombia, South America. *Genetic Psychology Monographs,* 1960, 61, 115–163.

FLEISHMAN, E. A., & BARTLETT, C. J. Human abilities. *Annual Review of Psychology,* 1969, 20, 349–380.

FLEISHMAN, E. A., & FRUCHTER, B. Factor structure and predictability of successive stages of learning Morse code. *Journal of Applied Psychology,* 1960, 44, 96–101.

FLEISHMAN, E. A., & HEMPEL, W. E., JR. Changes in factor structure of a complex psychomotor test as a function of practice. *Psychometrika,* 1954, 19, 239–252.

FLEISHMAN, E. A., & RICH, S. Role of kinesthetic and spatial-visual abilities in perceptual-motor learning. *Journal of Experimental Psychology,* 1963, 66, 6–11.

FREDERIKSEN, C. H. Abilities, transfer, and information retrieval in verbal learning. *Multivariate Behavioral Research Monographs,* No. 69-2, 1969.

FRENCH, J. W. The relationship of problem-solving styles to the factor com-position of tests. *Educational and Psychological Measurement,* 1965, 25, 9–28.

GAMES, P. A. A factorial analysis of verbal learning tasks. *Journal of Experimental Psychology,* 1962, 63, 1–11.

GARRETT, H. E. A developmental theory of intelligence. *American Psychologist,* 1946, 1, 372–378.

GREEN, R. F., & BERKOWITZ, B. Changes in intellect with age: II. Factorial analysis of Wechsler-Bellevue scores. *Journal of Genetic Psychology,* 1964, 104, 3–18.

GREENE, E. B. An analysis of random and systematic changes with practice. *Psychometrika,* 1943, 8, 37–52.

GUTHRIE, G. M. Structure of abilities in a non-Western culture. *Journal of Educational Psychology,* 1963, 54, 94–103.

GUTTMAN, R., & GUTTMAN, L. Cross-cultural stability of an intercorrelation pattern of abilities: A possible test for a biological basis. *Human Biology,* 1963, 35, 53–60.

HARLOW, H. F. The formation of learning sets. *Psychological Review,* 1949, 56, 51–65.

HARLOW, H. F. Learning set and error factor theory. In S. Koch (Ed.), *Psychology: A study of a science.* Vol. 2. New York: McGraw-Hill, 1960.

HEINONEN, V. A factor analytic study of transfer of training. *Scandinavian Journal of Psychology,* 1962, 3, 177–188.

HIRSCH, J., & TRYON, R. C. Mass screening and reliable individual measure-ment in the experimental behavior genetics of lower organisms. *Psychological Bulletin,* 1956, 53, 402–410.

HUNT, J. McV. *Intelligence and experience.* New York: Ronald Press, 1961.

IRVINE, S. H. Factor analysis of African abilities and attainments: Constructs across cultures. *Psychological Bulletin,* 1969, 71, 20–32.

KOHFELD, D. L. The prediction of perceptual-motor learning from indepen-dent verbal and motor measures. *Psychonomic Science,* 1966, 4, 413–414.

LESSER, G. S., FIFER, G., & CLARK, D. H. Mental abilities of children from different social-class and cultural groups, *Monographs of the Society for Research in Child Development,* 1965, 30(4), 1–115.

LIENERT, G. A. *Belastung und Regression: Versuch einer Theorie der systematischen Beeinträchtigung der intellektuellen Leistungsfähigkheit.* Meisen-heim am Glan: Hain, 1964.

LIENERT, G. A., & CROTT, H. W. Studies on the factor structure of intelli-gence in children, adolescents, and adults. *Vita Humana,* 1964, 7, 147–163.

LINDSEY, J. M. *The factorial organization of intelligence in children as related to the variables of age, sex, and subculture.* (Doctoral dissertation, Uni-versity of Georgia) Ann Arbor, Mich.: University Microfilms, 1966. No. 67-3567.

MACKINNEY, A. C. The assessment of performance change: An inductive ex-ample. *Organizational Behavior and Human Performance,* 1967, 2, 56–72.

MANLEY, M. B. A factor-analytic study of three types of concept attainment tasks. *Educational Testing Service Research Bulletin,* RB-65-31, 1965.

MELAMETSA, L. The influence of training on the level of test performance and the factor structure of intelligence tests. *Scandinavian Journal of Psychology,* 1965, 6, 19–25.

MITCHELL, J. V., JR. A comparison of the factorial structure of cognitive functions for a high and low status group. *Journal of Educational Psychology,* 1956, 47, 397–414.

MUKHERJEE, B. N. The factorial structure of aptitude tests at successive grade levels. *British Journal of Statistical Psychology,* 1962, 15, 59–65.

MYERS, C. E., ORPET, R. E., ATTWELL, A. A., & DINGMAN, H. F. Primary mental abilities at mental age six. *Monographs of the Society for Research in Child Development,* 1962, 27, No. 1.

OSBORNE, R. T., & LINDSEY, J. M. A longitudinal investigation of change in the factorial composition of intelligence with age in young school children. *Journal of Genetic Psychology,* 1967, 110, 49–58.

QUERESHI, M. Y. Patterns of psycholinguistic development during early and middle childhood. *Educational and Psychological Measurement,* 1967, 27, 353–365.

SEGEL, D. Intellectual abilities in the adolescent period. *Bulletin No. 6, United States Office of Education,* 1948.

SUTHERLAND, T. E. *The effect of school departmentalization on the organization of certain mental abilities.* (Doctoral dissertation, University of Kentucky) Ann Arbor, Mich.: University Microfilms, 1960. No. 60–708.

THOMSON, G. H. A hierarchy without a general factor. *British Journal of Psychology,* 1916, 8, 271–281.

THOMSON, G. H. *The factorial analysis of human ability.* (3rd ed.) Boston: Houghton Mifflin, 1948.

THURSTONE, L. L. Current issues in factor analysis. *Psychological Bulletin,* 1940, 37, 189–236.

TRYON, R. C. A theory of psychological components—an alternative to "mathematical factors." *Psychological Review,* 1935, 42, 425–454.

TRYON, R. C. *Cluster analysis.* Ann Arbor, Mich.: Edwards, 1939.

TRYON, R. C. Genetic differences in maze-learning ability in rats. *Thirty-ninth Yearbook, National Society for the Study of Education,* 1940, Part I, 111–119.

TRYON, R. C. Identification of social areas by cluster analysis. *University of California Publications in Psychology,* 1955, 8(1), 1–100.

TRYON, R. C. Experimental behavior genetics of maze ability and a sufficient polygenic theory. Paper presented at the meeting of the American Psychological Association, Philadelphia, September 1963.

TRYON, R. C. Person-clusters on intellectual abilities and on MMPI attributes. *Multivariate Behavioral Research,* 1967, 2, 5–34.

TRYON, R. C. Comparative cluster analysis of social areas. *Multivariate Behavioral Research,* 1968, 3, 213–232.

TYLER, L. E. The relationship of interests to abilities and reputation among first-grade children. *Educational and Psychological Measurement,* 1951, 11, 255–264.

VANDENBERG, S. G. The primary mental abilities of Chinese students: A comparative study of the stability of a factor structure. *Annals of the New York Academy of Sciences,* 1959, **79**, 257–304.

VANDENBERG, S. G. The primary mental abilities of South American students. *Research Reports, Louisville Twin Study (University of Louisville, Louisville, Ky.),* Report No. 9, 1966.

VERNON, P. E. *The structure of human abilities.* (Rev. ed.) London: Methuen, 1961.

VERNON, P. E. Ability factors and environmental influences. *American Psychologist,* 1965, **20**, 723–733.

VERNON, P. E. *Intelligence and cultural environment.* London: Methuen, 1969.

VERY, P. S. Differential factor structures in mathematical ability. *Genetic Psychology Monographs,* 1967, **75**, 169–207.

WEINER, M. Organization of mental abilities from ages 14 to 54. *Educational and Psychological Measurement,* 1964, **24**, 573–587.

WHIMBEY, A. E., & DENENBERG, V. H. Programming life histories: Creating individual differences by the experimental control of early experiences. *Multivariate Behavioral Research,* 1966, **1**, 279–286.

WHITEMAN, M. Intelligence and learning. *Merrill-Palmer Quarterly,* 1964, **10**, 297–309.

WOODROW, H. The relation between abilities and improvement with practice. *Journal of Educational Psychology,* 1938, **29**, 215–230.

WOODROW, H. Factors in improvement with practice. *Journal of Psychology,* 1939, **7**, 55–70.

7

Heredity and Environment: Diverse Approaches

My pervasive interest in the contributions of heredity and environment to the etiology of behavioral differences was discussed as a major theme in Chapter 1. There it was noted that this theme can be recognized in much of my work, as illustrated by several papers included in the preceding chapters. The papers reproduced in the present chapter, however, were chosen because they deal explicitly with research on the contributions of particular experiential variables to individual differences. The approaches followed and the specific behavior domains investigated are highly diversified. This diversification is apparent in the topics discussed in Chapter 1 under the heredity-environment theme; and it is fully evident in the selections reproduced in the present chapter.

The first paper summarizes a descriptive analysis of animal drawings by Indian schoolchildren of the North Pacific Coast. Published in the 1930s, it should be viewed against the prevailing climate of the period, when children's drawings were widely acclaimed as relatively "culture-free" indicators of intellectual development.

The article on tested intelligence and family size is based on an invited paper presented at the World Population Conference held in Rome from August 30 to September 10, 1954, under United Nations auspices. It was one of six conference papers chosen by the editor of the Eugenics Quarterly *for publication in the first volume of that journal. Because of the many methodological and interpretive problems encountered in research on this topic, the paper also exemplifies the "pitfall-questing" theme illustrated in Chapter 2.*

The study reported in the last paper was part of a four-year research project on the role of experiential factors in the development of creative thinking in children and adolescents. This project was conducted in collaboration with several of my graduate students and former students. Representing still another approach to the ubiquitous heredity-environment theme, the study also reflects an interest in the nature and cultivation of creativity (see Ch. 1) and in the use of biographical inventories as a technique for gathering data on an individual's experiential history. Both topics represented active areas of research in the 1960s.

A Study of Animal Drawings by Indian Children of the North Pacific Coast[1]

Psychologists have repeatedly investigated the drawing behavior of the child as a possible index of general developmental level. Specific characteristics of subject matter as well as technique have been laboriously catalogued for each age, and norms thereby established (3, 4, 5, 6, 8, 9). This procedure, however, has been largely restricted to children living within a single cultural group or similar groups. As in the case of other forms of psychological behavior, the resulting alleged generalizations are found to be inadequate or even false when the observations are repeated in another cultural milieu. Such comparative data serve a dual purpose. In the first place, the etiology of the behavior under consideration can best be studied by observing the varied manifestations of such behavior under differing stimulational circumstances. Thus a study of cultural differences in the subject matter and technique of children's drawings will contribute toward an understanding of the underlying factors conditioning drawing behavior. Secondly, such comparative investigations delimit the range of situations within which a given set of behavioral norms can be meaningfully and legitimately applied.

In an earlier article (1), the writers surveyed the available published material on drawings by children in different cultural groupings. In addition, 602 spontaneous drawings, representing the work of children between the ages of six and twelve from 41 countries, were analyzed. The basic conclusion suggested both by the literature and by the new data was, briefly, that the drawing behavior of children is intimately related to their experiential background. This is true of every phase of the drawings. Within any one age level, no one type of *subject matter* predominates universally. In one group, the human form may be the favorite subject drawn, in another animals, in still others landscapes with wide vistas, or industrial and mechanical objects, or symbolical representations. The relative frequency of

---

[1] The writers are indebted to Professor Franz Boas of the Department of Anthropology, Columbia University, who collected the present drawings in the field in 1931, and who generously turned them over to the writers for analysis and report.

A study of animal drawings by Indian children of the North Pacific Coast. *Journal of Social Psychology,* 1938, *9,* 363–374. (With J. P. Foley, Jr.) Reprinted by permission.

imaginative themes and of realistic portrayal seemed also to vary, not with age, but with the specific cultural group.

Equally pronounced differences were found in the *technique* of the drawings. Thus the *organization* of the picture may differ from group to group, in some a single unified scene being presented, in others a sequence of events, in still others isolated or randomly placed objects. The degree to which *color* is employed, as well as the choice of specific hues, seems to reflect the influence both of physical environment and of social tradition. In certain groups, *detail* is relatively poor, total impressions and panoramic views being emphasized; in others, the minutest features are painstakingly reproduced. An even more significant point is the *specificity* of detail, *i.e.,* the tendency to emphasize those characteristics which are specifically observed and which play an important part in the everyday activities of the group, and to ignore others. The portrayal of detail may be relatively poor in the drawings from a given group except when some special object is involved, whether it be the decoration of a peasant's gown, the elaboration of a ceremonial mask, the accurate depiction of a reindeer in flight, or the minutiae of a particular species of local plant life.

The present study is a somewhat more intensive analysis of children's drawings within a single cultural group. The subjects were 159 Indian children from the province of British Columbia on the northwest coast of Canada. All of the children were attending a single government school at Alert Bay. The instruction in this school followed the usual elementary school curriculum; drawing was taught in connection with the ordinary grade school requirements, but received no special emphasis. The pupils were all resident at the school, returning to their native villages only during the summer vacation. The age of admission varied considerably and, as a result, older children were frequently found in the lower grades; the age distribution occurring within any one grade group is therefore relatively wide.

The general characteristics of the subjects are summarized in Table 1. It will be noted that the ages range from 5 to 18. There is considerable clustering around the center of the distribution, however, the middle 50 per cent of the children falling within the limits of 10 and 14 years. The median age of the group is 12 years. Nearly half of the subjects belong to the Kwakiutl, the remainder being divided among five tribes, the Nass River, Bella Bella, Haida, Tsimshian, and Bella Coola. The two sexes are fairly evenly represented, the total number of boys being 90 and that of girls 69.

The drawings were collected in 1931 by Professor Franz Boas of the Department of Anthropology, Columbia University. The subjects

TABLE 1 Classification of Subjects

Age	Tribal Group							Total
	Kwakiutl	Nass River	Bella Bella	Tsimshian	Haida	Bella Coola	Unclassified	
5					1			1
6				1				1
7	3	1						4
8	2	3	4	3	1	1		11
9	8	2	2	1	3	2		20
10	10	4	3	2	3	2		23
11	6			1	1	1		12
12	11	10	1	2	1	1	1	26
13	6	3	1	2	1			13
14	8	2	4	1				17
15	5	1	3	3		1		12
16	3	4	3			2	1	14
17	1	1					1	3
18	2						1	2
Boys	43	21	11	6	5	3	1	90
Girls	22	10	10	10	8	7	2	69
Total	65	31	21	16	13	10	3	159

were furnished with paper and pencil and were directed simply to "draw an animal." One drawing was obtained from each child, although a few of the subjects drew several discrete objects on the single sheet of paper given them.

A classification of the drawings from the standpoint of *subject matter* will be found in Table 2. The data have been analyzed in respect to tribal group, age, and sex of each subject. The entries under each tribal heading in the table give the age of each individual child making the drawing described at the left. The ages of boys are given in roman type, those of girls in italics.

The most distinctive feature of these drawings, which differentiates them from drawings by children in other cultures, is the presence of certain *stylized representations* patterned after the traditional adult art of the northwest coast Indians. The drawings which clearly fall into this category are reported in section *A* of Table 2 and sample illustrations are reproduced in Figure 1. They include representations of the killer whale, thunder bird, sea lion, and the mythical double-headed serpent. In such drawings, the influence of tradition and cultural milieu is apparent not only in the particular choice of subject matter but also in the technique of representation. All details of the drawings are highly stylized and conventionalized, being portrayed by means of the traditional symbols employed by the group.[2] Thus the typical representation of the killer whale is characterized by a long dorsal fin, elongated head, large square mouth set with many teeth, a long eye, and a very large eyebrow; the sea lion has a rounded nose, large teeth, the eye near to the nose, and a small ear; the double-headed serpent has a small eye, a spiral nose, and a spiral plume. Among the Kwakiutl, special eye patterns are employed to differentiate one animal from another. In all tribes, characteristic styles are to be found in the representation of the tail of birds and sea mammals. Wings and fins likewise have their own special designs.

The remainder of the drawings are more or less realistic in style and seem to fall roughly into two general classes: those showing animals and events from the typical home environment of the Indian child, and those reflecting the influence of school experience. Among the latter may be mentioned several schematic drawings of cats and birds in the conventional school book or "kindergarten" fashion (cf. Figure 2), pictures of such animals as camel, elephant, and giraffe which the child may have seen in books, and the one drawing of a

---

[2] For a description of the adult art forms of this area, the reader is referred to Boas' *Primitive Art* (2), Chapter VI.

TABLE 2 Classification of Drawings According to Tribal Group, Age, and Sex of Subjects*

Drawing	Tribal Group						
	Kwakiutl	Nass River	Bella Bella	Tsimshian	Haida	Bella Coola	Un-classified
A. "Stylized"							
Double-headed serpent	11, 12						
Killer whale	11, 14, 14, 17, 18	*9, 12*	*9, 10, 12*	16			
Killer whale, thunder bird						*15*	
Sea lion	13		14				
Thunder bird	*13, 13, 14*						
B. "Realistic"							
Bear, showing teeth		10, 12					
Bear dancer	10						
Bird; birds	8, 9, *9, 9,* 10, 12	*10, 13, 16*	10, 14, 16	*9, 9, 11*	*10*	*9*	
Birds, men	10						
Bison			14	13			
Camel							
Camel with rider	15						
Cat; cats	7, 7, 8, *10,* 10, *12, 12,* 18	7, 8, 9, 12	7	*14*	*5, 9, 9, 10*	*8, 10*	
Cat and bird or birds	10, 10		8	*6*	*9*		
Cat, bird in mouth, another on tree					10		
Cat, dogs	*12*						
Cat, man in canoe							
Chicken or hen	7, 10	8		9		*15*	
Chicken, cow, dog, fish		*13*				*9*	
Cow	*14, 15, 16*		16	14			

*Numerical entries represent ages. Boys are indicated in roman type, girls in italics.

159

TABLE 2 Classification of Drawings According to Tribal Group, Age, and Sex of Subjects* (Continued)

Drawing	Tribal Group						
	Kwakiutl	Nass River	Bella Bella	Tsimsbian	Haida	Bella Coola	Un-classified
Cow, man leading horse		10					
Deer	12			15			
Deer, man shooting					9		
Deer, salmon			15				
Dog	9, *9, 12, 14, 14,15*		8	12, 16		10, *11, 12*	
Elephant	10, 11, 12				11		
Fish (3 show salmon)	*11,*	*12, 14*		*16*			
Giraffe		12					
Goat, pig	14						
Horse	9, 12	10, 12, 12, 14, 16, 16,	*9, 13, 15*			*14*	17
Horse, man	14, 15						
Hunting scene	12, 13						
Native canoes				10			
Owl	9	*12, 12*	*15*				
Pig	*11*	8	8		12		
Pig, bird	*13*				*11*		
Rabbit; rabbits	13			11	*11*		
Rabbit, owl					*11*		
School boy at his desk	10						
Series of small animal pictures	12						
Sheep	*13, 16*				13		12
Squirrel (one on fence)	15, 16	*15*	16				*16*
Whales, men harpooning	11		14				
Wolf		16, 17	10				
Blank		*12, 13*		*13*			

*Numerical entries represent ages. Boys are indicated in roman type, girls in italics.

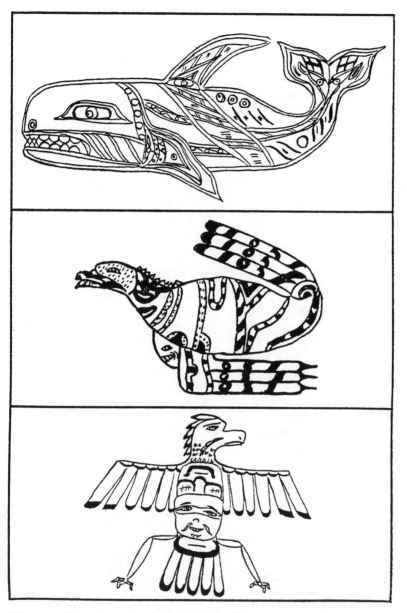

Figure 1 Examples of stylized drawings: killer whale, sea lion, thunder bird.

Figure 2 Examples of realistic drawings: cat and bird, salmon, horse.

school boy at his desk. It should be added that this type of drawing is in the minority. The larger portion of realistic animal drawings seem to have been suggested by the activities and contacts of daily life in an Indian village. Thus we find hunting scenes, deer, wolf, rabbits, squirrel, men harpooning whales, and fish, three of the drawings clearly portraying the salmon which abounds in the waters of the northwest. Among the domestic animals drawn are to be found horse, dog, cat, cow, chicken, pig, goat, sheep, and several species of birds.

Although not exhibiting the distinctly stylized features of the drawings in Group *A*, these more or less realistic representations often showed the influence of local traditions, customs, and habits. Noteworthy examples of such influence are the "bear dancer" drawn by one child and the special type of native canoes depicted by another. In two drawings of bears the teeth are clearly portrayed, a detail which is part of the conventional symbolism of the bear within these tribes. Among the objects included in the two drawings which have been listed in Table 2 as "series of small animal pictures" are two representations of the stylized killer whale and one of a "supernatural serpent." In a number of drawings, the path of motion is clearly indicated. The trajectory of a bullet, for example, is regularly shown by a line extending from the gun to the hunted animal. This practice may reflect the interest of a group accustomed to hunting, for whom the exact path followed by the bullet would represent an important detail of the situation. Similarly, the close association with animals characteristic of a rural community may account for the frequent designation of the sex of the animals drawn. This is particularly demonstrated by the labels written on the pictures, among which are "billy goat," "a dog boy," "a sheep girl," and "mother deer and father deer." In the last, the antlers are correctly drawn on the male and omitted on the female.

Wide *individual differences* are exhibited by the drawings, no two being identical. The range of subject matter is fairly wide in view of the specific directions given. In technique, the differences are very pronounced, extending from the crude and almost unrecognizable efforts to draw a schematic cat or bird to very accurate realistic portrayals of horse, wolf, and deer, and beautifully executed stylized drawings. These differences in technique seem not to be very closely associated with *age*. Only certain general trends can be detected in the comparison of age groups. Thus there is a slightly greater frequency of schematic drawings (such as the cat and bird illustrated in Figure 2) among the younger children, but such drawings are not absent among the older subjects. Similarly, the stylized drawings are produced chiefly by the older children, although some are found among 9-, 10-, and 11-year-olds. It should be recalled in this connection that owing to the variation in age of admission to the school, wide grade differences exist within a single age level. This would also mean that the relative length of time during which the individual has been exposed to the school environment and to his native home environment differs significantly within any one age group.

Sex differences are somewhat more distinct than the differences among age levels, and seem to be closely linked with the traditional activities and everyday associations of the sexes within these tribes. Thus stylized drawings are more common among the boys, only 5 having been made by girls as contrasted to 15 by boys. It should be noted in this connection that among the north Pacific coast Indians, painting and wood carving are conducted exclusively by the men. The style represented by these art forms is symbolic and resembles closely the type of stylized drawings obtained in the present investigation. The embroidery of the women is always based upon the symbolic patterns originated by the men, and this is likewise true of much of their weaving. The only patterns originated by the women are those employed in basketry and matting; the style of these, however, is formal and geometric and quite distinct from the symbolic patterns devised by the men (cf. 2).

Certain sex differences are also indicated by the subject matter of the more realistic drawings. Thus the animal form most commonly drawn by the boys was the horse, appearing in 13 individual drawings by boys; only 4 drawings by girls, on the other hand, show horses. Similarly, hunting scenes, deer, wolf, and whales, are more frequent in the boys' drawings. A slight predominance of such animals as sheep, cows, rabbits, and birds is to be seen in the girls' drawings. It is interesting to note in this connection that in a previous investigation by McDermott (7) on the spontaneous drawings of Indian children between the ages of 5 and 16, the horse was likewise found to be the most common animal form pictured by the boys. McDermott attributes this to the Indian boy's close association with horses. Among the girls' drawings, animal forms in general were much less varied, the most popular being birds.

For various reasons, *inter-tribal comparisons* cannnot be expected to yield very marked differences. It must be borne in mind that all of the subjects were attending a single school and had thus been exposed to a similar environment for a period which in the majority of cases covered several years. The same artistic style and type of symbolism, furthermore, is universal throughout the north Pacific coast; the art forms do not differ in any essential way from tribe to tribe. In general culture and in physical surroundings the tribes are likewise very similar. Only minor differences can therefore be noticed in the drawings. In reference to the relatively large number of stylized drawings submitted by the Kwakiutl children, it should be noted that at the present time the Kwakiutl have a more highly developed art in their villages than do any of the other tribes. The Bella Bella, although somewhat more highly assimilated than the other groups, still retain in their graveyards stone carvings which embody the stylistic features of their traditional art. The frequent contacts of the children with these art forms during the time spent in their own villages may account for the somewhat greater relative frequency of stylized drawings among the Bella Bella than among the remaining four tribes.

In general, the results of the present investigation corroborate the conclusions reached in the writers' earlier analysis of drawings by children in different cultures (1). Both the subject matter and the technique of the drawings reflect specific cultural and experiential factors rather than age differences or developmental stages. Any attempt to employ specific features of the child's drawing as an index of developmental level independently of the child's experiential background is doomed to failure. An Indian child of the north Pacific coast, when directed to draw an animal, may produce a symbolical representation rich in stylized details which it would be futile to evaluate in terms of norms established elsewhere. The fact that in response to the request to draw an animal, some of the children drew mythical creatures is itself significant and quite unlike results which would be obtained under similar conditions with children in our own culture.

REFERENCES

1. ANASTASI, A., & FOLEY, J. P., JR. An analysis of spontaneous drawings by children in different cultures. *J. Appl. Psychol.,* 1936, 20, 689–726.
2. BOAS, F. Primitive Art. Cambridge, Mass.: Harvard Univ. Press, 1927. Pp. 376.
3. GOODENOUGH, F. L. Measurement of Intelligence by Drawings. Yonkers, N.Y.: World Book, 1926. Pp. 177.
4. KERCHENSTEINER, D. G. Die Entwickelung der zeichnerischen Begabung. Munich: Gerber, 1905. Pp. 508.
5. LEVINSTEIN, S. Kinderzeichnungen bis zum 14 Lebensjahr. Leipzig: Voigtlander, 1905. Pp. 169.
6. LUQUET, G. H. Le Dessin Enfantin. Paris: Alcan, 1927. Pp. 260.
7. MCDERMOTT, L. Favorite drawings of Indian children. *Northwestern Mo.,* 1897, 8, 134–137.

8. PIAGET, J. The Language and Thought of the Child. New York: Harcourt Brace, 1926. Pp. 246.
9. ROUMA, G. Le Langage Graphique de L'Enfant. Paris: Alcan, 1913. Pp. 284.

Tested Intelligence and Family Size: Methodological and Interpretive Problems

Within the past three decades, the relationship between intelligence test scores and family size has been repeatedly investigated. Among such studies, the outstanding examples are the surveys conducted on nearly complete samples of 11-year-old Scottish children (22, 23). In all investigations in which the intelligence test scores of unselected school children were correlated with number of *siblings,* the results have been quite consistent. The correlations are invariably negative and cluster numerically in the .20's or low .30's (4, 5, 6, 7, 8, 10, 14, 17, 21, 22, 23, 26). Within certain more narrowly defined sub-samples of the general population, results vary. For example, among college students, nearly all surveys agree in finding no significant correlation between intelligence and size of sibship (12, 18, 25, 29, 30). Similarly, there is some evidence that within the professional class the correlation may be zero or even positive, while within other occupational categories it is negative (cf. 5). On the other hand, the usual negative correlation in the .20's was found within a group of intellectually superior children tested at the elementary school level (27).

Data on the relation between parental intelligence and number of *offspring* are very meager, but suggest an absence of significant correlation, especially when completed families are studied (9) or when amount of parental education is ruled out (32).[1] It cannot be assumed that the relationship between intelligence and number of siblings is the same as that between intelligence and number of offspring. In this connection, it should be recalled that the correlation between parental and child intelligence is only about .50, thus leaving room for considerable variation. Moreover, we cannot assume that children coming from larger families will themselves have correspondingly large families. Among other factors, social mobility will affect the fertility pattern of such individuals. More direct informa-

---

[1] In a critique of this study (20), there appears to be a misunderstanding of the data reported. Subjects' intelligence correlated −.02 with number of *offspring,* but −.12 with number of *siblings.*

Tested intelligence and family size: Methodological and interpretive problems. *Eugenics Quarterly,* 1954, *1,* 155–160. Reprinted by permission.

tion on the relationship between parental intelligence and number of offspring would be helpful in disentangling the causal interrelations of factors.

THEORETICAL ANALYSIS OF CAUSAL RELATIONS

The problem of causal relations is a far more difficult one than that of determining correlations. It is especially important in this connection to differentiate clearly between plausible hypotheses and empirically established facts, and to ferret out tacit assumptions which may underlie our interpretations. For example, if we define intelligence in terms of hereditary predispositions, we shall logically preclude the possibility of discovering that certain individual differences in intelligence may be unrelated to gene constitution. It is more consistent with scientific method to employ definitions which do not prejudge the data but which permit the maximum freedom of interpretation.

We may, of course, define the word "intelligence" to mean anything we choose. All studies on intelligence and family size, however, have employed intelligence test scores as their index of intelligence. It is evident, therefore, that our interpretations must take intelligence test scores as their point of departure.

When intelligence is defined in such terms, we may recognize three distinct etiological mechanisms whereby the obtained correlations between intelligence and family size might result. It is understood, of course, that the actual causal relations may involve any combination of two or all three of these mechanisms. First, there may be inherited structural factors (neural, glandular, etc.) which limit the sort of intellectual development measured by current intelligence tests. The less intelligent parents would thus transmit their structural limitations to their offspring. The obtained correlations would then result from the fact that, within a given culture, persons with inferior heredity tended to have more offspring.

A second familiar explanation attributes individual differences in children's intelligence to psychological differences in the environments provided by parents of varying intellectual levels. In this case, the correlations between family size and intelligence of offspring would again result from a tendency for the less intelligent parents to have more children, but heredity would not be involved. It should be added that the child's intellectual development may be influenced, not only by the nature and extent of direct intellectual stimulation afforded by his home, but also by emotional and motivational factors deriving from the "social climate" of the home. There is a growing body of data pertaining to differences in child-rearing practices in various socio-economic levels and other sub-cultures (3, Ch. 23 and p. 734). Some of these differences, such as the degree to which verbalization and exploratory behavior are encouraged or discouraged, are likely to influence the child's intellectual development.

A third possible interpretation is based upon size of family itself as a causal factor. For example, a larger family—at least in certain socio-economic levels—would reduce the per capita funds available for education, recreation, suitable housing, proper food, medical attention, and other environmental requisites. From a psychological viewpoint, another important factor is the degree of adult contact provided in families of different sizes. Available evidence suggests, for example, that such contact may be the most important single factor in linguistic development (3, pp. 335–339; 16). And it is well known that verbal ability plays a major role both in educational progress and in intelligence test performance. Whatever the specific factors involved, the causal mechanism under consideration is independent of the intellectual level of parents. A crucial test of this hypothesis would thus be found in the correlation between size of sibship and intelligence of offspring, when intellectual level of parents is held constant.

It is clear that the three hypotheses differ significantly in both their theoretical and practical implications. One fact remains, however, regardless of which hypothesis, or combination of hypotheses, may ultimately prove to be correct. Insofar as a significant negative correlation is conclusively established between intelligence test performance and family size, it follows that mean intelligence test scores of the population should decline slowly in successive generations, unless other counterbalancing influences operate. Theoretically, such counteracting factors might be genetic (cf., e.g., 19). It is more likely, however, that they would be environmental.

IMPLICATIONS OF FOLLOW-UP SURVEYS

In an effort to obtain direct evidence regarding the predicted decline, follow-up procedures have been employed, whereby comparable samples are tested under similar conditions after a lapse of several years. Again the most notable example of such a study is to be found in the Scottish survey (23, 24), in which a second approximately complete sample of 11-year-old Scottish children was given the same group intelligence test 15 years after the testing of the initial sample. As is now well known, this survey revealed a small but significant rise in mean score, rather than a decline. Similar gains have been found in other surveys. Although not so extensive or so well controlled as the Scottish survey, especially with regard to comparability of samples, these other surveys have yielded consistent results.[2]

Reference may likewise be made to certain relevant data gathered incidentally, as by-products from other types of testing programs. Thus an analysis of the intelligence test performance of American soldiers in World Wars I and II indicated that the level of performance had improved to such an extent that the median score of the later sample corresponded to the 83rd percentile of the earlier sample (28). This rise in score paralleled an increase in amount of education, the mean being at the 8th grade for the first sample and at the 10th grade for the second. It is also noteworthy that a survey of the intelligence test performance of American high school students over a 20-year period suggested that this, too, had improved, despite the marked increase in the proportion of students enrolled in high school (11). Since a larger proportion of the total population was attending high school at the end than at the beginning of this 20-year period, a decrease in mean score would be expected, unless the total population had improved sufficiently to counteract such a drop.

When educational and other environmental conditions within a given community improve conspicuously, larger rises in test scores may be observed over even shorter intervals. Thus a 10-year follow-up conducted in a relatively isolated mountainous region of Eastern Tennessee showed a 10-point rise in median IQ (31). During this interval, the socio-economic and educational conditions of this region had greatly improved. The second sample tested in this survey was closely comparable to the first, the children coming largely from the same families in the two cases.

That intelligence test performance is susceptible to improvement as a result of education has been more directly demonstrated in at least two investigations in which persons who had been tested following a uniform period of universal education were retested after 10 years in one case and after 20 years in the other (13, 15). In the intervening years, members of these groups had received varying amounts of further education. Both studies report significant relationships between amount of subsequent schooling and retest performance, when initial scores are held constant.

---

[2] In the relatively few instances in which discrepant findings are reported, lack of comparability of samples seems to provide an adequate explanation.

A question that is frequently raised in connection with all such improvements in test performance pertains to the role of test sophistication and other conditions which might spuriously raise test scores. Fundamentally, the answer to this question depends upon the *breadth* of the effect (1; 2, pp. 52–56). Any influence which is restricted to the test performance itself and does not correspondingly affect the criterion behavior which the test is designed to predict would of course reduce the validity of the test. But the broad educational and social conditions under consideration can be expected to affect the individual's overall intellectual development, rather than being restricted to the particular samples of behavior included in psychological tests.

METHODOLOGICAL PROBLEMS

Apart from questions of interpretation, investigations of the relationship between family size and intelligence are beset with methodological pitfalls. Since the obtained correlations are so low, the operation of *selective factors,* however slight, may produce a completely spurious result. An example of such a selective factor is provided by a study conducted within an American women's college (25). Within the entire group of 2261 entering students for whom test scores were available, a significant inverse relation was found between test scores and number of siblings. This relationship disappeared, however, when the records of those whose older sisters had attended the same college were excluded. Presumably somewhat lower entrance requirements had been applied to those whose siblings had previously matriculated. Such students would also be likely to come from larger families. Many other examples of institutional selective factors could readily be cited. It is when such factors affect the correlation between the variables under consideration that they create a particularly serious problem.

Nor are more general samples free from selective factors. Thus in a sample of children between, let us say, the ages of 8 and 14, individual large families will appear repeatedly within the sample, the number of re-appearances being directly proportional to the size of the family. A family containing five school-age children, for example, would appear five times in the sample. Any chance conditions characterizing individual large families would thus be spuriously magnified in the sample. Nor would ordinary sampling statistics be strictly applicable to such samples. It is partly to avoid such difficulties that single-age samples, such as 11-year-olds, have been utilized. Even in such a carefully chosen sample, however, certain selective factors will operate. For example, large families will be over-represented, since by chance a child of any specified age is more likely to be found in a large family than in a small one. Such a sample is therefore not representative of existing families, nor of the parental populations. With regard to the child population, it can be argued that large families should be over-represented, since they contribute more members to the population. Nevertheless, certain types of comparisons may be distorted through the use of a single-age sample.[3]

In the case of follow-up studies conducted within a limited area, such as a single city or county, any *selective migration* which may have occurred in the interim will reduce the comparability of initial and subsequent samples. Similarly, differences in thoroughness of sampling procedures on successive testings may introduce differential selection. For example, subjects in lower socio-economic levels or those who are physically less fit are more likely to be excluded when sampling coverage is less adequate.

Another recurrent difficulty arises from the presence of *incomplete families* in the sample. This factor may operate in a number of different and not entirely predictable ways. All children from such incomplete families are, of course, classified as coming from somewhat smaller families than will eventually be the case. This may have the effect of classifying lower test-scorers (from the ultimately larger families) into a category of higher test-scorers (from smaller families). Such a procedure would thus reduce the obtained differences in test scores between the various family-size categories. On the other hand, when a negative correlation is found between intelligence and family size in a sample of incomplete families, it may simply reflect the tendency for persons of lower intelligence to begin having children earlier. Should such persons also stop having children earlier than the more intelligent members of the community, the correlation would disappear when completed families are studied. There is evidence that, at least in one rural American community, such was actually the case (9).

It should be noted, of course, that if the less intelligent parents begin having children earlier than the more intelligent parents, they will contribute more individuals to the population in the long run, through more frequent generations. For example, if each successive generation begins to bear children at age 20, there will be five generations per century; while if childbearing begins at age 25, there will be only four generations. Nevertheless, the effect upon the intelligence level of the population would be less if the duller parents

---

[3] See, e.g., the analyses of order of birth and of maternal age reported in 23 and 24, respectively.

merely began to have children earlier than the brighter, than it would be if the duller also had larger completed families than the brighter.

Age of parents is a factor which needs to be considered in its own right. The smaller families in a sample may include a relatively large proportion of incomplete families of younger parents. Such parents are likely to be better educated than the older parents of the completed families, owing to the progressive rise in educational level of the population. The better educated parents would in turn provide a more favorable environment for their offspring. *Thus when incomplete families are included in the sample, the differences in parental age, coupled with the rising level of general education, might be sufficient to account for the negative correlation found between family size and intelligence.*

As we pass from sampling problems to testing problems, we must consider such questions as the *reliability* of the measuring instrument, a question which assumes special importance in view of the small group differences in scores which must be detected in such studies. It is also desirable that the test cover an *adequate difficulty range,* to permit a proper determination of the ability of persons at the extremes of the distribution.

The use of *different tests,* or different forms of the same test, in follow-up studies presents a number of problems, such as variation in functions tested, differences in standardization samples, and lack of comparability of units. A particularly dangerous practice, which should be avoided if at all possible, is that of converting scores from one test to another. Nor is it advisable in precise studies to use the traditional *ratio IQ.* This measure has many disadvantages which can be avoided by employing standard scores or deviation IQ's.

Finally, it must be noted that "intelligence" is not a unitary function. Research on the organization of abilities has revealed a number of relatively independent traits or *group factors* (cf. 2, 3). As examples may be mentioned verbal comprehension, word fluency, speed and accuracy of numerical computation, spatial visualization, perceptual speed, associative memory, and numerical reasoning. A single global score, such as an IQ on an intelligence test, measures a conglomerate of heterogeneous abilities combined in unknown proportions. Let us suppose that two individuals obtain an IQ of 120 on the same intelligence test. The first may have done so because he excels markedly in verbal comprehension, is about average in numerical reasoning, and is slightly inferior in spatial visualization. The second may have obtained the identical score by virtue of a superior performance in numerical reasoning and spatial visualization and a low average performance in verbal comprehension. Such a state of affairs obviously makes for ambiguity. It is certainly more precise to describe the individual's intellectual status in terms of a profile of scores on the traits identified through factor analysis, rather than in terms of a single, hodgepodge IQ.

In conclusion, it may be well to consider the sort of experimental design suggested by the theoretical and methodological questions which have been discussed. The ideal investigation should begin with the testing of young people prior to their educational and vocational differentiation, *i.e.*, after all have completed a uniform period of required schooling. Preferably the tests should consist of a differential aptitude battery yielding a profile of scores rather than a single global score. The subjects should be followed up until the age when all, or nearly all, of their families are completed. Age of both parents at the birth of their first and last child should be noted. Records should also show deaths, unmarried persons, and childless marriages. Information should likewise be gathered on occupation, income level, and amount of subsequent education for each member of the group.

Additional questions can be answered if test scores of the children of these persons are studied. But many problems can be solved even prior to this step. From a practical viewpoint, such a program is not too unrealistic, especially in nations where uniform psychological tests are administered in the school system and where detailed census data are regularly collected. From a theoretical standpoint, this approach would help to separate the many interrelated variables which are now so intricately intertwined.

REFERENCES

1. ANASTASI, ANNE, The concept of validity in the interpretation of test scores, *Educ. Psychol. Measmnt.*, 1950, **10**, 67–78.
2. ——, "Psychological Testing," New York, Macmillan, 1954.
3. ——, and FOLEY, J. P., JR., "Differential Psychology" (Rev. Ed.), New York, Macmillan, 1949.
4. BRADFORD, E. J. G., Can present scholastic standards be maintained?, *Forum of Education*, 1925, 3, 186–198.
5. BURT, C., "Intelligence and Fertility," London, Hamilton, 1946.
6. CATTELL, R. B., "The Fight for our National Intelligence," London, King, 1937.
7. ——, The fate of national intelligence; test of a thirteen-year prediction, *Eugen. Rev.*, 1951, 42, 136–148.
8. CHAPMAN, J. C., and WIGGINS, D. M., Relation of family size to intelligence of offspring and socio-economic status of family. *J. Genet. Psychol.*, 1925, 32, 414–421.

9. CONRAD, H. S., and JONES, H. E., A field study of the differential birth rate, *J. Amer. Stat. Assoc.,* 1932, 27, 153–159.
10. DAWSON, S., Intelligence and fertility, *Brit. J. Psychol.,* 1932, 23, 42–51.
11. FINCH, F. H., Enrollment increases and changes in the mental level, *Appl. Psychol. Monogr.,* 1946, No. 10, pp. 75.
12. HIMMELWEIT, H. T., Intelligence and size of family; their relationship in an adult group of high educational standard, *Eugen. Rev.,* 1948, 40, 77–88.
13. HUSÉN, T., The influence of schooling upon IQ, *Theoria,* 1951, 17, 61–88.
14. LENTZ, T., JR., Relation of IQ to size of family, *J. Educ. Psychol.,* 1927, 18, 486–496.
15. LORGE, I., Schooling makes a difference, *Teachers Coll. Rec.,* 1945, 46, 483–492.
16. MCCARTHY, DOROTHEA, Language Development in Children, in L. Carmichael (Ed.), "Manual of Child Psychology," New York, Wiley, 1954.
17. MACMEEKEN, A. M. "The Intelligence of a Representative Group of Scottish Children," London, Univer. London Press, 1940.
18. MAXWELL, J., Intelligence and family size of college students, *Eugen. Rev.,* 1951, 42, 209–210.
19. PENROSE, L. S., The supposed threat of declining intelligence, *Amer. J. Ment. Def.,* 1948, 53, 114–118.
20. ROBERTS, J. A. F., The negative association between intelligence and fertility, *Human Biol.,* 1941, 13, 410–412.
21. ——, et al., Studies on a child population, III: Intelligence and family size, *Ann. Eugen.,* 1938, 8, 178–215.
22. SCOTTISH COUNCIL FOR RESEARCH IN EDUCATION, "The Intelligence of Scottish Children: A National Survey of an Age Group," London, Univer. London Press, 1933.
23. ——, "The Trend of Scottish Intelligence," London, Univer. London Press, 1949.
24. ——, "Social Implications of the 1947 Scottish Mental Survey," London, Univer. London Press, 1953.
25. SHUEY, AUDREY M., Intelligence of college women as related to family size, *J. Educ. Psychol.,* 1951, 42, 215–222.
26. SUTHERLAND, H. E. G., and THOMSON, G. H., The correlation between intelligence and size of family, *Brit. J. Psychol.,* 1926, 17, 81–92.
27. TERMAN, L. M., et al., "Genetic Studies of Genius," Vol. I, Stanford, Calif., Stanford Univer. Press, 1925.
28. TUDDENHAM, R. D., Soldier intelligence in World Wars I and II, *Amer. Psychologist,* 1948, 3, 54–56.
29. WARBURTON, F. W., Relationship between intelligence and size of family, *Eugen. Rev.,* 1951, 43, 36–37.
30. ——, Relationship between the intelligence of students and size of family, *Eugen. Rev.,* 1952, 43, 188.
31. WHEELER, L. R., A comparative study of the intelligence of East Tennessee mountain children, *J. Educ., Psychol.,* 1942, 33, 321–334.
32. WILLOUGHBY, R. R., and COOGAN, MARGUERITE, The correlation between intelligence and fertility, *Human Biol.,* 1940, 12, 114–119.

Biographical Correlates of Artistic and Literary Creativity in Adolescent Girls[1]

Research on the nature and correlates of creativity has been accumulating at an increasing rate. Golann (1963) classified the various approaches with reference to their emphasis on products, process, measurement, or personality. Methodologically, investigations differ in their use of evaluated achievement (which focuses on products) or test performance as *criteria of creativity*. The test criterion is open to criticism because of limitations of test coverage and inadequate or inconsistent validation data. For these reasons, the criterion employed in this study was evaluated achievement. More specifically, the present criterion reflected the essential conditions of creativeness proposed by MacKinnon (1962), which include (*a*) novelty, originality, or statistical infrequency; (*b*) adaptiveness to reality, involving the achievement of some reality-oriented goal, such as the solution of a scientific or aesthetic problem; and (*c*) sustained activity leading to the development, evaluation, and elaboration of the original idea. It is apparent that tests concentrate on the first of these conditions, largely neglecting the last two.

In the effort to identify the *correlates of creativity,* different investigators have employed aptitude and personality tests, interviews, and biographical inventories. The biographical inventory provides a standardized group procedure for gathering information about the individual's experiential history and about relevant aspects of the psychological environment in which he developed. Insofar as environment may play a significant role in the development of creativity, the biographical inventory technique should serve a dual function: (*a*) prediction of subsequent creative achievement in individuals, (*b*) identification of environmental variables conducive to the development of creative behavior.

[1] This study is part of a larger project supported by Subcontract No. 2 of the Center for Urban Education, Contract OEC-1-7-062868-3060 with the United States Office of Education.

Biographical correlates of artistic and literary creativity in adolescent girls. *Journal of Applied Psychology,* 1969, 53, 267–273. (With C. E. Schaefer) Copyright 1969 by the American Psychological Association. Reprinted by permission.

As predictive instruments, biographical inventories have repeatedly demonstrated satisfactory validity against complex industrial, military, and educational criteria (Freeberg, 1967; Henry, 1966). With regard to creative achievement, they have proved effective in differentiating between levels of creativity in several groups of scientific research workers. Such results have been obtained with petroleum research scientists (Morrison, Owens, Glennon & Albright, 1962; Smith, Albright, Glennon, & Owens, 1961), with a variety of research personnel in a pharmaceutical company (Buel, 1965; Tucker, Cline, & Schmitt, 1967), with engineers (McDermid, 1965), and with psychologists and chemists (Chambers, 1964). In a series of studies of scientists in the National Aeronautics and Space Administration (NASA), Taylor, Ellison, and Tucker (1966) obtained validity coefficients in the .40s and .50s when biographical inventory keys were cross-validated against several criteria of creative achievement. It is also noteworthy that such biographical inventory keys have shown substantial validity generalization when applied to research scientists in other fields (Buel, Albright, & Glennon, 1966; Cline, Tucker, & Anderson, 1966).

Investigations at the high school and college level have usually employed tests as criteria, predictors, or both. Few studies have utilized biographical inventories and still fewer have done so against a criterion of evaluated achievement. Taylor, Cooley, and Nielson (1963) applied a modified version of the biographical inventory developed on NASA scientists to high school students participating in a summer science program supported by the National Science Foundation. This biographical inventory proved to be the best overall predictor of creative research performance in these students, its validity being as high as .47 in one of the groups. Parloff and Datta (1965) compared contrasted groups of participants in the Westinghouse Science Talent Search, selected on the basis of judges' ratings of their research projects. However, these groups were compared chiefly in personality test scores, the only background items reported being father's occupation, socioeconomic level, and intactness of family. Dauw (1966) successfully differentiated between highly creative and less creative adolescents by means of a biographical inventory, but his Ss were chosen on the basis of creativity tests only.

A series of studies conducted for the National Merit Scholarship Corporation report significant relationships between biographical data and subsequent creative achievement in college (Holland & Nichols, 1964; Nichols & Holland, 1963). That the obtained relationships are often low may result in part from the highly selected nature of the samples. It is of particular interest that among the many predictors investigated—including aptitude and personality tests—the best predictor of creative achievement in college was creative achievement in the same area in high school (Holland & Astin, 1962; Nichols & Holland, 1964). Even more striking is the finding that, in a large and representative sample of college freshmen, it was the students with superior high school grades who had most often won distinction for creative achievement in high school extracurricular activities (Werts, 1966). Contrary to a prevalent view, academic aptitude was closely related to creativity, especially in scientific and literary fields.

Relevant biographical data have also been obtained in studies employing interviewing or other intensive individual assessment procedures with adults who have made creative contributions in the arts or sciences (MacKinnon, 1962; Roe, 1951a, 1951b, 1953). Similar assessment techniques were utilized by Helson (1967) with college women identified through faculty nominations and ratings of creative achievement in college. In the same series of studies, Helson (1965, 1966, 1967) gathered questionnaire data regarding childhood interests and activities as recalled by her Ss. Finally, parental characteristics have been investigated in relation to children's creativity as determined by either creativity tests or evaluated achievement (Domino, 1969; Dreyer & Wells, 1966; Helson, 1966, 1967; Weisberg & Springer, 1961). The Ss of these studies included school children, high school students, and college women.

In an earlier study by the present writers (Schaefer & Anastasi, 1968), biographical inventory keys were developed in a group of 400 high school boys against criteria of creative achievement in (a) science and (b) art or creative writing. Cross-validation yielded validity coefficients of .35 and .64 for the science and art-writing keys, respectively, both significant at the .001 level. In the present study, the same basic procedures were followed in developing biographical inventory keys for high school girls in creative art and creative writing. These two fields were chosen for further exploration because in the earlier study differentiation between creative and control groups was greater in the combined art and writing group than in the science group. Among high school girls, moreover, outstanding creative achievement in art or writing is more frequent than it is in science. As in the earlier study, a second major objective of the present investigation was to utilize the differentiating biographical inventory items in formulating a description of the antecedents and correlates of creativity in this population.

METHOD

Subjects

The Ss employed in the principal data analyses were 400 female students from seven public high schools in greater New York.[2] These schools were chosen, first, because they offer courses or programs providing opportunities for creative activities and, second, because they have outstanding records of awards, prizes, and other indications of creative student achievement in art or writing. Of the 400 Ss, 246 were seniors, 128 juniors, and 26 sophomores. The group as a whole was superior with regard to educational level of parents, slightly more than one-half of the fathers and one-third of the mothers having attended college for one or more years. While over half of the parents were born in New York City, nearly one-third were foreign-born. The most frequent national ancestries were Russian, Polish, and German, in that order; 24 Ss were Negro.

The total sample comprises four criterion groups of 100 students each, designated as follows: Creative-Art (CrA), Control-Art (CoA), Creative-Writing (CrW), and Control-Writing (CoW). For inclusion in a *creative* group, S had to meet two criteria: (*a*) teacher nomination on the basis of one or more creative products to be listed on a teacher nomination form—any type of visual art or creative writing was acceptable for this purpose; (*b*) score above a minimum cutoff on Guilford Alternate Uses and Consequences tests. The *control* Ss were enrolled in the same courses from which the creative Ss were selected and were nominated by the same teachers as having provided no evidence of creative achievement. They also scored below a maximum cutoff on the two Guilford screening tests. Within each field, creative and control groups were matched in school attended, class, and grade-point average. The 400 Ss in the four criterion groups were selected from an initial pool of 1,114 nominees in the seven schools.

It should be noted that the Guilford tests were employed only as a check on irrelevant factors that might have influenced the nomination of creative or control Ss. The scores on these tests were employed only to exclude cases, never to admit them. Moreover, the two cutoff scores were sufficiently extreme as to exclude only those students whose test performance was highly discordant with their reported achievement. In terms of available published norms, the mean scores of the creative students on the two Guilford tests are approximately equal to those of college students, while the mean scores of the control groups fall close to the ninth grade mean.

---

[2] The authors gratefully acknowledge the cooperation of J. Wayne Wrightstone, Assistant Superintendent, Board of Education of the City of New York, Nathan Brown, then with the Center for Urban Education, and the principals and participating teachers of the following high schools: Abraham Lincoln, Art and Design, Erasmus Hall, Forest Hills, Jamaica, Midwood, and Music and Art.

Biographical Inventory

Except for minor changes, the biographical inventory employed in this study
was the same as that prepared in the earlier study of high school boys (Schaefer
& Anastasi, 1968). The questions were originally formulated on the basis of hypotheses and published research findings regarding the correlates of creativity.
The 166 questions of this inventory are grouped into five sections designated as
physical characteristics, family history, educational history, leisure-time activities, and miscellaneous. Most of the questions cover objective facts regarding
present or past activities and experiences; some call for expressions of preference
and others pertain to plans and goals.

The inventory contains some multiple-choice and checklist items; but many
questions are open-ended. Even with the objective items, moreover, there is
usually provision for additional unlisted responses. Although scoring and data
analysis are more difficult under these conditions, these types of items yield a
richer return of information and are especially appropriate in an exploratory
study. All responses were coded prior to tabulation. For each question, there
were several possible responses, the number being quite large for some questions.
In addition, several questions yielded responses that could be classified from different viewpoints to test different hypotheses. For example, a response to "List
your present hobbies" could be scored with reference to number of hobbies or
type of hobbies; and hobbies could be sorted into types according to several
different schemas. As a result, the 166 questions yielded a total of 3,962 "scorable items" or individual response alternatives employed in the item analysis.

Procedure

The biographical inventory, together with three tests employed in another part
of the project, was administered by the same E to groups of 110–256 students
during a 2-hr. session held in the school buildings outside of school hours. The
Ss were paid for participating in this testing session. Identification numbers were
assigned to provide anonymity, and students were assured of the confidentiality
of their responses.

In the analysis of biographical inventory data, each of the four criterion
groups was subdivided into two subgroups of 50, employed for development of
scoring keys and cross-validation, respectively. Each pair of subgroups was
equated in number of students from each school, class distribution, grade-point
average, and mean score on the screening tests. For each of the 3,962 scorable
items, classified as present or absent, a phi coefficient was computed against
the dichotomous criterion of creative versus control. These coefficients were
computed separately in art and writing criterion groups. All items with phi
coefficients at the significance level of $p < .20$ or better were considered for
inclusion in the *initial CrA and CrW scoring keys*. Some of these items were
excluded because they duplicated other items, were checked by fewer than
four Ss in either subgroup, or were inconsistent with other responses or with
hypotheses and hence likely to have yielded isolated chance correlations.

In the initial scoring keys, a weight of 1 was assigned to items discriminating between the $p < .20$ and $p < .05$ levels, and a weight of 2 to items discriminating at the $p < .05$ level or better. Items with higher frequencies in the creative group received positive weights; those with higher frequencies in the control group received negative weights. The initial CrA and CrW scoring keys were used in scoring the biographical inventories of the corresponding creative and control Ss in the cross-validation samples. The scorers were unaware of the criterion status of Ss. The scores thus obtained were correlated with the dichotomous criterion to provide an estimate of the validity of the scoring keys.

In order to utilize all the data in the selection of items for *final scoring keys,* item analyses were carried out independently in initial and cross-validation samples and those items were selected that differentiated between creative and control groups with a compound probability of .05 or better (Baker, 1952).

RESULTS

Application of the initial CrA and CrW biographical inventory keys to the appropriate cross-validation samples yielded the data summarized in Table 1. Although there is considerable overlapping between the scores of creative and control groups, the means of both creative groups are significantly higher than those of the corresponding control groups at the .001 level. Point-biserial correlations between biographical inventory scores and the dichotomous criterion are .34 in the art group and .55 in the writing group.

At least two conditions imposed upon the selection of Ss tend to reduce the differences between creative and control groups. First, creative and control Ss were equated in grade-point average, although there is evidence that high school grades are in fact related to creative achievement (e.g., Werts, 1966). Second, the creative and control Ss were enrolled in the same courses in art or writing and attended high schools noted for the creative achievement of their students.

The second condition applies more strongly to the art than to the writing group, since a large proportion of Ss in the art sample were in special high schools whose students are selected on the basis of superior artistic talents. This fact is consistent with the finding that differentiation between creatives and controls was less sharp in the art than in the writing group. Not only were the mean difference and the criterion correlation higher in the writing than in the art group, but the number of significantly differentiating items was also larger in the CrW key than in the CrA key—a difference that is reflected in the higher scores obtained with this key. In the light of these sample characteristics, it should be noted that the present study is concerned with the differentiating biographical characteristics of the more highly creative *S*s within an academically superior and talented population.

After the cross-validation of the initial biographical inventory keys, final keys were constructed with items whose compound probability was derived from both initial and cross-validation samples. The CrA key thus developed contains 40 items, the CrW key 82 items. An examination of these items provides a description of the biographical correlates of creativity as revealed within the conditions of this study.

DISCUSSION

Correlates of Creativity Across Both Fields

The most conspicuous characteristic of the creatives in both fields is a *pervasive and continuing interest* in their chosen field and absorption in its pursuit. Items in this category include those dealing with favorite subjects in elementary school and high school; subjects found easy and those found difficult; nature of extracurricular activities in elementary school and high school, as well as anticipated extracurricular activities in college; concentration of hobbies in one's field of interest, as well as hobbies bearing a close relation to vocational goal; and reported career plans. Strength of interest is also indicated by the significantly greater number of creatives than controls in both fields reporting that they frequently became so absorbed in a project that they missed a meal or stayed up late.

Typically, the highly creative adolescent girl in this study had manifested an absorbing interest in her field since childhood and her creative activities had received recognition through exhibitions, publication, prizes, or awards. Her initial interest was thus rewarded and reinforced early in life by persons in authority, such as parents and elementary school teachers. The continuity of creative achievement over time is corroborated by the findings of other investigations, notably Helson's (1965, 1967) research with college women, the surveys of National Merit Scholarship finalists (Holland & Astin, 1962; Nichols & Holland, 1964), and our own earlier study of creative high school boys (Schaefer & Anastasi, 1968).

Several significantly differentiating items suggest a predominance of *unusual experiences* in the backgrounds of the creatives as contrasted with the controls. Thus the creatives were more likely than the controls to have had a variety of unusual experiences, to day-

TABLE 1 Biographical Inventory Scores of Criterion Groups in Cross-Validation Samples

Score	Creative Art Key		Creative Writing Key	
	Creative Art	Control Art	Creative Writing	Control Writing
141–150	0	0	1	0
131–140	0	0	6	1
121–130	0	0	6	1
111–120	0	0	5	2
101–110	0	0	11	4
91–100	1	0	10	1
81–90	7	1	4	10
71–80	3	5	3	8
61–70	12	7	3	11
51–60	19	11	1	8
41–50	4	13	0	3
31–40	1	8	0	1
21–30	3	5	0	0
N	50	50	50	50
M	61.26	50.00	104.40	76.24
σ	15.65	15.04	21.57	20.87
Range	24–94	23–89	54–149	39–136
z	3.67*		6.63*	
r_{pbis}	.34*		.55*	

Note.—In order to eliminate negative scores, 50 was added to each raw score. This adjustment, however, does not exclude negative scores from the total possible range, which is −87 to 248 for the CrA key and −60 to 370 for the CrW key.

*$p < .001$.

dream about unusual things, to have collections of an unusual nature (such as ant pictures, mushrooms, and mobiles), and to have experienced eidetic imagery or had imaginary companions in childhood. To some extent, these differences may indicate greater readiness to acknowledge unusual experiences on the part of the creatives and less reluctance to report them. It is also interesting to note that more creatives than controls in both fields reported unusual types of paternal discipline, other than those listed on the inventory form. One could speculate that the prevalence of atypical experiences in their early life may contribute to the low level of conformity and conventionality generally found to characterize creative persons at all ages.

Because of the selection procedures employed, both creative and control groups tended to come from intellectually superior homes. Nevertheless, certain significant differences were found in the *familial backgrounds* of creatives and controls. In both creative groups, significantly more fathers had attended college, graduate school, or professional schools than was true in the corresponding control groups. More controls than creatives reported that no musical instrument was played in the family. Since Ss were not selected for this study on the basis of musical achievement, this difference probably reflects the general cultural level of the home. Also relevant to general home conditions may be the fact that significantly more creatives than controls reported having two or more collections.

Earlier investigations have repeatedly found creativity to be related to parental educational and occupational level and to socioeconomic level of the home, whether Ss be distinguished scientists (Chambers, 1964) or creative high school students (Schaefer & Anastasi, 1968). Nor is the relationship limited to full-fledged creative achievement. Using performance on the Minnesota Tests of Creative Thinking as a criterion, Dauw (1966) found that high-scoring high school seniors had parents with better educational backgrounds and more professional and managerial occupations than did the low scorers. Similarly, in a study of seventh grade children subdivided on the basis of scores on an originality battery, socioeconomic status yielded the largest group difference of all variables investigated (Anderson & Cropley, 1966). In explaining this finding, the authors refer first to typical lower-class parental attitudes that tend to evoke anxiety toward school learning and hence encourage convergent rather than divergent thinking. As a second reason, they cite the more varied and stimulating environment provided by homes at higher socioeconomic levels. In Parloff and Datta's (1965) study of highly selected participants in the Westinghouse Science Talent Search, the entire sample averaged above the general population in socioeconomic level and in parental educational and occupational level, although these variables were unrelated to the rated creativity of projects within the sample.

With regard to parental influence on the creative high school girls in our study, the majority of items differentiating between creatives and controls refer to the *father* rather than to the mother. In our earlier study of high school boys, the reverse was true, more of the differentiating items pertaining to the mother. These findings are consistent with those reported by Dauw (1966) for high school seniors, by MacKinnon (1962) for creative male architects, and by Helson (1966, 1967) for creative women mathematicians and creative college women. In the study of women mathematicians, moreover, Helson (1966, p. 21) reports that "the creative women were judged by interviewers to have had more identification with their fathers than comparison subjects." If such results truly indicate a greater influence of the opposite-sex parent on creative children, they may help to explain the finding that in their attitudes, interests, and problem-solving styles creative individuals show more traits of the opposite sex than do controls and generally conform less closely to sex stereotypes (see e.g., MacKinnon, 1962).

Differences Between Creativity Correlates in Art and Writing Groups

The CrA and CrW groups are not directly comparable because of differences in school and class distribution and grade-point average. As might be anticipated, the grades in the CrW group average significantly higher than those in the CrA group. In the present experimental design, each creative group was equated with its own control group in these variables. The question now to be considered is whether the characteristics that significantly differentiate CrA Ss from their own controls differ in any systematic way from those that significantly differentiate the CrW Ss from their controls. This question can be answered by examining the items in the final CrA and CrW keys.

As previously noted, the CrW key contains about twice as many items as the CrA key. With few exceptions, these additional items fall into a cluster indicative of strong intellectual and "cultural" orientation and breadth of interests, both in the student herself and in her home background. The fathers of the CrW girls, as compared with those of the controls, are more likely to have one or more hobbies, frequently of an artistic or literary nature. Magazines regularly available at home are more likely to be of the cultural-intellectual types. The student herself is more likely to own classical records, attend concerts, and read more than 10 books a year, preferably in science, science fiction, philosophy, languages, or history. She regularly reads more than two sections of a newspaper, including editorials. She frequently visits art museums and galleries, has received lessons in arts or crafts, and has a large number of hobbies, beginning in childhood, to which she now devotes over 5 hr. a week. She reports owning a microscope more often than do the controls. In high school, she participates more extensively in extracurricular activities and anticipates more participation in college. Her college plans are more fully developed and ambitious. In comparison to the controls, the CrW student is more often considering two or more colleges, usually including an Ivy League or small private college, and is less often considering a public city college.

It is noteworthy that the breadth of interests and intellectual orientation characterizing the CrW girls was found in *both* creative groups of boys in our earlier study (Schaefer & Anastasi, 1968). One of these groups was selected because of creative achievement in science, the other because of creative achievement in art or writing. The latter group, however, included 76 boys in creative writing and only 24 in art. It is thus likely that the similarity of this group to the CrW girls resulted from the predominance of creative writing cases within it.

When the results of the two studies are considered together, they indicate that the biographical correlates of creativity are closely similar for boys and girls, with the possible exception of the reversal of role model and the greater influence of the opposite-sex parent upon the creative offspring. With regard to field of creative achievement, certain characteristic differences emerge among science, writing, and art. Cutting across both sex and field, however, are certain common characteristics of creative adolescents: continuity and pervasiveness of interest in chosen field; prevalence of unusual, novel, and diverse experiences; and educational superiority of familial background.

REFERENCES

ANDERSON, C. C., & CROPLEY, A. J. Some correlates of originality. *Australian Journal of Psychology*, 1966, **18**, 218–227.

BAKER, P. C. Combining tests of significance in cross-validation. *Educational and Psychological Measurement*, 1952, **12**, 300–306.

BUEL, W. D. Biographical data and the identification of creative research personnel. *Journal of Applied Psychology*, 1965, **49**, 318–321.

BUEL, W. D., ALBRIGHT, L. E., & GLENNON, J. R. A note on the generality and cross-validity of personal history for identifying creative research scientists. *Journal of Applied Psychology*, 1966, **50**, 217–219.

CHAMBERS, J. A. Relating personality and biographical factors to scientific creativity. *Psychological Monographs*, 1964, **78**, No. 7 (Whole No. 584).

CLINE, V. B., TUCKER, M. F., & ANDERSON, D. R. Psychology of the scientist: XX. Cross-validation of biographical information predictor keys across diverse samples of scientists. *Psychological Reports*, 1966, **19**, 951–954.

DAUW, D. C. Life experiences of original thinkers and good elaborators. *Exceptional Children*, 1966, **32**, 433–440.

DOMINO, G. Maternal personality correlates of sons' creativity. *Journal of Consulting and Clinical Psychology*, 1969, **33**, 180–183.

DREYER, A., & WELLS, M. Parental values, parental control, and creativity in young children. *Journal of Marriage and the Family,* 1966, 28, 83–88.

FREEBERG, N. E. The biographical information blank as a predictor of student achievement. *Psychological Reports,* 1967, 20, 911–925.

GOLANN, S. E. Psychological study of creativity. *Psychological Bulletin,* 1963, 60, 548–565.

HELSON, R. Childhood interest clusters related to creativity in women. *Journal of Consulting Psychology,* 1965, 29, 352–361.

HELSON, R. Personality of women with imaginative and artistic interests: The role of masculinity, originality, and other characteristics in their creativity. *Journal of Personality,* 1966, 34, 1–25.

HELSON, R. Personality characteristics and developmental history of creative college women. *Genetic Psychology Monographs,* 1967, 76, 205–256.

HENRY, E. R. Conference on the use of biographical data in psychology. *American Psychologist,* 1966, 21, 247–249.

HOLLAND, J. L., & ASTIN, A. W. The prediction of the academic, artistic, scientific, and social achievement of undergraduates of superior scholastic aptitude. *Journal of Educational Psychology,* 1962, 53, 132–143.

HOLLAND, J. L., & NICHOLS, R. C. Prediction of academic and extracurricular achievement in college. *Journal of Educational Psychology,* 1964, 55, 55–65.

MACKINNON, D. W. The nature and nurture of creative talent. *American Psychologist,* 1962, 17, 484–495.

MCDERMID, C. D. Some correlates of creativity in engineering personnel. *Journal of Applied Psychology,* 1965, 49, 14–19.

MORRISON, R. F., OWENS, W. A., GLENNON, J. R., & ALBRIGHT, L. E. Factored life history antecedents of industrial research performance. *Journal of Applied Psychology,* 1962, 46, 281–284.

NICHOLS, R. C., & HOLLAND, J. L. Prediction of the first year college performance of high aptitude students. *Psychological Monographs,* 1963, 77, No. 7 (Whole No. 570).

NICHOLS, R. C., & HOLLAND, J. L. The selection of high aptitude high school graduates for maximum achievement in college. *Personnel and Guidance Journal,* 1964, 43, 33–40.

PARLOFF, M. B., & DATTA, L. E. Personality characteristics of the potentially creative scientist. *Science and Psychoanalysis,* 1965, 8, 91–106.

ROE, A. A psychological study of eminent biologists. *Psychological Monographs,* 1951, 65, No. 14 (Whole No. 331). (a)

ROE, A. A psychological study of physical scientists. *Genetic Psychology Monographs,* 1951, 43, 121–235. (b)

ROE, A. A psychological study of eminent psychologists and anthropologists, and a comparison with biologists and physical scientists. *Psychological Monographs,* 1953, 67, No. 2 (Whole No. 287).

SCHAEFER, C. E., & ANASTASI, A. A biographical inventory for identifying creativity in adolescent boys. *Journal of Applied Psychology,* 1968, 52, 42–48.

SMITH, W. J., ALBRIGHT, L. E., GLENNON, J. R., & OWENS, W. A. The prediction of research competence and creativity from personal history. *Journal of Applied Psychology,* 1961, 45, 59–62.

TAYLOR, C. W., COOLEY, G. N., & NIELSEN, E. C. Identifying high school students with characteristics needed in research work. NSF-G17543, University of Utah, 1963. (Mimeograph)

TAYLOR, C. W., ELLISON, R. L., & TUCKER, M. F. *Biographical information and the prediction of multiple criteria of success in science.* Greensboro, N.C.: Richardson Foundation, 1966.

TUCKER, M. F., CLINE, V. B., & SCHMITT, J. R. Prediction of creativity and other performance measures from biographical information among pharmaceutical scientists. *Journal of Applied Psychology,* 1967, 51, 131–138.

WEISBERG, P. S., & SPRINGER, K. J. Environmental factors in creative function. *Archives of General Psychiatry,* 1961, 5, 555–564.

WERTS, C. E. The many faces of intelligence. *National Merit Scholarship Corporation Research Reports,* 1966, 2, No. 5.

8

Heredity and Environment: Theoretical Considerations

In the 1958 paper reproduced in this chapter, I proposed that, as traditionally formulated, the heredity-environment problem may have been asking the wrong questions; and, for this reason, it had gradually come to be regarded as a pseudoproblem. A more meaningful question, I maintained, is the question "How?" What are the specific causal mechanisms and chains of events whereby hereditary and environmental conditions combine to influence behavioral development? In the effort to provide a systematic framework for this question, the paper describes and illustrates a continuum of indirectness along which hereditary influences can be ordered. Environmental influences of an organic nature can be similarly ordered. Behavioral or experiential influences can be arranged along a continuum of breadth. Cultural differentials may affect behavioral development through either organic or experiential mechanisms. It may be noted that, in subsequent decades, some provocative answers to the question "How?" have been formulated, and a considerable body of supportive data has accumulated (e.g., Hayes, 1962; Scarr, 1981).

Addressing the heredity-environment question within a different context, an article by Jensen (1969) aroused a storm of controversy which still lingers on. Although there are several aspects to this controversy and the issues are complicated (see, e.g., Cronbach, 1975), a major substantive source of disagreement pertains to the interpretation of heritability estimates. Specifically, a heritability index shows the proportional contribution of genetic or hereditary factors to the total variance of a particular trait in a given population under existing conditions. In an early article cited in Chapter 1, Hebb

*(1953) had addressed this point, although not using the term "herita-
bility" but referring to it as an application of analysis of variance to
the heredity-environment question. Essentially the same critique of
the possible misuses of this procedure was reiterated by Hebb (1970)
in a brief comment on Jensen's conclusions about the heritability
of intelligence. Even before the publication of Jensen's reply and of
Hebb's rejoinder, others had joined the fray (Einhorn, 1970; Gordon,
1970). Two of my comments, published at different stages in this
interchange, are reproduced at the end of this chapter.*

REFERENCES

Cronbach, L. J. Five decades of public controversy over mental testing. *American Psychologist,* 1975, *30,* 1–14.

Einhorn, H. J. On Hebb's criticism of Jensen. *American Psychologist,* 1970, *25,* 1173–1174.

Gordon, R. A. Concerning Hebb's criticism of Jensen and the heredity-environment argument. *American Psychologist,* 1970, *25,* 1172–1173.

Hayes, K. J. Genes, drives, and intellect. *Psychological Reports,* 1962, *10,* 299–342.

Hebb, D. O. Heredity and environment in mammalian behaviour. *British Journal of Animal Behaviour,* 1953, *1,* 43–47.

Hebb, D. O. A return to Jensen and his social science critics. *American Psychologist,* 1970, *25,* 568.

Jensen, A. R. How much can we boost IQ and scholastic achievement? *Harvard Educational Review,* 1969, *39,* 1–123.

Scarr, S. *On the development of competence and the indeterminate boundaries between cognition and motivation: A genotype-environment correlation theory.* Invited address presented at the meeting of the Eastern Psychological Association, New York, April 1981.

Heredity, Environment, and the Question "How?"[1]

Two or three decades ago, the so-called heredity-environment question was the center of lively controversy. Today, on the other hand, many psychologists look upon it as a dead issue. It is now generally conceded that both hereditary and environmental factors enter into all behavior. The reacting organism is a product of its genes and its past environment, while present environment provides the immediate stimulus for current behavior. To be sure, it can be argued that, although a given trait may result from the combined influence of hereditary and environmental factors, a specific difference in this trait between individuals or between groups may be traceable to either hereditary or environmental factors alone. The design of most traditional investigations undertaken to identify such factors, however, has been such as to yield inconclusive answers. The same set of data has frequently led to opposite conclusions in the hands of psychologists with different orientations.

Nor have efforts to determine the proportional contribution of hereditary and environmental factors to observed individual differences in given traits met with any greater success. Apart from difficulties in controlling conditions, such investigations have usually been based upon the implicit assumption that hereditary and environmental factors combine in an additive fashion. Both geneticists and psychologists have repeatedly demonstrated, however, that a more tenable hypothesis is that of interaction (15, 22, 28, 40). In other words, the nature and extent of the influence of each type of factor depend upon the contribution of the other. Thus the proportional contribution of heredity to the variance of a given trait, rather than being a constant, will vary under different environmental conditions. Similarly, under different hereditary conditions, the relative contribution of environment will differ. Studies designed to estimate the proportional contribution of heredity and environment, however, have rarely included measures of such interaction. The only possible conclusion from such research would thus seem to be that both

[1] Address of the President, Division of General Psychology, American Psychological Association, September 4, 1957.

Heredity, environment, and the question "How?" *Psychological Review*, 1958, *65*, 197–208. Copyright 1958 by the American Psychological Association. Reprinted by permission.

heredity and environment contribute to all behavior traits and that the extent of their respective contributions cannot be specified for any trait. Small wonder that some psychologists regard the heredity-environment question as unworthy of further consideration!

But is this really all we can find out about the operation of heredity and environment in the etiology of behavior? Perhaps we have simply been asking the wrong questions. The traditional questions about heredity and environment may be intrinsically unanswerable. Psychologists began by asking *which* type of factor, hereditary or environmental, is responsible for individual differences in a given trait. Later, they tried to discover *how much* of the variance was attributable to heredity and how much to environment. It is the primary contention of this paper that a more fruitful approach is to be found in the question *"How?"* There is still much to be learned about the specific *modus operandi* of hereditary and environmental factors in the development of behavioral differences. And there are several current lines of research which offer promising techniques for answering the question "How?"

VARIETY OF INTERACTION MECHANISMS

Hereditary Factors

If we examine some of the specific ways in which hereditary factors may influence behavior, we cannot fail but be impressed by their wide diversity. At one extreme, we find such conditions as phenyl-pyruvic amentia and amaurotic idiocy. In these cases, certain essential physical prerequisites for normal intellectual development are lacking as a result of hereditary metabolic disorders. In our present state of knowledge, there is no environmental factor which can completely counteract this hereditary deficit. The individual will be mentally defective, regardless of the type of environmental conditions under which he is reared.[a]

A somewhat different situation is illustrated by hereditary deafness, which may lead to intellectual retardation through interference with normal social interaction, language development, and schooling. In such a case, however, the hereditary handicap can be offset by appropriate adaptations of training procedures. It has been said, in fact, that the degree of intellectual backwardness of the deaf is an

---

[a]When this paper was prepared, the dietary treatment for PKU (phenylketonuria) had not yet become available for large-scale operational use.—Ed.

index of the state of development of special instructional facilities. As the latter improve, the intellectual retardation associated with deafness is correspondingly reduced.

A third example is provided by inherited susceptibility to certain physical diseases, with consequent protracted ill health. If environmental conditions are such that illness does in fact develop, a number of different behavioral effects may follow. Intellectually, the individual may be handicapped by his inability to attend school regularly. On the other hand, depending upon age of onset, home conditions, parental status, and similar factors, poor health may have the effect of concentrating the individual's energies upon intellectual pursuits. The curtailment of participation in athletics and social functions may serve to strengthen interest in reading and other sedentary activities. Concomitant circumstances would also determine the influence of such illness upon personality development. And it is well known that the latter effects could run the gamut from a deepening of human sympathy to psychiatric breakdown.

Finally, heredity may influence behavior through the mechanism of social stereotypes. A wide variety of inherited physical characteristics have served as the visible cues for identifying such stereotypes. These cues thus lead to behavioral restrictions or opportunities and—at a more subtle level—to social attitudes and expectancies. The individual's own self concept tends gradually to reflect such expectancies. All of these influences eventually leave their mark upon his abilities and inabilities, his emotional reactions, goals, ambitions, and outlook on life.

The geneticist Dobzhansky illustrates this type of mechanism by means of a dramatic hypothetical situation. He points out that, if there were a culture in which the carriers of blood group AB were considered aristocrats and those of blood group O laborers, then the blood-group genes would become important hereditary determiners of behavior (12, p. 147). Obviously the association between blood group and behavior would be specific to that culture. But such specificity is an essential property of the causal mechanism under consideration.

More realistic examples are not hard to find. The most familiar instances occur in connection with constitutional types, sex, and race. Sex and skin pigmentation obviously depend upon heredity. General body build is strongly influenced by hereditary components, although also susceptible to environmental modification. That all these physical characteristics may exert a pronounced effect upon behavior within a given culture is well known. It is equally apparent, of course, that in different cultures the behavioral correlates of such hereditary physical traits may be quite unlike. A specific physical cue may be completely unrelated to individual differences in psychological traits in one culture, while closely correlated with them in another. Or it may be associated with totally dissimilar behavior characteristics in two different cultures.

It might be objected that some of the illustrations which have been cited do not properly exemplify the operation of hereditary mechanisms in behavior development, since hereditary factors enter only indirectly into the behavior in question. Closer examination, however, shows this distinction to be untenable. First it may be noted that the influence of heredity upon behavior is always indirect. No psychological trait is ever inherited as such. All we can ever say directly from behavioral observations is that a given trait shows evidence of being influenced by certain "inheritable unknowns." This merely defines a problem for genetic research; it does not provide a causal explanation. Unlike the blood groups, which are close to the level of primary gene products, psychological traits are related to genes by highly indirect and devious routes. Even the mental deficiency associated with phenylketonuria is several steps removed from the chemically defective genes that represent its hereditary basis. Moreover, hereditary influences cannot be dichotomized into the more direct and the less direct. Rather do they represent a whole "continuum of indirectness," along which are found all degrees of remoteness of causal links. The examples already cited illustrate a few of the points on this continuum.

It should be noted that as we proceed along the continuum of indirectness, the range of variation of possible outcomes of hereditary factors expands rapidly. At each step in the causal chain, there is fresh opportunity for interaction with other hereditary factors as well as with environmental factors. And since each interaction in turn determines the direction of subsequent interactions, there is an ever-widening network of possible outcomes. If we visualize a simple sequential grid with only two alternatives at each point, it is obvious that there are two possible outcomes in the one-stage situation, four outcomes at the second stage, eight at the third, and so on in geometric progression. The actual situation is undoubtedly much more complex, since there will usually be more than two alternatives at any one point.

In the case of the blood groups, the relation to specific genes is so close that no other concomitant hereditary or environmental conditions can alter the outcome. If the organism survives at all, it will have the blood group determined by its genes. Among psychological traits, on the other hand, some variation in outcome is always possible as a result of concurrent circumstances. Even in cases of phenylketonuria, intellectual development will exhibit some relationship with the type of care and training available to the individual. That behavioral outcomes show progressive diversification as we proceed along the continuum of indirectness is brought out by the other examples which were cited. Chronic illness *can* lead to scholarly renown or to intellectual immaturity; a mesomorphic physique *can* be a contributing factor in juvenile delinquency or in the attainment of a college presidency! Published data on Sheldon somatotypes provide some support for both of the latter outcomes.

Parenthetically, it may be noted that geneticists have sometimes used the term "norm of reaction" to designate the range of variation of possible outcomes of gene properties (cf. 13, p. 161). Thus heredity sets the "norm" or limits within which environmental differences determine the eventual outcome. In the case of some traits, such as blood groups or eye color, this norm is much narrower than in the case of other traits. Owing to the rather different psychological connotations of both the words "norm" and "reaction," however, it seems less confusing to speak of the "range of variation" in this context.

A large portion of the continuum of hereditary influences which we have described coincides with the domain of somatopsychological relations, as defined by Barker et al. (6). Under this heading, Barker includes "variations in physique that affect the psychological situation of a person by influencing the effectiveness of his body as a tool for actions or by serving as a stimulus to himself or others" (6, p. 1). Relatively direct neurological influences on behavior, which have been the traditional concern of physiological psychology, are excluded from this definition, Barker being primarily concerned with what he calls the "social psychology of physique." Of the examples cited in the present paper, deafness, severe illness, and the physical characteristics associated with social stereotypes would meet the specifications of somatopsychological factors.

The somatic factors to which Barker refers, however, are not limited to those of hereditary origin. Bodily conditions attributable to environmental causes operate in the same sorts of somatopsychological relations as those traceable to heredity. In fact, heredity-environment distinctions play a minor part in Barker's approach.

Environmental Factors: Organic

Turning now to an analysis of the role of environmental factors in behavior, we find the same etiological mechanisms which were observed in the case of hereditary factors. First, however, we must differentiate between two classes of environmental influences: (*a*) those producing organic effects which may in turn influence behavior and (*b*) those serving as direct stimuli for psychological reactions. The former may be illustrated by food intake or by exposure to bacterial infection; the latter, by tribal initiation ceremonies or by a course in algebra. There are no completely satisfactory names by which to designate these two classes of influences. In an earlier paper by Anastasi and Foley (4), the terms "structural" and "functional" were employed. However, "organic" and "behavioral" have the advantage of greater familiarity in this context and may be less open to misinterpretation. Accordingly, these terms will be used in the present paper.

Like hereditary factors, environmental influences of an organic nature can also be ordered along a continuum of indirectness with regard to their relation to behavior. This continuum closely parallels that of hereditary factors. One end is typified by such conditions as mental deficiency resulting from cerebral birth injury or from prenatal nutritional inadequacies. A more indirect etiological mechanism is illustrated by severe motor disorder—as in certain cases of cerebral palsy—*without* accompanying injury to higher neurological centers. In such instances, intellectual retardation may occur as an indirect result of the motor handicap, through the curtailment of educational and social activities. Obviously this causal mechanism corresponds closely to that of hereditary deafness cited earlier in the paper.

Finally, we may consider an environmental parallel to the previously discussed social stereotypes which were mediated by hereditary physical cues. Let us suppose that a young woman with mousy brown hair becomes transformed into a dazzling golden blonde through environmental techniques currently available in our culture. It is highly probable that this metamorphosis will alter, not only the reactions of her associates toward her, but also her own self concept and subsequent behavior. The effects could range all the way from a rise in social poise to a drop in clerical accuracy!

Among the examples of environmentally determined organic influences which have been described, all but the first two fit Barker's definition of somatopsychological factors. With the exception of birth injuries and nutritional deficiencies, all fall within the social psychology of physique. Nevertheless, the individual factors exhibit wide diversity in their specific *modus operandi*—a diversity which has important practical as well as theoretical implications.

Environmental Factors: Behavioral

The second major class of environmental factors—the behavioral as contrasted to the organic—are by definition direct influences. The immediate effect of such environmental factors is always a behavioral change. To be sure, some of the initial behavioral effects may themselves indirectly affect the individual's later behavior. But this relationship can perhaps be best conceptualized in terms of breadth and permanence of effects. Thus it could be said that we are now dealing, not with a continuum of indirectness, as in the case of hereditary and organic-environmental factors, but rather with a continuum of breadth.

Social class membership may serve as an illustration of a relatively broad, pervasive, and enduring environmental factor. Its influence upon behavior development may operate through many channels. Thus social level may determine the range and nature of intellectual stimulation provided by home and community through books, music, art, play activities, and the like. Even more far-reaching may be the effects upon interests and motivation, as illustrated by the desire to perform abstract intellectual tasks, to surpass others in competitive situations, to succeed in school, or to gain social approval. Emotional and social traits may likewise be influenced by the nature of interpersonal relations characterizing homes at different socioeconomic levels. Somewhat more restricted in scope than social class, although still exerting a relatively broad influence, is amount of formal schooling which the individual is able to obtain.

A factor which may be wide or narrow in its effects, depending upon concomitant circumstances, is language handicap. Thus the bilingualism of an adult who moves to a foreign country with inadequate mastery of the new language represents a relatively limited handicap which can be readily overcome in most cases. At most, the difficulty is one of communication. On the other hand, some kinds of bilingualism in childhood may exert a retarding influence upon intellectual development and may under certain conditions affect personality development adversely (2, 5, 10). A common pattern in the homes of immigrants is that the child speaks one language at home and another in school, so that his knowledge of each language is limited to certain types of situations. Inadequate facility with the language of the school interferes with the acquisition of basic concepts, intellectual skills, and information. The frustration engendered by scholastic difficulties may in turn lead to discouragement and general dislike of school. Such reactions can be found, for example, among a number of Puerto Rican children in New York City schools (3). In the case of certain groups, moreover, the child's foreign language background may be perceived by himself and his associates as a symbol of minority group status and may thereby augment any emotional maladjustment arising from such status (34).

A highly restricted environmental influence is to be found in the opportunity to acquire specific items of information occurring in a particular intelligence test. The fact that such opportunities may vary with culture, social class, or individual experiential background is at the basis of the test user's concern with the problem of coaching and with "culture-free" or "culture-fair" tests (cf. 1, 2). If the advantage or disadvantage which such experiential differences confer upon certain individuals is strictly confined to performance on the given test, it will obviously reduce the validity of the test and should be eliminated.

In this connection, however, it is essential to know the breadth of the environmental influence in question. A fallacy inherent in many attempts to develop culture-fair tests is that the breadth of cultural differentials is not taken into account. Failure to consider breadth of effect likewise characterizes certain discussions of coaching. If, in coaching a student for a college admission test, we can improve his knowledge of verbal concepts and his reading comprehension, he will be better equipped to succeed in college courses. His performance level will thus be raised, not only on the test, but also on the criterion which the test is intended to predict. To try to devise a test which is not susceptible to such coaching would merely reduce the effectiveness of the test. Similarly, efforts to rule out cultural differentials from test items so as to make them equally "fair" to subjects in different social classes or in different cultures may merely limit the usefulness of the test, since the same cultural differentials may operate within the broader area of behavior which the test is designed to sample.

METHODOLOGICAL APPROACHES

The examples considered so far should suffice to highlight the wide variety of ways in which hereditary and environmental factors may interact in the course of behavior development. There is clearly a need for identifying explicitly the etiological mechanism whereby any given hereditary or environmental condition ultimately leads to a behavioral characteristic—in other words, the "how" of heredity and environment. Accordingly, we may now take a quick look at some promising methodological approaches to the question "how."

Within the past decade, an increasing number of studies have been designed to trace the connection between specific factors in the hereditary backgrounds or in the reactional biographies of individuals and their observed behavioral characteristics. There has been a definite shift away from the predominantly descriptive and correlational approach of the earlier decades toward more deliberate attempts to verify explanatory hopotheses. Similarly, the cataloguing of group differences in psychological traits has been giving way gradually to research on *changes* in group characteristics following altered conditions.

Among recent methodological developments, we have chosen seven as being particularly relevant to the analysis of etiological mechanisms. The first represents an extension of selective breeding investigations to permit the identification of specific hereditary conditions underlying the observed behavioral differences. When early selective breeding investigations such as those of Tryon (36) on rats indicated that "maze learning ability" was inherited, we were still a long way from knowing what was actually being transmitted by the genes. It was obviously not "maze learning ability" as such. Twenty— or even ten—years ago, some psychologists would have suggested that it was probably general intelligence. And a few might even have drawn a parallel with the inheritance of human intelligence.

But today investigators have been asking: Just what makes one group of rats learn mazes more quickly than the other? Is it differences in motivation, emotionality, speed of running, general activity level? If so, are these behavioral characteristics in turn dependent upon group differences in glandular development, body weight, brain size, biochemical factors, or some other organic conditions? A number of recent and ongoing investigations indicate that attempts are being made to trace, at least part of the way, the steps whereby certain chemical properties of the genes may ultimately lead to specified behavior characteristics.

An example of such a study is provided by Searle's (31) follow-up of Tryon's research. Working with the strains of maze-bright and maze-dull rats developed by Tryon, Searle demonstrated that the two strains differed in a number of emotional and motivational factors, rather than in ability. Thus the strain differences were traced one step further, although many links still remain to be found between maze learning and genes. A promising methodological development within the same general area is to be found in the recent research of Hirsch and Tryon (18). Utilizing a specially devised technique for measuring individual differences in behavior among lower organisms, these investigators launched a series of studies on selective breeding for behavioral characteristics in the fruit fly, *Drosophila.* Such research can capitalize on the mass of available genetic knowledge regarding the morphology of *Drosophila,* as well as on other advantages of using such an organism in genetic studies.

Further evidence of current interest in the specific hereditary

factors which influence behavior is to be found in an extensive research program in progress at the Jackson Memorial Laboratory,
under the direction of Scott and Fuller (30). In general, the project
is concerned with the behavioral characteristics of various breeds and
cross-breeds of dogs. Analyses of some of the data gathered to date
again suggest that "differences in performance are produced by differences in emotional, motivational, and peripheral processes, and
that genetically caused differences in central processes may be either
slight or non-existent" (29, p. 225). In other parts of the same project, breed differences in physiological characteristics, which may in
turn be related to behavioral differences, have been established.

A second line of attack is the exploration of possible relationships between behavioral characteristics and physiological variables
which may in turn be traceable to hereditary factors. Research on
EEG, autonomic balance, metabolic processes, and biochemical factors illustrates this approach. A lucid demonstration of the process of
tracing a psychological condition to genetic factors is provided by
the identification and subsequent investigation of phenylpyruvic
amentia. In this case, the causal chain from defective gene, through
metabolic disorder and consequent cerebral malfunctioning, to
feeblemindedness and other overt symptoms can be described step
by step (cf. 32; 33, pp. 389–391). Also relevant are the recent researches on neurological and biochemical correlates of schizophrenia
(9). Owing to inadequate methodological controls, however, most of
the findings of the latter studies must be regarded as tentative (19).

Prenatal environmental factors provide a third avenue of fruitful
investigation. Especially noteworthy is the recent work of Pasamanick and his associates (27), which demonstrated a tie-up between
socioeconomic level, complications of pregnancy and parturition,
and psychological disorders of the offspring. In a series of studies on
large samples of whites and Negroes in Baltimore, these investigators
showed that various prenatal and paranatal disorders are significantly
related to the occurrence of mental defect and psychiatric disorders
in the child. An important source of such irregularities in the process
of childbearing and birth is to be found in deficiencies of maternal
diet and in other conditions associated with low socioeconomic
status. An analysis of the data did in fact reveal a much higher frequency of all such medical complications in lower than in higher
socioeconomic levels, and a higher frequency among Negroes than
among whites.

Direct evidence of the influence of prenatal nutritional factors
upon subsequent intellectual development is to be found in a recent,
well controlled experiment by Harrell et al. (16). The subjects were

pregnant women in low-income groups, whose normal diets were generally quite deficient. A dietary supplement was administered to some of these women during pregnancy and lactation, while an equated control group received placebos. When tested at the ages of three and four years, the offspring of the experimental group obtained a significantly higher mean IQ than did the offspring of the controls.

Mention should also be made of animal experiments on the effects of such factors as prenatal radiation and neonatal asphyxia upon cerebral anomalies as well as upon subsequent behavior development. These experimental studies merge imperceptibly into the fourth approach to be considered, namely, the investigation of the influence of early experience upon the eventual behavioral characteristics of animals. Research in this area has been accumulating at a rapid rate. In 1954, Beach and Jaynes (8) surveyed this literature for the *Psychological Bulletin,* listing over 130 references. Several new studies have appeared since that date (e.g., 14, 21, 24, 25, 35). The variety of factors covered ranges from the type and quantity of available food to the extent of contact with human culture. A large number of experiments have been concerned with various forms of sensory deprivation and with diminished opportunities for motor exercise. Effects have been observed in many kinds of animals and in almost all aspects of behavior, including perceptual responses, motor activity, learning, emotionality, and social reactions.

In their review, Beach and Jaynes pointed out that research in this area has been stimulated by at least four distinct theoretical interests. Some studies were motivated by the traditional concern with the relative contribution of maturation and learning to behavior development. Others were designed in an effort to test certain psychoanalytic theories regarding infantile experiences, as illustrated by studies which limited the feeding responses of young animals. A third relevant influence is to be found in the work of the European biologist Lorenz (23) on early social stimulation of birds, and in particular on the special type of learning for which the term "imprinting" has been coined. A relatively large number of recent studies have centered around Hebb's (17) theory regarding the importance of early perceptual experiences upon subsequent performance in learning situations. All this research represents a rapidly growing and promising attack on the *modus operandi* of specific environmental factors.

The human counterpart of these animal studies may be found in the comparative investigation of child-rearing practices in different cultures and subcultures. This represents the fifth approach in our list. An outstanding example of such a study is that by Whiting and Child (38), published in 1953. Utilizing data on 75 primitive societies from the Cross-Cultural Files of the Yale Institute of Human Relations, these investigators set out to test a number of hypotheses regarding the relationships between child-rearing practices and personality development. This analysis was followed up by field observations in five cultures, the results of which have not yet been reported (cf. 37).

Within our own culture, similar surveys have been concerned with the diverse psychological environments provided by different social classes (11). Of particular interest are the study by Williams and Scott (39) on the association between socioeconomic level, permissiveness, and motor development among Negro children, and the exploratory research by Milner (26) on the relationship between reading readiness in first-grade children and patterns of parent-child interaction. Milner found that upon school entrance the lower-class child seems to lack chiefly two advantages enjoyed by the middle-class child. The first is described as "a warm positive family atmosphere or adult-relationship pattern which is more and more being recognized as a motivational prerequisite of any kind of adult-controlled learning." The lower-class children in Milner's study perceived adults as predominantly hostile. The second advantage is an extensive opportunity to interact verbally with adults in the family. The latter point is illustrated by parental attitudes toward mealtime conversation, lower-class parents tending to inhibit and discourage such conversation, while middle-class parents encourage it.

Most traditional studies on child-rearing practices have been designed in terms of a psychoanalytic orientation. There is need for more data pertaining to other types of hypotheses. Findings such as those of Milner on opportunities for verbalization and the resulting effects upon reading readiness represent a step in this direction. Another possible source of future data is the application of the intensive observational techniques of psychological ecology developed by Barker and Wright (7) to widely diverse socioeconomic groups.

A sixth major approach involves research on the previously cited somatopsychological relationships (6). To date, little direct information is available on the precise operation of this class of factors in psychological development. The multiplicity of ways in which physical traits—whether hereditary or environmental in origin—may influence behavior thus offers a relatively unexplored field for future study.

The seventh and final approach to be considered represents an adaptation of traditional twin studies. From the standpoint of the question "How?" there is need for closer coordination between the usual data on twin resemblance and observations of the family interactions of twins. Available data already suggest, for example, that closeness of contact and extent of environmental similarity are greater in the case of monozygotic than in the case of dizygotic twins (cf. 2). Information on the social reactions of twins toward each other and the specialization of roles is likewise of interest (2). Especially useful would be longitudinal studies of twins, beginning in early infancy and following the subjects through school age. The operation of differential environmental pressures, the development of specialized roles, and other environmental influences could thus be more clearly identified and correlated with intellectual and personality changes in the growing twins.

Parenthetically, I should like to add a remark about the traditional applications of the twin method, in which persons in different degrees of hereditary and environmental relationships to each other are simply compared for behavioral similarity. In these studies, attention has been focused principally upon the amount of resemblance of monozygotic as contrasted to dizygotic twins. Yet such a comparison is particularly difficult to interpret because of the many subtle differences in the environmental situations of the two types of twins. A more fruitful comparison would seem to be that between dizygotic twins and siblings, for whom the hereditary similarity is known to be the same. In Kallmann's monumental research on psychiatric disorders among twins (20), for example, one of the most convincing bits of evidence for the operation of hereditary factors in schizophrenia is the fact that the degrees of concordance for dizygotic twins and for siblings were practically identical. In contrast, it will be recalled that in intelligence test scores dizygotic twins resemble each other much more closely than do siblings—a finding which reveals the influence of environmental factors in intellectual development.

SUMMARY

The heredity-environment problem is still very much alive. Its viability is assured by the gradual replacement of the questions, "Which one?" and "How much?" by the more basic and appropriate question, "How?" Hereditary influences—as well as environmental factors of an organic nature—vary along a "continuum of indirectness." The more indirect their connection with behavior, the wider will be the range of variation of possible outcomes. One extreme of the continuum of indirectness may be illustrated by brain damage leading to mental deficiency; the other extreme, by physical characteristics associated with social stereotypes. Examples of factors falling at intermediate points include deafness, physical diseases, and motor disorders. Those environmental factors which act directly upon behavior can be ordered along a continuum of breadth or permanence of effect, as exemplified by social class membership, amount of formal schooling, language handicap, and familiarity with specific test items.

Several current lines of research offer promising techniques for exploring the *modus operandi* of hereditary and environmental factors. Outstanding among them are investigations of: (*a*) hereditary conditions which underlie behavioral differences between selectively bred groups of animals; (*b*) relations between physiological variables and individual differences in behavior, especially in the case of pathological deviations; (*c*) role of prenatal physiological factors in behavior development; (*d*) influence of early experience upon eventual behavioral characteristics; (*e*) cultural differences in child-rearing practices in relation to intellectual and emotional development; (*f*) mechanisms of somatopsychological relationships; and (*g*) psychological development of twins from infancy to maturity, together with observations of their social environment. Such approaches are extremely varied with regard to subjects employed, nature of psychological functions studied, and specific experimental procedures followed. But it is just such heterogeneity of methodology that is demanded by the wide diversity of ways in which hereditary and environmental factors interact in behavior development.

REFERENCES

1. ANASTASI, ANNE. *Psychological testing.* New York: Macmillan, 1954.
2. ANASTASI, ANNE. *Differential psychology.* (3rd ed.) New York: Macmillan, 1958.
3. ANASTASI, ANNE, & CORDOVA, F. A. Some effects of bilingualism upon the intelligence test performance of Puerto Rican children in New York City. *J. educ. Psychol.,* 1953, **44,** 1–19.
4. ANASTASI, ANNE, & FOLEY, J. P., JR. A proposed reorientation in the heredity-environment controversy. *Psychol. Rev.,* 1948, **55,** 239–249.
5. ARSENIAN, S. Bilingualism in the postwar world. *Psychol. Bull.,* 1945, **42,** 65–86.
6. BARKER, R. G., WRIGHT, BEATRICE A., MYERSON, L., & GONICK, MOLLIE R. Adjustment to physical handicap and illness: A survey of the social psychology of physique and disability. *Soc. Sci. Res. Coun. Bull.,* 1953, No. 55 (Rev.).

7. BARKER, R. G., & WRIGHT, H. F. *Midwest and its children: The psychological ecology of an American town,* Evanston, Ill.: Row, Peterson, 1955.
8. BEACH, F. A., & JAYNES, J. Effects of early experience upon the behavior of animals. *Psychol. Bull.,* 1954, 51, 239–263.
9. BRACKBILL, G. A. Studies of brain dysfunction in schizophrenia. *Psychol. Bull.,* 1956, 53, 210–226.
10. DARCY, NATALIE T. A review of the literature on the effects of bilingualism upon the measurement of intelligence. *J. genet. Psychol.,* 1953, 82, 21–57.
11. DAVIS, A., & HAVIGHURST, R. J. Social class and color differences in child rearing. *Amer. sociol. Rev.,* 1946, 11, 698–710.
12. DOBZHANSKY, T. The genetic nature of differences among men. In S. Persons (Ed.), *Evolutionary thought in America.* New Haven: Yale Univer. Press, 1950. Pp. 86–155.
13. DOBZHANSKY, T. Heredity, environment, and evolution. *Science,* 1950, 111, 161–166.
14. FORGUS, R. H. The effect of early perceptual learning on the behavioral organization of adult rats. *J. comp. physiol. Psychol.,* 1954, 47, 331–336.
15. HALDANE, J. B. S. *Heredity and politics.* New York: Norton, 1938.
16. HARRELL, RUTH F., WOODYARD, ELLA, & GATES, A. I. *The effect of mothers' diets on the intelligence of the offspring.* New York: Bur. Publ., Teach. Coll., Columbia Univer., 1955.
17. HEBB, D. O. *The organization of behavior.* New York: Wiley, 1949.
18. HIRSCH, J., & TRYON, R. C. Mass screening and reliable individual measurement in the experimental behavior genetics of lower organisms. *Psychol. Bull.,* 1956, 53, 402–410.
19. HORWITT, M. K. Fact and artifact in the biology of schizophrenia. *Science,* 1956, 124, 429–430.
20. KALLMANN, F. J. *Heredity in health and mental disorder; Principles of psychiatric genetics in the light of comparative twin studies.* New York: Norton, 1953.
21. KING, J. A., & GURNEY, NANCY L. Effect of early social experience on adult aggressive behavior in C57BL10 mice. *J. comp. physiol. Psychol.,* 1954, 47, 326–330.
22. LOEVINGER, JANE. On the proportional contributions of differences in nature and in nurture to differences in intelligence. *Psychol. Bull.,* 1943, 40, 725–756.
23. LORENZ, K. Der Kumpan in der Umwelt des Vogels. Der Artgenosse als auslösendes Moment sozialer Verhaltungsweisen. *J. Orn., Lpz.,* 1935, 83, 137–213; 289–413.
24. LUCHINS, A. S., & FORGUS, R. H. The effect of differential postweaning environment on the rigidity of an animal's behavior. *J. genet. Psychol.,* 1955, 86, 51–58.
25. MELZACK, R. The genesis of emotional behavior: An experimental study of the dog. *J. comp. physiol. Psychol.,* 1954, 47, 166–168.
26. MILNER, ESTHER A. A study of the relationships between reading readiness in grade one school children and patterns of parent-child interaction. *Child Develpm.,* 1951, 22, 95–112.

27. PASAMANICK, B., KNOBLOCH, HILDA, & LILIENFELD, A. M. Socio-economic status and some precursors of neuropsychiatric disorder. *Amer. J. Orthopsychiat.*, 1956, **26**, 594–601.
28. SCHWESINGER, GLADYS C. *Heredity and environment.* New York: Macmillan, 1933.
29. SCOTT, J. P., & CHARLES, MARGARET S. Some problems of heredity and social behavior. *J. gen. Psychol.*, 1953, **48**, 209–230.
30. SCOTT, J. P., & FULLER, J. L. Research on genetics and social behavior at the Roscoe B. Jackson Memorial Laboratory, 1946–1951—A progress report. *J. Hered.*, 1951, **42**, 191–197.
31. SEARLE, L. V. The organization of hereditary maze-brightness and maze-dullness. *Genet. Psychol. Monogr.*, 1949, **39**, 279–325.
32. SNYDER, L. H. The genetic approach to human individuality. *Sci. Mon., N.Y.*, 1949, **68**, 165–171.
33. SNYDER, L. H., & DAVID, P. R. *The principles of heredity.* (5th ed.) Boston: Heath, 1957.
34. SPOERL, DOROTHY T. Bilinguality and emotional adjustment. *J. abnorm. soc. Psychol.*, 1943, **38**, 37–57.
35. THOMPSON, W. R., & MELZACK, R. Early environment. *Sci. Amer.*, 1956, **194** (1), 38–42.
36. TRYON, R. C. Genetic differences in maze-learning ability in rats. *Yearb. nat. Soc. Stud. Educ.*, 1940, **39**, Part I, 111–119.
37. WHITING, J. W. M., et al. *Field guide for a study of socialization in five societies.* Cambridge, Mass.: Harvard Univer., 1954 (mimeo.).
38. WHITING, J. W. M., & CHILD, I. L. *Child training and personality: A cross-cultural study.* New Haven: Yale Univer. Press, 1953.
39. WILLIAMS, JUDITH R., & SCOTT, R. B. Growth and development of Negro infants: IV. Motor development and its relationship to child rearing practices in two groups of Negro infants. *Child Develpm.*, 1953, **24**, 103–121.
40. WOODWORTH, R. S. Heredity and environment: A critical survey of recently published material on twins and foster children. *Soc. Sci. Res. Coun. Bull.*, 1941, No. 47.

More on Heritability: Addendum to the Hebb and Jensen Interchange

The recent comments by Hebb (1970, 1971a) and Jensen (1970), as well as those of others who joined the argument (Einhorn, 1970; Gordon, 1970), illustrate once more the fact that several different questions may be asked about the role of heredity and environment in behavior development. When one person's answer is attached to another's question, the resulting juxtaposition may make little sense. Many of the confusions and controversies regarding heredity and environment arise from the failure to differentiate among these diverse questions.

Hebb (1970) argued that the concept of heritability (or amount of population variance attributable to heredity) "cannot show how important heredity (or environment) is in determining an aspect of behavior [p. 568]." To dramatize this point, he cited Mark Twain's humorous proposal that boys be raised in barrels to the age of 12. While the heritability ratio of IQ computed within such a population of boys would be close to .1.00, because of the negligible environmental variance among them, environment would obviously account for the major intellectual retardation displayed by these boys. Jensen (1970) correctly replied that, in order to assess the contribution of heredity and environment to such retardation, it would be necessary to compute a new heritability ratio in a population comprising both barrel-reared and normally reared boys. (Essentially the same point was made by Gordon, 1970.) In his one-paragraph reply, Hebb (1971a) put his finger on the crux of the difficulty. Because there is so much confusion and misunderstanding in this area, however, it may not be amiss to risk some redundancy and spell out the points more fully.[1]

In his analysis of heritability in the original article, Jensen (1969, pp. 33–46) gave a lucid and thorough explanation of this concept, together with its limitations (see especially pp. 42–46). Three of these

---

[1] A further comment by Hebb (1971b), in direct response to Jensen's (1970) reply, appeared after the present note had been accepted for publication. In it Hebb explains more fully the point made in his earlier reply to Gordon (Hebb, 1971a).

More on heritability: Addendum to the Hebb and Jensen interchange. *American Psychologist*, 1971, *26*, 1036–1037. Copyright 1971 by the American Psychological Association. Reprinted by permission.

limitations have particular relevance to the present controversy. First, heritability refers only to population variance in a trait and is inapplicable to individuals. For example, in identifying the etiology of severe mental retardation in a child with PKU or in one of Mark Twain's barrel-reared boys, data on the heritability of intelligence would be of no use whatever.

Second, a heritability ratio pertains to a specified population under existing conditions. It is not generalizable to other populations nor to the same population under altered conditions of heredity or environment. Heritability ratios are not characteristic of traits but are descriptive of a particular population. As Jensen (1969) correctly stated,

> All the major heritability studies reported in the literature are based on samples of white European and North American populations, and our knowledge of the heritability of intelligence in different racial and cultural groups within these populations is nil. For example, no adequate heritability studies have been based on samples of the Negro population of the United States [pp. 64–65].

Thus, available heritability ratios tell us no more about Negro–white differences in intelligence than a heritability ratio computed on Hebb's barrel-reared boys would tell us about the differences between these boys and a normative sample. To be sure, in a later section of his article dealing with race differences, Jensen (1969), pp. 78–88) made no direct reference to heritability ratios (although there is a vague, indirect allusion to "a large genetic component of intelligence [p. 82]"). Nevertheless, the inclusion of the sections on heritability and race differences within the same article may account for some of the misconceptions and non sequiturs characterizing popular citations of the article.

Third, heritability does not indicate the degree of modifiability of a trait. As Jensen (1969) put it: "High heritability by itself does not necessarily imply that the characteristic is immutable [p. 45]." The same point was made more explicit by the population geneticist, Crow (1969), in his comments on the original Jensen article, when he wrote, "High heritability of intelligence does not mean that a program of compensatory education is destined to fail [p. 307]." The fact that Jensen drew just the reverse conclusion in his article again compounds the confusion about the concept of heritability.

In summary, available heritability data do not provide a proper answer to such questions as the etiology of an individual's handicaps, the origin of ethnic differences in test performance, or the anticipated benefits of compensatory education or other programs of environmental intervention. The question they *are* designed to answer is much more limited in scope, namely, What is the proportional contribution of heredity to the variance of a specified trait in a given population under existing conditions?

REFERENCES

CROW, J. F. Genetic theories and influences: Comments on the value of diversity. *Harvard Educational Review*, 1969, **39**, 301–309.

EINHORN, H. J. On Hebb's criticism of Jensen. *American Psychologist,* 1970, **25**, 1173–1174.

GORDON, R. A. Concerning Hebb's criticism of Jensen and the heredity-environment argument. *American Psychologist,* 1970, **25**, 1172–1173.

HEBB, D. O. A return to Jensen and his social science critics. *American Psychologist,* 1970, **25**, 568.

HEBB, D. O. Response to Gordon by Hebb. *American Psychologist,* 1971, **26**, 665. (a)

HEBB, D. O. Whose confusion? *American Psychologist,* 1971, **26**. 736. (b)

JENSEN, A. R. How much can we boost IQ and scholastic achievement? *Harvard Educational Review*, 1969, **39**, 1–123.

JENSEN, A. R. Hebb's confusion about heritability. *American Psychologist,* 1971, **26**, 394–395.

Interpretation of Heritability:
A Rejoinder

After reading Jensen's (1972) latest discussion of heritability, I would repeat all of the points I made in my earlier comment (Anastasi, 1971). With a lingering hope of further clarifying communication, I shall add just three points. First, it was not the statistical procedures but the empirical data to which they were applied that led me to question Jensen's original conclusions. Second, the probabilistic argument, to which Jensen's present comment addresses itself in large part, is of primary interest when no other information is available regarding the origins of particular differences between individuals or groups. In Hebb's (1970) example of Mark Twain's boys-in-barrels, as in the case of several minority groups, we do have information regarding environmental sources of interpopulation differences. To draw conclusions regarding such group differences from probabilities estimated from intragroup heritability ratios is logically equivalent to diagnosing a child's brain damage in terms of the base rate, with no attempt to obtain a case history or other pertinent data about the individual. Finally, the sort of environmental interventions generally considered in relation to minority group status do not represent simply a reshuffling of environmental variations already existing within such groups (or within *other* groups). Rather what is envisaged are massive changes in the physical or psychological environments of a population as a whole.

REFERENCES

ANASTASI, A. More on heritability: Addendum to the Hebb and Jensen interchange. *American Psychologist,* 1971, **26**, 1036–1037.
HEBB, D. O. A return to Jensen and his social science critics. *American Psychologist,* 1970, **25**, 568.
JENSEN, A. R. Interpretation of heritability. *American Psychologist,* 1972, **27**, 973–975.

9
Current Trends and Future Prospects

Some of the current developments within differential psychology and psychometrics reflect trends that are discernible in American psychology generally. Notable among these trends is the increasing concern with theory and a continuing movement away from the blind empiricism of earlier decades. The growing emphasis on constructs in analyses of personality and aptitudes, as well as the increasing use of construct validation in test construction, illustrates this theoretical orientation. Another—possibly related—trend is reflected in the efforts toward integration of different areas of inquiry and a merging of extreme positions. A provocative demonstration of a broadly unifying theory-building system is provided by Staats (1981). Designated as "social behaviorism," this system is similar to social learning theory (Bandura, 1977), but broader in coverage. With this system, Staats illustrates the possible integration of multiple approaches, ranging from clinical and developmental to psychometric and experimental. Some of Staats's long-term research within this framework has a direct bearing on questions of trait formation, the nature of intelligence, test construction, and the heredity-environment relation (Staats, 1963, pp. 407–411; 1975, Ch. 12; 1981; Staats, Staats, Heard, & Finley, 1962).

Evidence for both the theoretical and the unifying trends can be found in several of the topics discussed in this chapter. These topics were chosen because they represent conspicuous ongoing developments in concepts, methodology, or applications of differential psychology. At this stage, they seem to indicate directions in which significant movement is occurring.

NATURE AND ORGANIZATION OF FACTORS

The overview of factor-analytic trait research in Chapter 1 brought us through the 1940s, with the development of Thurstone's techniques of multiple factor analysis and his identification of some ten "primary mental abilities." The next decades saw a rapid proliferation of factors, in which several of Thurstone's primary abilities were broken down into narrower group factors. One way of coping with this multiplicity of factors was followed by Guilford, with his cubical, structure-of-intellect model (Guilford, 1967; Guilford & Hoepfner, 1971). The three dimensions of this model correspond to operations, content, and products. Any test can be classified along all three dimensions. The model provides a total of 120 cells, in each of which at least one factor or differentiable ability is expected, while some may contain more than one. The number of anticipated factors in this model is admittedly large; but Guilford argued that human nature is exceedingly complex and a few factors could not be expected to describe it adequately.

Another schema for classifying factors uses a hierarchical model. This type of trait organization was proposed by several British psychologists, including Burt (1949) and Vernon (1960), and by Humphreys (1962) in the United States. These models resemble an inverted genealogical tree: at the top is a general factor (which could represent Spearman's g); at the next level are broad group factors, similar to some of Thurstone's primary mental abilities; these major factors subdivide into narrower group factors at one or more levels; the specific (s) factors are found at the bottom level.

Different theories focus on one or another level of this hierarchy, such as g or broad group factors. Humphreys (1962), however, proposed that no level should be regarded as necessarily of primary importance; rather, each test constructor or user should select the level that is most appropriate for his or her purpose. This solution fits what is generally done in practice. For example, if we want to select applicants for a difficult and highly specialized mechanical job, we would probably test fairly narrow perceptual and spatial factors that closely match the job requirements. In selecting college students, however, a few broad factors, such as verbal comprehension, numerical facility, and general reasoning would be most relevant. That different investigators may arrive at dissimilar models of trait organization becomes less perplexing when we recognize that the traits identified through factor analysis are simply an expression of correlation among behavior measures. They are not underlying entities or causal factors; they are descriptive categories. Hence, it is conceivable that different principles of classification may be applicable to the same data.

Factor analysis is no longer regarded as a means of searching for *the* primary, fixed, universal units of behavior, but rather as a method of organizing empirical data into useful categories through an analysis of behavioral uniformities. There is also an increasing interest in exploring the mechanisms whereby both cognitive and personality traits are formed, as through transfer of training (Ferguson, 1956), operant conditioning (Staats et al., 1962), or generalizability of cognitive skills and of learning sets, among others (see Anastasi, 1970).

REANALYSES OF INTELLIGENCE

An outstanding example of the rapprochement between psychometrics and experimental psychology is provided by the contributions of cognitive psychology to an understanding of what intelligence tests measure. Some of the investigations in this area represent the work of psychologists trained in both fields; others result from the auspicious collaboration of specialists in the two areas.

Beginning in the 1950s, cognitive psychologists had been applying the concepts of information processing to describe what occurs in human problem solving. Some designed computer programs that carry out these processes and thereby simulate human thought. The "basic units" of thought identified by these procedures consist of processes and knowledge. The cognitive models specify the intellectual processes used to perform the task, the way the processes are organized, the relevant knowledge store, and how this knowledge is represented in memory and retrieved when needed. Increasing attention is also being given to what has been called an "executive process," which refers to the control the individual exerts over his or her own choices of processes, representations, and strategies for carrying out the task.

In the 1970s, a few psychologists began to apply these information-processing and computer-simulation techniques to an exploration of what intelligence tests measure (see Resnick, 1976). Individual investigators approached this goal from various angles. One of the most ambitious and systematic efforts to relate intelligence test performance to cognitive psychology is to be found in the research of Sternberg (1979) on what he calls componential analysis. This type of analysis has been used with tasks that resemble complex intelligence test materials more closely than do the usual simplified and somewhat artificial laboratory tasks. The tasks employed by Sternberg include such familiar types as analogies, classifications, series completions, and syllogisms. His experimental procedures involve principally the systematic alteration of both task variables and subject variables. An example of the latter is provided by age differences in performance of the same task. The experimental manipulation of task variables can be illustrated by task decomposition, whereby parts of tasks are presented separately or in succession.

What can we conclude about the contributions that cognitive psychology has made thus far to a clarification of intelligence test performance? It must be recognized, of course, that efforts to bridge the gap between psychometrics and cognitive psychology in this area are still in an exploratory stage. Information-processing approaches have contributed heuristic concepts to guide further research and have focused attention clearly on processes rather than end-products in problem solving. Analyzing intelligence test performance in terms of basic cognitive processes should certainly strengthen and enrich our understanding of what the tests measure. Moreover, describing the performances of individuals at the level of component processes should eventually make it possible to pinpoint each person's sources of weakness and strength and thus enhance the diagnostic use of tests. This, in turn, should facilitate the tailoring of training programs to the individual's needs.

At the same time, we should not be carried away by the heady promise of these new vistas. It is unlikely that intelligence tests will change drastically in content as a result of information-processing analyses. If these tests are to continue to serve practical ends, they must maintain a firm hold on the intellectual demands of real life. We should also guard against attaching excess meanings to the emerging terms. Basic cognitive skills do not necessarily represent fixed or innate properties of the organism, any more than do IQs or primary mental abilities. Let me emphasize, however, that these cautions are not intended to diminish the contributions of cognitive psychologists or to imply that they have succumbed to any of these pitfalls. On the contrary, some investigators have themselves called attention to these potential hazards and to the limitations of their procedures for investigating intelligence (e.g., Sternberg, 1981). Once the concepts become widely publicized, however, popular misinterpretations are all too likely to follow.

TRAITS AND SITUATIONS

The merging and reconciliation of opposing views is illustrated by the controversy regarding the generalizability of personal traits versus the situational specificity of behavior. This long-standing controversy reached a peak in the late 1960s and the 1970s. Several developments in the 1960s focused attention on narrowly defined "behaviors of interest" and away from broadly defined traits. In the cognitive domain, this focus is to be found in individualized instructional programs and criterion-referenced testing, as well as in the diagnosis and treatment of learning disabilities.

In the noncognitive or personality domain, the strongest impetus toward behavioral specificity in testing came from social learning theory and the general orientation characterizing behavior modification and behavior therapy (Bandura, 1977; Bandura & Walters, 1963; Goldfried & Kent, 1972; Mischel, 1968, 1969, 1973). Criticism was directed especially toward the traditional view of traits as fixed, unchanging, underlying causal entities. This kind of criticism had been anticipated in the earlier research and writings of several psychologists, with regard to all traits—cognitive as well as noncognitive (see Chs. 5 and 6). In fact, few psychologists today would argue for perpetuating this early view of traits. In commenting on the current rarity of this extreme type of "trait theorist," Jackson and Paunonen (1980, p. 523) wrote: "Like witches of 300 years ago, there is confidence about their existence, and even possibly their sinister properties, although one is hard pressed to find one in the flesh or even meet someone who has."

It should also be noted that situational specificity is much more characteristic of personality traits than it is of abilities. For example, a person might be sociable and outgoing at the office, but shy and retiring at social gatherings; or a student who cheats on examinations might be scrupulously honest in money matters. An extensive body of empirical evidence was assembled by Mischel (1968) and others showing that individuals do exhibit considerable situational specificity in many nonintellective dimensions, such as aggression, social conformity, dependency, rigidity, honesty, and attitudes toward authority.

In part, the explanation for the higher cross-situational consistency of cognitive than of noncognitive functions may be found in the greater standardization of the individual's reactional biography in the intellectual than in the personality domain (see Ch. 6). The formal school curriculum, for example, fosters the development of widely applicable cognitive skills in the verbal and numerical areas. In contrast, personality development occurs under far less uniform conditions. Moreover, in the personality domain, the same response may lead to social consequences that are positively reinforcing in one situation and negatively reinforcing in another. The individual may thus learn to respond in quite different ways in different contexts. Such dissimilarities in experiential history, across individuals as well as across situations, also lead to more ambiguity in personality test items than is found in cognitive test items. Thus, the same response to a given question on a personality inventory may have a different diagnostic significance from one person to another.

With regard to testing methodology, the impact of situational specificity was most clearly evident among researchers identified with social learning theory (e.g., Endler & Hunt, 1968; Goldfried & D'Zurilla, 1969; Kjerulff & Wiggins, 1976). Special instruments were developed to assess the behavior of individuals in different types of situations. Analysis of the results showed the extent to which behavior variance depended upon persons, situations, and the interaction between the two.

Both the theoretical discussions and the research on person-by-situation analyses have undoubtedly enriched our understanding of the many conditions that determine individual behavior and have contributed to the development of sophisticated research designs. At the same time, there has been a growing consensus among the proponents of contrasting views. This rapprochement was especially evident in several well-balanced and thoughtful discussions of the problem published in the late 1970s and early 1980s (e.g., Mischel, 1977, 1979; Endler & Magnusson, 1976; Epstein, 1979, 1980). Several noteworthy points emerged from these discussions. Behavior exhibits considerable temporal stability when measured reliably, that is, by summing repeated observations and thereby reducing the error of measurement. When random samples of persons and situations are studied, individual differences contribute more to total behavior variance than do situational differences. Interaction between persons and situations contributes as much as do individual differences, or slightly more. To identify broad personality traits, we need to measure the individual across many situations and aggregate the results (Epstein, 1980). While recognizing that the study of persons-in-situations adds an important dimension to the assessment of individual differences, psychologists on both sides of the controversy now agree that properly defined and interpreted trait constructs are needed for the systematic and orderly description of behavior.

CONSTRUCT VALIDATION OF TESTS

A clear example of the shift away from the early atheoretical orientation is provided by the increasing emphasis on construct validation in test development. The construct validity of a test is the extent to which the test may be said to measure a theoretical construct or trait. Examples of such constructs are intelligence, mechanical comprehension, verbal fluency, speed of walking, neuroticism, and anxiety. Each construct is developed to explain and organize observed response consistencies. It derives from established interrelationships among behavioral measures (Cronbach & Meehl, 1955; Messick, 1975, 1980, 1981). Focusing on a broader, more enduring, and more abstract kind of behavioral description than the traditional, criterion-related validation procedures, construct validation requires the gradual accumulation of information from a variety of sources. Any data throwing light on the nature of the trait under consideration and the conditions affecting its development and manifestations are grist for this validity mill.

The term "construct validity" was officially introduced into the psychometrician's lexicon in 1954 in the *Technical Recommendations for Psychological Tests and Diagnostic Techniques,* which constitute the first edition of the current test *Standards* (1974). The first detailed exposition of construct validity appeared the following year in an article by Cronbach and Meehl (1955). The discussions of construct validation that followed—and that are continuing with renewed vigor—have served to make the implications of its procedures more explicit and to provide a systematic rationale for their use. Construct validation has centered attention on the role of psychological theory in test construction and on the need to formulate hypotheses that can be proved or disproved in the validation process.

On the negative side, superficial adoption of the concept of construct validity presents certain hazards. Because it is a broad and complex concept, it has not always been clearly understood by those who employed the term. Some test developers apparently regarded it as content validity expressed in terms of psychological trait names. Hence, they offered as construct validity purely subjective accounts of what they believed (or hoped) their test measured. Actually, constructs are useful if they generate testable hypotheses and are linked to observable behavior. It is only through the empirical investigation of the relationships of test scores to other, external data that we can ascertain what a test measures.

It is being increasingly recognized that all test uses and all interpretations of test scores imply construct validity (Guion, 1977; Messick, 1980; Tenopyr, 1977). Since tests are rarely, if ever, used under conditions that are identical with those under which validity data are gathered, some degree of generalizability of results is inevitably involved. Thus, the interpretive meaning of test scores is almost always based on constructs, which may vary widely in breadth or generalizability with regard to behavior domains, populations, and situations.

Messick (1980) has argued convincingly that the term "validity," insofar as it designates the interpretive meaningfulness of a test, should be reserved for construct validity. Other procedures with which the term "validity" has been traditionally associated should, he maintains, be designated by more specifically descriptive labels. Thus, content validity can be labeled content relevance and content coverage, to refer to domain specifications and domain representativeness, respectively. Criterion-related validity can be labeled predictive utility and diagnostic utility, to correspond to predictive and concurrent validation. These more clearly descriptive labels undoubtedly enhance our understanding of what the various procedures actually accomplish. It is likely, however, that the traditional terms will linger through a lengthy transition period, because of their long-established usage and their inclusion in currently available test manuals.

With regard to actual test-construction procedures, the increasing concern with theoretical constructs can be seen most clearly in the evolving methodology of personality inventory development. The Minnesota Multiphasic Personality Inventory (MMPI) is the classic example of empirical criterion keying, whereby the selection of individual items to be retained, their sorting into separate scales, and the assignment of scoring weights are based on the relation of each item to an external criterion (Hathaway & McKinley, 1943; see also Anastasi, 1982, Ch. 17). In the construction of the MMPI, items for each scale were selected on the basis of the responses of patients classified according to traditional psychiatric syndromes, in comparison with the responses of a normal control sample. Although this procedure is limited and crude when judged by current test-construction standards, the MMPI maintains its clinical popularity largely because of the rich store of interpretive research data that has accumulated over the intervening years. The individual scales are now treated as linear measures of personality traits, rather than as indicators of the original diagnostic categories. Through subsequent research, the construct validity of different MMPI profiles, or "codes," has gradually been built up. There are now a vast number of publications and a growing array of handbooks, codebooks, atlases, and other guides to facilitate these broader score interpretations.

The early factor-analytic personality inventories also relied principally on empirically established item relationships. Although the scales were given factor names, and such factors were often regarded as theoretical constructs, the factors were derived solely from item intercorrelations and were uninfluenced by personality theory. The Guilford-Zimmerman Personality Survey illustrates this early factor-analytic methodology (Guilford & Zimmerman, 1949). The more recently developed Comrey Personality Scales (Comrey, 1970) foreshadowed current methodology in at least two ways: (1) greater concern for constructs as illustrated by assigning items to clusters (and item clusters to scales) on the basis of logical as well as factor-analytic homogeneity; and (2) utilization of multiple procedures at different stages in test construction.

Current trends in personality inventory construction are well illustrated in the Personality Research Form (PRF) developed by Jackson (1970, 1974). The PRF reflects several technical advances in test construction, including item-selection procedures that would have been virtually impossible before the availability of high-speed computers. This inventory exemplifies Jackson's fundamental approach to personality test development, which begins with explicit, detailed descriptions of the constructs to be assessed. These descriptions form the basis for item writing, as well as for defining the traits to be rated in validation studies. Empirical statistical procedures are then followed at several later stages to refine the scales and to corroborate item selection and placement.

The PRF was designed principally for research uses with essentially normal populations. In contrast, the Millon Clinical Multiaxial Inventory (MCMI) was designed chiefly for the same populations for which the MMPI was developed. Although following the MMPI tradition in several ways, the MCMI introduced significant methodological innovations (Millon, 1977). In fact, its development was deliberately undertaken to meet the criticisms of the older instrument and to utilize intervening advances in psychopathology and test construction. Item development followed the multiple approach characteristic of recent practice in the construction and validation of personality inventories. The procedure included a sequence of three major steps: (1) theoretical-substantive (i.e., writing and selecting items to fit clinically relevant constructs); (2) internal-structural (e.g., item-scale correlations, endorsement frequencies); and (3) external-criterion (e.g., differentiation of diagnostic groups from reference group, cross-validation on new samples).

LONGITUDINAL STUDY OF POPULATIONS

What happens to the intelligence test performance of a population over long time periods? This question pertains to what I have designated as the longitudinal study of populations (Anastasi, 1958, pp. 209–211; 1962; 1982, Ch. 12). The usual application of the longitudinal method in psychological research involves the repeated testing of the same persons over time. In the longitudinal study of populations, the comparison is between cohorts of persons born at different times but tested at the same ages. Several large-scale investigations conducted during the first fifty years of the twentieth century revealed a rising intellectual level in the population, as measured by standardized intelligence tests. With increasing literacy, higher educational levels, and other cultural changes, it was evident that the mean tested intelligence of the general population of all ages exhibited a steady rise over several decades. Some of the implications of these progressive population changes were discussed in my 1954 paper that is reproduced in Chapter 7.

Various procedures have been employed in these comparative studies over time. One procedure is to administer the identical test after a lapse of time, as was done in surveys of 11-year-old Scottish children in 1932 and 1947 (Scottish Council, 1949). Another is to give two tests to a representative sample of persons in order to establish the correspondence between the two sets of scores and thereby "translate" performance from one test to the other. This was done in comparing the performance of soldiers in the U.S. Army in World Wars I and II, who had been examined with the Army Alpha in the first instance and with the Army General Classification Test in the second (Tuddenham, 1948). A third and technically superior approach is based on the establishment of an absolute, sample-free scale through the use of common anchor items, as is done with the College Board tests (Angoff, 1971). Further refinements of this approach are provided by the recent applications of item response theory (also known as latent trait theory and item characteristic curve theory).

Population changes in test performance may affect the interpretation of test scores in various ways. One example, discussed in my 1956 paper in Chapter 2, pertains to age differences within the standardization sample of the Wechsler Adult Intelligence Scale (WAIS). The older members of the normative sample for this test had completed less schooling, on the average, than had the younger members; accordingly, they scored lower on the test than did the younger members. As a result, intelligence appeared to decline with age.

A different sort of misinterpretation may occur through the use of tests that were standardized at different times. In both the restandardization of the Stanford-Binet (1937 versus 1972) and the revision of the Wechsler Intelligence Scale for Children (1949 versus 1974), the later normative sample performed substantially better than did the earlier sample. Consequently, the same children would receive lower IQs if tested with the revised edition than they would on the earlier edition, simply because their performance was evaluated against higher norms. At the adult level, a preliminary comparison of the 1977 WAIS with the 1981 WAIS-R given to 72 persons aged 35 to 44 yielded a higher mean IQ on the earlier form. This finding again suggests that the earlier norms were lower than those established more recently.

Whether the intelligence test performance of a given population rises, declines, or remains stable over time depends on many conditions. Among them are the time period covered, with its concomitant cultural changes; the age level of the persons examined; and changes in the composition, or degree of selection, of the particular population. The number and complexity of conditions that may account for a population rise or decline in tested intelligence are well illustrated by an analysis of the highly publicized score decline in the College Board's Scholastic Aptitude Test (SAT) between 1963 and 1977. In an effort to understand this steady 14-year score decline, a specially appointed panel commissioned 38 studies by experts in various areas and considered an impressive array of causal hypotheses (Wirtz, 1977).

The results of these studies indicated that, during the first half of this 14-year period, the score decline could be attributed predominantly to a compositional change in the sample taking the SAT. Because of continuing increase in the proportion of high school graduates going to college over this period, the sampling became progressively less highly selected in the cognitive skills measured by the SAT. During the second half of the period, however, the college-going population had become largely stabilized, and the explanation for the continuing score decline had to be sought principally in conditions in the home, the school, and society at large. It should be added that the score decline, while most thoroughly investigated with reference to the SAT, was not limited to this instrument. Not only did it occur in other college admission tests, but there was also evidence of a corresponding decline in test performance at the high school and elementary school levels.

An early study by Pressey and Jones (1955) explored population changes in emotional and attitudinal responses. Their procedure represented a rudimentary form of a sophisticated experimental design first fully described by Schaie (1965), who called it the cross-sequential method. Essentially, this method involves the testing of a representative sample of different age groups on two or more occasions. It thus permits (1) *cross-sectional* comparisons of different age groups tested at one time period; (2) *longitudinal* comparisons of the same individuals retested at two or more time periods; and (3) *time-lag* comparisons of samples of equal age drawn from different cohorts and tested at different time periods—for instance, 30-year-olds tested in 1950 could be compared with 30-year-olds tested in 1960. The third comparison corresponds to the longitudinal study of populations.

A large-scale pioneer application of the complete cross-sequential model is illustrated by a 14-year investigation conducted by Schaie and his co-workers (Schaie, Labouvie, & Buech, 1973; Schaie & Labouvie-Vief, 1974; Schaie & Strother, 1968). This carefully designed study began in 1956 with the administration of the SRA Primary Mental Abilities tests and Schaie's Test of Behavioral Rigidity to a stratified-random sample of 500 persons ranging in age from 20 to 70 years. The cross-sequential method is being used increasingly by researchers in the emerging field of life-span developmental psychology.

BROADENING ADOPTION OF PSYCHOMETRIC METHODOLOGY

There has been growing recognition of the need for sound psychometric methodology in all aspects of the assessment of persons. This evolving orientation is especially evident in fields that began with a qualitative focus, uncontrolled procedures, and subjective interpretations. These operating conditions characterized much of the assessment conducted by clinical psychologists and psychiatrists prior to the 1970s. My 1960 paper urging the establishment of behavioral norms against which pathological deviations could be evaluated (Ch. 2) was stimulated by those prevailing conditions. Today there are numerous indications that clinical researchers and practitioners are becoming aware, not only of the need for empirical norms, but also of the advantages of testing their techniques for such psychometric properties as reliability, validity, and statistical significance of score differences.

Projective Techniques

Some clear examples of this trend are provided by projective techniques. Prior to the 1970s, there were only scattered efforts to strengthen the psychometric quality of these instruments. One of the earliest quantification attempts is to be found in the Rosenzweig Picture-Frustration Study (P-F Study). Being more limited in coverage, more highly structured, and relatively objective in scoring, the P-F Study lent itself better to statistical analysis than did most other projective techniques. From the outset, systematic efforts were made to gather norms and to check the instrument's reliability and validity. Over some forty years, considerable research has been conducted, by both the test author and other investigators, which bears on the psychometric properties of the P-F Study (Rosenzweig, 1978).

The more recently developed Holtzman Inkblot Technique represents a major attempt to meet technical psychometric standards in the development of a projective technique of the Rorschach type (Holtzman, 1968, 1975). With regard to the Rorschach itself, repeated efforts have been made over the years to gather norms on special groups, including children, adolescents, and persons over 70. The most ambitious project to put the Rorschach on a psychometrically sound basis, however, was undertaken by Exner (1974, 1978). First, Exner developed a comprehensive Rorschach system, incorporating elements culled from the extensive clinical and research literature; for this comprehensive system, he provides standardized administration, scoring, and interpretive procedures. Second, using this system, Exner and his co-workers have begun to collect a considerable body of psychometric data, including adult and child norms on many Rorschach variables, obtained from both patient and nonpatient samples. Retest reliability and construct validity of Rorschach variables are also being investigated.

Intelligence Tests

A promising approach, integrating individualized clinical exploration with the use of psychometric data, is described by Kaufman (1979), with special reference to the diagnostic interpretation of intelligence test performance. In a book entitled *Intelligent Testing with the WISC-R*, Kaufman demonstrates how the clinician can combine statistical information about test scores, such as significance of differences and the results of factor analysis, with knowledge about human development, personality theory, and other areas of psychological research. The test scores, in combination with background data from other sources, lead to the formulation of hypotheses about the individual. These hypotheses can then be tested as more information is obtained to round out the picture, in a continuing spiral of data gathering and interpretation.

Behavioral Assessment

Another clinical area that began in an antitesting mood and has moved toward the recognition of psychometric standards is that of behavioral assessment. Because of the rapid growth of behavior therapy and behavior modification programs, the development of assessment techniques to meet the needs of these programs had lagged far behind. Makeshift procedures and crude techniques were prevalent. Many practitioners, moreover, regarded behavioral assessment as fundamentally irreconcilable with the traditional psychometric approach. In the 1970s, however, several leaders in behavior therapy presented thoughtful and convincing arguments demonstrating that behavioral assessment must meet traditional psychometric standards with regard to standardization of materials and procedures, normative data, reliability, and validity (Goldfried & Linehan, 1977; Hartman, Roper, & Bradford, 1979).

Health Psychology

Still wider applications of psychometric methodology are to be found in the burgeoning field of health psychology. New types of psychometric instruments are being developed to aid in general medical practice and in public health programs. In their construction, some of these instruments have employed psychometric procedures of high technical quality. Their wide diversity in purpose and nature can be illustrated with three recently developed instruments. The Jenkins Activity Survey (Jenkins, Zyzanski, & Rosenman, 1979) is a self-report inventory designed to assess Type-A personality. This personality construct was identified through laboratory, clinical, and epidemiological investigations as characterizing persons who are prone to coronary heart disease. Research is in progress on the generalizability of the findings to different populations, as well as on the nature of the Type-A personality construct.

From a different angle, the Millon Health Behavior Inventory (Millon, Green, & Meagher, 1979) was designed to provide medical practitioners with information about a patient's characteristic coping styles, attitudes toward illness and treatment, and other personality tendencies that may significantly influence the patient's reaction to treatment and the course of his or her illness. Although much research remains to be done on this inventory, it has already proved useful in several medical settings, such as pain clinics, cancer centers, renal dialysis programs, and health maintenance organizations.

Still another application of psychometric techniques to medical problems is illustrated by the development of health status measures. An example of such a measure is provided by the Sickness Impact Profile (Bergner, Bobbitt, et al., 1981). Developed by an interdisciplinary team, this instrument exemplifies an effective cooperative enterprise of high technical quality. It consists of a detailed inventory that can be filled out by the respondent or by an interviewer. In either case, the patient indicates which statements describe his or her actual performance or state of health *on that day.* The instrument yields scores in 12 categories: sleep and rest, eating, work, home management, recreation and pastimes, ambulation, mobility, body care and movement, social interaction, alertness behavior, emotional behavior, and communication. Items within each category extend over the full range of possible response, from normal behavior to extreme dysfunction. Instruments such as the Sickness Impact Profile are beginning to serve a useful function, not only in health research, but also in the treatment of individual patients and in the administration and evaluation of public health programs.

REFERENCES

Anastasi, A. *Differential psychology* (3rd ed.). New York: Macmillan, 1958.
——. The longitudinal study of populations. *Indian Psychological Bulletin*, 1962, 7 (Part II), 25–28.
——. On the formation of psychological traits. *American Psychologist*, 1970, 25, 899–910.
——. *Psychological testing* (5th ed.). New York: Macmillan, 1982.
Angoff, W. H. (Ed.). *College Board Admission Testing Program: A technical report on research and development activities relating to the Scholastic Aptitude Test and achievement tests.* New York: College Entrance Examination Board, 1971.

Bandura, A. *Social learning theory.* Englewood Cliffs, N.J.: Prentice-Hall, 1977.

Bandura, A., & Walters, R. H. *Social learning and personality development.* New York: Holt, Rinehart & Winston, 1963.

Bergner, M., Bobbitt, R. A., et al. The Sickness Impact Profile: Development and final revision of a health status measure. *Medical Care, 1981, 19*(8).

Burt, C. The structure of the mind: A review of the results of factor analysis. *British Journal of Educational Psychology, 1949, 19,* 110–111; 176–199.

Comrey, A. L. *Comrey Personality Scales: Manual.* San Diego: Educational and Industrial Testing Service, 1970.

Cronbach, L. J., & Meehl, P. E. Construct validity in psychological tests. *Psychological Bulletin, 1955, 52,* 281–302.

Endler, N. S., & Hunt, J. McV. S-R inventories of hostility and comparisons of proportions of variance from persons, responses, and situations for hostility and anxiousness. *Journal of Personality and Social Psychology, 1968, 9,* 309–315.

Endler, N.S., & Magnusson, D. Toward an interactional psychology of personality. *Psychological Bulletin, 1976, 83,* 956–974.

Epstein, S. The stability of behavior: I. On predicting most of the people much of the time. *Journal of Personality and Social Psychology, 1979, 37,* 1097–1121.

Epstein, S. The stability of behavior: II. Implications for psychological research. *American Psychologist, 1980, 35,* 790–806.

Exner, J. E., Jr. *The Rorschach: A comprehensive system.* New York: Wiley, 1974.

Exner, J. E., Jr. *The Rorschach: A comprehensive system, Vol. 2: Current research and advanced interpretations.* New York: Wiley-Interscience, 1978.

Ferguson, G. A. On transfer and the abilities of man. *Canadian Journal of Psychology, 1956, 10,* 121–131.

Goldfried, M. R., & D'Zurilla, T. J. A behavioral-analytic model for assessing competence. In C. D. Spielberger (Ed.), *Current topics in clinical psychology* (Vol. 1). New York: Academic Press, 1969. Pp. 151–196.

Goldfried, M. R., & Kent, R. N. Traditional versus behavioral personality assessment: A comparison of methodological and theoretical assumptions. *Psychological Bulletin, 1972, 77* 409–420.

Goldfried, M. R., & Linehan, M. M. Basic issues in behavioral assessment. In A. R. Ciminero, K. S. Calhoun, & H. E. Adams (Eds.), *Handbook of behavioral assessment.* New York: Wiley, 1977. Ch. 2.

Guilford, J. P. *The nature of human intelligence.* New York: McGraw-Hill, 1967.

Guilford, J. P., & Hoepfner, R. *The analysis of intelligence.* New York: McGraw-Hill, 1971.

Guilford, J. P., & Zimmerman, W. S. *The Guilford-Zimmerman Temperament Survey: Manual.* Orange, Calif.: Sheridan Psychological Services, 1949.

Guion, R. M. Content validity: Three years of talk—what's the action? *Public Personnel Management, 1977, 6,* 407–414.

Hartman, D. P., Roper, B. L., & Bradford, D. C. Some relationships between behavioral and traditional assessment. *Journal of Behavioral Assessment, 1979, 1,* 3–21.

Hathaway, S. R., & McKinley, J. C. *Manual for the Minnesota Multiphasic Personality Inventory.* New York: Psychological Corporation, 1943.

Holtzman, W. H. Holtzman Inkblot Technique. In A. I. Rabin (Ed.), *Projective techniques in personality assessment.* New York: Springer, 1968. Pp. 136–170.

Holtzman, W. H. New developments in Holtzman Inkblot Technique. In P. Mc-Reynolds (Ed.), *Advances in psychological assessment* (Vol. 3). San Francisco: Jossey-Bass, 1975. Ch. 6.

Humphreys, L. G. The organization of human abilities. *American Psychologist,* 1962, *17*, 475–483.

Jackson, D. N. A sequential system for personality scale development. In C. D. Spielberger (Ed.), *Current topics in clinical and community psychology* (Vol. 2). New York: Academic Press, 1970. Pp. 61–96.

Jackson, D. N. *Personality Research Form: Manual.* Port Huron, Mich.: Research Psychologists Press, 1974.

Jackson, D. N., & Paunonen, S. V. Personality structure and assessment. *Annual Review of Psychology,* 1980, *31*, 503–551.

Jenkins, C. D., Zyzanski, S. J., & Rosenman, R. H. *Jenkins Activity Survey: Manual.* New York: Psychological Corporation, 1979.

Kaufman, A. S. *Intelligent testing with the WISC-R.* New York: Wiley, 1979.

Kjerulff, K., & Wiggins, N. H. Graduate student styles for coping with stressful situations. *Journal of Educational Psychology,* 1976, *68*, 247–254.

Messick, S. The standard problem: Meaning and values in measurement and evaluation. *American Psychologist,* 1975, *30*, 955–966.

Messick, S. Test validity and the ethics of assessment. *American Psychologist,* 1980, *35*, 1012–1027.

Messick, S. Constructs and their vicissitudes in educational and psychological measurement. *Psychological Bulletin,* 1981, *89*, 575–588.

Millon, T. *Millon Clinical Multiaxial Inventory: Manual.* Minneapolis: NCS Interpretive Scoring Systems, 1977.

Millon, T., Green, C. J., & Meagher, R. B., Jr. *Millon Behavioral Health Inventory: Manual.* Minneapolis: NCS Interpretive Scoring Systems, 1979.

Mischel, W. *Personality and assessment.* New York: Wiley, 1968.

Mischel, W. Continuity and change in personality. *American Psychologist,* 1969, *24*, 1012–1018.

Mischel, W. Toward a cognitive social learning reconceptualization of personality. *Psychological Review,* 1973, *80*, 252–283.

Mischel, W. On the future of personality measurement. *American Psychologist,* 1977, *32*, 246–254.

Mischel, W. On the interface of cognition and personality: Beyond the person-situation debate. *American Psychologist,* 1979, *34*, 740–754.

Pressey, S. L., & Jones, A. W. 1923–1953 and 20–60 age changes in moral codes, anxieties, and interests, as shown by the "X-O Tests," *Journal of Psychology,* 1955, *39*, 485–502.

Resnick, L. B. (Ed.). *The nature of intelligence.* Hillsdale, N.J.: Erlbaum, 1976.

Rosenzweig, S. *Aggressive behavior and the Rosenzweig Picture-Frustration Study.* New York: Praeger, 1978.

Schaie, K. W. A general model for the study of developmental problems. *Psychological Bulletin*, 1965, *64*, 92–107.

Schaie, K. W., Labouvie, G. V., & Buech, B. U. Generational and cohort-specific differences in adult cognitive functioning: A fourteen-year study of independent samples. *Developmental Psychology*, 1973, *9*, 151–166.

Schaie, K. W., & Labouvie-Vief, G. Generational versus ontogenetic components of change in cognitive behavior: A fourteen-year cross-sequential study. *Developmental Psychology*, 1974, *10*, 305–320.

Schaie, K. W., & Strother, C. R. A cross-sequential study of age changes in cognitive behavior. *Psychological Bulletin*, 1968, *70*, 671–680.

Scottish Council for Research in Education. *The trend of Scottish intelligence.* London: University of London Press, 1949.

Staats, A. W. *Complex human behavior.* New York: Holt, Rinehart & Winston, 1963.

Staats, A. W. *Social-behaviorism.* Homewood, Ill.: Dorsey Press, 1975.

Staats, A. W. Paradigmatic behaviorism, unified theory, unified theory construction methods, and the Zeitgeist of separatism. *American Psychologist*, 1981, *36*, 239–256.

Staats, A. W., Staats, C. K., Heard, W. G., & Finley, J. R. Operant conditioning of factor analytic personality traits. *Journal of General Psychology*, 1962, *66*, 101–114.

Standards for educational and psychological tests. Washington, D.C.: American Psychological Association, 1974.

Sternberg, R. J. The nature of mental abilities. *American Psychologist*, 1979, *34*, 214–230.

Sternberg, R. J. Nothing fails like success: The search for an intelligent paradigm for studying intelligence. *Journal of Educational Psychology*, 1981, *73*, 142–155.

Tenopyr, M. L. Content-construct confusion. *Personnel Psychology*, 1977, *30*, 47–54.

Tuddenham, R. D. Soldier intelligence in World Wars I and II. *American Psychologist*, 1948, *3*, 54–56.

Vernon, P. E. *The structure of human abilities* (rev. ed.). London: Methuen, 1960.

Wirtz, W. (Chair). *On further examination: Report of the Advisory Panel on the Scholastic Aptitude Test Score Decline.* New York: College Entrance Examination Board, 1977.

10

Autobiography

This autobiography is a condensation of two longer biographical sketches published in other sources (Anastasi, 1972, 1980). Since those earlier accounts differ substantially from each other in purpose and orientation, they cover somewhat different content. Hence, in combination, they provide fairly full coverage of material that was necessarily excluded from this brief summary.

EARLY EDUCATION

Born in New York City on December 19, 1908, I was educated at home until the age of ten, when I entered a neighborhood public school. I was enrolled in the second semester of the fourth grade, designated 4B. After subsequently "skipping" 5A and 6A, I continued through the eighth grade without further readjustments. I graduated from elementary school at the top of my class and was awarded the gold medal for general excellence. Together with many of my classmates, I then entered a large public high school in our neighborhood. Because the school had outgrown its own building, the entire entering class was assigned to temporary quarters in an ancient elementary school building, which probably had been—and certainly should have been—condemned as unfit for human use. In order to accommodate more students, classes were held on a double shift. My routine on three out of five school days was to leave home at 10:30 A.M., ride a trolley car to the school, engage in a physical education period at 11:00, eat a box lunch in the school yard, and then attend classes from 1:00 to 5:00. There were no lockers, no showers, and meager washing facilities of any sort. Classes were overcrowded, teachers were overworked, and the whole environment was most unattractive. I stood all this for just two months.

During my dropout phase, there were many family conferences about what to do next. The final solution was reached with the help of a loyal family friend, herself a brilliant and dedicated teacher. Upon hearing about my grim high school experiences, she offered the bold suggestion that what I should really do was go to college, not high school. There were alternative routes, she explained, such as the series of examinations administered by the College Entrance Examination Board. At that time, these examinations were designed for specific courses, such as elementary algebra, solid geometry, or third-year French. There were, in addition, certain special schools that offered courses in just those subjects required for college admission, with no such "frills" as extracurricular activities, physical education, or high school diplomas. Through a careful selection of the required subjects in such a school, I was able to qualify for admission to Barnard College in only two years. As a result, I entered college at the age of fifteen, graduated at nineteen, and received the Ph.D. degree from Columbia University at twenty-one.

A further bonus of this unorthodox education was that I was admitted to Barnard with advanced college credits in mathematics. On the basis of such credits and my performance on entrance examinations, I was placed in advanced classes, not only in mathematics but also in French literature and Latin poetry. My Barnard years picked up where elementary school had left off: classes were fun again, and on graduation I won the Caroline Duror Memorial Fellowship, "awarded to that member of the graduating class showing greatest promise of distinction in her chosen line of work." To this day, I am not convinced that high school is necessary!

ON BECOMING A PSYCHOLOGIST

When I entered Barnard in 1924, I was certain that I would major in mathematics, which had been my first love since elementary school days. Although told I did not need to decide yet, I filled out forms for a BS degree with a major in mathematics and a double minor in physics and chemistry. In my freshman year, I took a required course in philosophy in the fall semester, followed by a required psychology course in the spring. Although both were taught by the same instructor, whose degree was in philosophy, the psychology course did offer solid scientific fare. The text was by Pillsbury (1921), and we covered it quite fully. I enjoyed the course thoroughly and felt more at home in it than I had in the philosophy course. But I certainly did not, at that time, entertain the idea that I might find my life work in psychology.

Two significant events occurred in my sophomore year: I took a course in developmental psychology with Harry L. Hollingworth, then chairman of Barnard's Psychology Department; and I happened to read an article by Charles Spearman (1904). Hollingworth was a fascinating lecturer, with a lively curiosity about all natural phenomena. He was an individualist who pursued his own theoretical bent with vigor and independence. At that time, his redintegration theory was just taking shape, and he sought applications of it in all behavior domains. He was also one of the last of the generalists in psychology. Years later, a classmate reminded me that after one of "Holly's" classes I remarked, "Once I get my Ph.D. in math, I'm going back to take some more psych. courses." Then the Spearman article really clinched matters. In it I learned not only about correlations but also about some fascinating relationships among correlation coefficients that later led Spearman (1927) to develop his rationale for the tetrad equation, itself an early step toward modern techniques of factor analysis. Here, then, I saw a way of enjoying the best of two possible worlds: I could remain faithful to my first love and espouse the newcomer too. I filled out new forms for a major in psychology and embarked upon the work of a lifetime.

Thus far I have singled out two psychologists, Hollingworth and Spearman, because their influence happened to come at a critical stage in my career choice. Obviously, my subsequent development in psychology, my eventual concentration on certain areas of specialization, and my theoretical orientation have been shaped by many other contacts in graduate school and throughout my career. At the time when I was a graduate student at Columbia (and during the following years when I was an instructor "across the street" at Barnard), the Columbia Psychology Department was one of the most active in the country. I owe much to my contacts with faculty and fellow students; several of the latter went on to become distinguished colleagues in many parts of the country. As for faculty influences, I had courses with each of the four senior professors then in the Psychology Department, H. E. Garrett, A. T. Poffenberger, C. J. Warden, and R. S. Woodworth, as well as with Gardner Murphy and Otto Klineberg, among others.

The psychology students also took advantage of off-campus facilities. I enrolled in a course entitled Clinical Psychology, which today would undoubtedly be called Individual Intelligence Testing. It covered chiefly the Stanford-Binet, also including some practice with a few other instruments such as the Pintner-Paterson and the Porteus Mazes. The course was given by Louise Poull at the Randall's Island Children's Hospital, where she was the only psychologist. This was a municipal institution for the mentally retarded of all ages and all degrees of intellectual disability. Dr. Poull explained that it had originally been named a "children's hospital" because the residents were all children in mental age. Housed in dilapidated wooden buildings, this institution has long since disappeared. Randall's Island is now accessible by the Triboro Bridge; at that time, it could be reached only by a diminutive ferry operated by the city. Another form of transportation was represented by a weekly subway ride that several psychology students took to the Columbia Medical Center, to attend courses at the College of Physicians and Surgeons. One term, the course I took was a survey of neuranatomy given by Adolph Elwyn, with occasional lectures by Frederick Tilney. Another term, it was an intensive course on the physiology of the nervous system conducted by F. H. Pike.

Those were exciting times in the burgeoning science of psychology. The journals bristled with vigorous controversies on topics ranging from Gestalt psychology to factor analysis. The New York State Psychiatric Institute had just been established in its new quarters in the Columbia Medical Center, and it offered great promise of interdisciplinary research. The Institute of Human Relations had recently been opened at nearby Yale University, with such leaders as Gesell, Hull, and Yerkes. There was much commuting between New York and New Haven by faculty, students, and postdoctorals. In 1929, as a second-year graduate student, I enjoyed the heady privilege of attending the International Congress of Psychology at Yale. This congress was the first to be held in the United States, and it would be over three decades before another was convened in this country. The 1929 congress met jointly with the American Psychological Association. Karl S. Lashley was president of the APA and James McKeen Cattell was president of the congress. For us graduate students, it was a rare opportunity to hear and meet psychologists whose work we had been studying, including not only most of the leading American psychologists but also the live persons attached to such familiar names as Spearman, McDougall, Piéron, and Pavlov.

The summer of 1929 was truly memorable for me. It began with a research assistantship at the Carnegie Institution of Washington in Cold Spring Harbor, Long Island, under Charles B. Davenport, who had taught biology in college to R. S. Woodworth. It ended with the International Congress at Yale. And sandwiched in between were six weeks of summer school in which I took one course with R. M. Elliott of Minnesota and two courses with Clark Hull. At that time, Hull was just moving from Wisconsin to Yale, and on the way he taught summer school at Columbia. My contact with Hull continued long after the completion of those summer courses, through correspondence, exchange of reprints, meetings, and personal conferences.

Another influence that I consider of primary importance was more indirect. It is the influence of J. R. Kantor of Indiana University. In some ways, Kantor resembles Hollingworth. He, too, is one of the last of the generalists in psychology, with a remarkable breadth of knowledge extending over psychology and related fields. He, too, formulated a comprehensive theoretical system for psychology. And he, too, pursued his interests with vigor and independence. It is, however, his emphasis on the role of environment and his explication of the specific operation of environmental factors in individual development that I recognize as the predominant influence on my own work.

My special interest in studying Kantor's published works and my opportunities for personal contacts with him stem from an event in my personal life. In the summer of 1933 I married one of Kantor's former students, John Porter Foley, Jr., of Bloomington, Indiana. After receiving the Bachelor's degree in psychology from Indiana University, John obtained the Ph.D. degree at Columbia, where we met. In many ways, John's experiential background complemented and thereby enriched mine. His Indiana upbringing and I.U. degree certainly provided the much-needed broadening of my ultralimited New York City environment. Within psychology itself, John not only stimulated my exploration of Kantor's ideas but also encouraged my interest in areas in which I had had limited preparation. For example, as a graduate student at Columbia and for several years in his own subsequent research and teaching, he worked largely in animal psychology, a specialty I had touched upon only lightly in my own training. Similarly, his studies in anthropology and his research with Franz Boas strengthened my own interest in a field that is most relevant to differential psychology. Professionally, my marriage has thus meant that I have had the benefit of not one but two Ph.D.'s in psychology.

PROFESSIONAL CAREER

Teaching and Administration

During my two years of graduate work, I held an assortment of assistantships: grading examinations and term papers for two of Hollingworth's large lecture courses, serving as laboratory assistant in Garrett's course on psychological testing, and conducting the laboratory sessions in the Barnard course on experimental psychology. In the fall of 1930, I was appointed instructor in psychology at Barnard, a post I held until 1939. At that time, the Ph.D. was required for appointment as a full-time instructor at Barnard. By present standards, both the rank and salary of my Barnard position seem incredibly low. During those Depression years, however, just having an academic job was considered an enviable achievement. At Barnard, I taught courses in general, experimental, applied, and differential psychology—the last introduced to fit my own developing interests.

In 1939, I was appointed assistant professor, sole member, and "chairman" of the newly established Psychology Department at Queens College of the City University of New York. The college itself had opened in 1938. During the department's first year, of course, only introductory psychology was taught. Gradually, my own offerings were expanded to include courses in statistics, testing, differential psychology, and applied psychology. The faculty also grew until, by the time World War II broke out, we had six full-time members. I remained as chairman during this period.

Although in those early years many of us had joined the newly founded college with great expectations about what could be accomplished, our hopes went unfulfilled. By 1946, the administrative climate at Queens College had become such as to make it well-nigh impossible for anyone seriously interested in teaching and research to function effectively. Too many hours were spent in futile committee meetings that led to little or no action. And too much time was absorbed in coping with the crises precipitated by a few unscrupulous persons who tried to pervert the system to their own ends. Within that year, four of the six department members left. I was one of the four. The others, together with their eventual academic positions, were: S. D. S. Spragg, chairman of the Psychology Department and dean of the Graduate School, University of Rochester; Benjamin McKeever, professor of psychology, University of Washington; and John I. Lacey, chief, Section of Behavioral Psychology, Fels Research Institute, and 1976 recipient (jointly with Beatrice C. Lacey) of an APA Award for Distinguished Scientific Contribution. It was apparently a wise move for all of us to leave Queens College when we did.

In 1947, I was appointed associate professor of psychology in the graduate school of Fordham University, where I remained until my retirement in 1979, having been advanced to the rank of professor in 1951. All my previous teaching, at Barnard and Queens, had been at the undergraduate level. At the time of my appointment, the only liberal arts college at Fordham University was exclusively male in both its student population and its faculty. Hence, I taught only in the graduate school, an arrangement that certainly had its advantages and was, in fact, one of the features that made the offer attractive to me. Eventually, when the college was sexually desegregated, I did teach one undergraduate course for a few years. The areas in which I taught at Fordham included statistics, psychological testing, applied psychology, test construction, factor analysis, differential psychology, and intellectual deviates (covering both the retarded and the gifted). I also served as chairman of the combined graduate and undergraduate Psychology Department from 1968 to 1974.

Research and Publication

Throughout my academic career, research and writing remained continuing interests and occupied much of my time. My principal areas of research are adequately sampled in the selected papers reproduced in this volume and are discussed in Chapters 1 and 9. The complete publication list includes also minor scattered studies that do not fall into any broadly conceived programs. These were undertaken to satisfy my curiosity about specific questions and may reflect, in part, a reaction against undue specialization arising from my generalist orientation. Examples range from an investigation of the effect of shape on the perceived area of two-dimensional figures (Anastasi, 1936) and a survey of fear and anger among college women by the diary method (Anastasi, 1948; Anastasi, Cohen, & Spatz, 1948) to a factor analysis of learning behavior in several breeds of dogs (Anastasi, Fuller, Scott, & Schmitt, 1955) and a case study of a musically gifted "idiot savant" (Anastasi & Levee, 1959).

A major category of my publications, not elsewhere discussed in this volume, consists of textbooks. As is often the case, these books grew out of courses I began to teach early in my career and continued to teach over the years. They include *Differential Psychology* (1937, 1949, 1958), *Psychological Testing* (1954, 1961, 1968, 1976, 1982), and *Fields of Applied Psychology* (1964, 1979). All three books have been widely used in foreign countries, both in the original English-language editions and in translations. Various editions of one or another of these books have been translated into Chinese, Dutch, German, Italian, Japanese, Portuguese, Spanish, and Thai; Hebrew and Russian translations of the fifth edition of my *Psychological Testing* are in progress. A word about my use of the term "differential psychology" may be in order. Prior to 1937, when my book by this title was first published, this area was commonly designated as "individual differences." Because I felt that a broader term was desirable, I chose a literal translation of the German term introduced by William Stern (1900) in the first edition of his book and retained in subsequent German editions. It was interesting to see that the German translation of my own book, published in 1976, was titled *Differentielle Psychologie*. We had now come full circle!

Mention may also be made of two books I edited: *Testing Problems in Perspective* (1966), comprising a selection of significant papers presented over a 25-year period at the ETS Invitational Conference on Testing Problems; and *Individual Differences* (1965), a book of readings in a series on historical antecedents of modern psychology, under the general editorship of William Kessen and George Mandler. Another related category, spanning several decades, includes chapters in edited books and survey articles in various encyclopedias on topics related to my three textbooks.

Academic Potpourri[1]

One of the attractions of the academic life is the diversity of activities it permits and encourages. Over the years, I have served as an individual consultant or as a member of advisory committees for various government agencies at the federal, state, and municipal levels; for educational, industrial, and other types of private organizations; and in association with lawyers in the preparation of cases involving the use of tests or other assessment procedures. In my service on a succession of panels, boards, commissions, and committees, I have had an opportunity to work closely with members of other disciplines, ranging from mathematics and engineering to the humanities, educational administration, and military leadership. With few exceptions, communication across disciplines did not prove to be a significant difficulty in these contexts, and I found such interdisciplinary contacts personally gratifying. Another favorite activity of those in academic life is the invited lecture delivered to groups of diverse sizes and degrees of heterogeneity, from small specialized seminars, institutes, or workshops to association-wide or university-wide audiences. I have had my share of these experiences, which have taken me to some well-traveled, cosmopolitan sites and prestigious university centers, as well as to some intriguing out-of-the-way places.

Participation in association activities has also represented an enduring interest throughout my professional life. The first APA meet-

---

[1] This section is reprinted with minor changes from Lindzey, G. (Ed.), *A history of psychology in autobiography*, Vol. VII (San Francisco: Freeman, © 1980, pp. 30–32), by permission of the publisher.

ing I attended was held at Columbia University in 1928, the year I graduated from Barnard. It was at this meeting that I first encountered the two women who preceded me as presidents of the APA and who were to remain, for fifty years, the sole representatives of their sex to hold this office. One of the sessions at the convention was chaired by Mary W. Calkins (president, 1905) and included a paper presented by Margaret Floy Washburn (president, 1921). In introducing Dr. Washburn, Dr. Calkins said, "I shall now call upon our past president to deliver the next paper." As a first-year graduate student, I found all this quite impressive.

The first office I held in any scientific society was the secretaryship of the Psychology Section of the New York Academy of Sciences in the mid-1930s, followed a couple of years later by the chairmanship of the section. Over the years, I have been a member of and served in various capacities in several other associations, including the American Psychological Association, the Eastern Psychological Association, the New York State Psychological Association, the Psychometric Society, the Psychonomic Society, the Psychology Section of the National Research Council, the Board of Trustees of the American Psychological Foundation, and local university chapters of Phi Beta Kappa and Sigma Xi. Among the offices I have held are the presidencies of the EPA (1946–1947), the APA Division of General Psychology (1956–1957), the APA Division of Evaluation and Measurement (1965–1966), the American Psychological Foundation (1965–1967), and the APA (1972).

Since I certainly consider it an honor to have been elected by my colleagues to these various offices, it may be appropriate at this point to mention some other items in the general category of "honors and awards." I have received honorary degrees from the University of Windsor in Canada (Litt.D., 1967), Villanova University (Paed.D., 1971), Cedar Crest College (Sc.D., 1971), Fordham University (Sc.D., 1979), and LaSalle College (Sc.D., 1979). At the 1977 ETS Invitational Conference, I was the recipient of the Educational Testing Service Award for Distinguished Service to Measurement, "presented annually to an individual whose work and career have had a major impact on the developments in educational and psychological measurement." In 1981, I received the American Psychological Association Distinguished Scientific Award for the Applications of Psychology.

"Honors and awards" provide a pleasant note on which to end one's autobiography. But it is an intrinsic limitation of autobiographies that they can never be complete. To be sure, from my personal standpoint, I would not want it to be otherwise! In the interest of fuller coverage, however, I must add that I am currently engaged in a wide diversity and staggering number of professional projects, and I still see many more lining up for the future.

REFERENCES

Anastasi, A. The estimation of area. *Journal of General Psychology*, 1936, *14*, 201–225.

——. *Differential psychology*, New York: Macmillan, 1937 (later eds., 1949, 1958).

——. A methodological note on the controlled diary technique. *Journal of Genetic Psychology*, 1948, *73*, 237–241.

——. *Psychological testing*, New York: Macmillan, 1954 (later eds., 1961, 1968, 1976, 1982).

——. *Fields of applied psychology*. New York: McGraw-Hill, 1964 (later ed., 1979).

——. (Ed.). *Individual differences*. New York: Wiley, 1965.

——. (Ed.). *Testing problems in perspective*. Washington, D.C.: American Council on Education, 1966.

——. Reminiscences of a differential psychologist. In T. S. Krawiec (Ed.), *The psychologists*. New York: Oxford University Press, 1972. Pp. 3–37.

——. Anne Anastasi. In G. Lindzey (Ed.), *A history of psychology in autobiography* (Vol. VII). San Francisco: Freeman, 1980. Pp. 1–37.

——, Cohen, N., & Spatz, D. A study of fear and anger in college students through the controlled diary method. *Journal of Genetic Psychology*, 1948, *73*, 243–249.

——, Fuller, J. L., Scott, J. P., & Schmitt, J. R. A factor analysis of the performance of dogs on certain learning tests. *Zoologica*, 1955, *40*(3), 33–46.

—— & Levee, R. F. Intellectual defect and musical talent. *American Journal of Mental Deficiency*, 1959, *64*, 695–703.

Pillsbury, W. B. *Essentials of psychology* (rev. ed.). New York: Macmillan, 1921.

Spearman, C. "General intelligence" objectively determined and measured. *American Journal of Psychology*, 1904, *15*, 201–293.

Spearman, C. *The abilities of man*. New York: Macmillan, 1927.

Stern, W. *Über Psychologie der individuellen Differenzen: Ideen zur einer "Differentielle Psychologie."* Leipzig: Barth, 1900 (later editions, 1911, 1921).

Publications: A Comprehensive Bibliography

1928

With F. H. Lund. An interpretation of esthetic experience. *American Journal of Psychology, 40,* 434–448.

1930

A group factor in immediate memory. *Archives of Psychology,* No. 120. Pp. 61.

1932

Further studies on the memory factor. *Archives of Psychology,* No. 142. Pp. 60.

Review of H. B. Reed, The influence of training on changes in variability in achievement. *American Journal of Psychology, 44,* 842–843.

With H. E. Garrett. The tetrad difference criterion and the measurement of mental traits. *Annals of the New York Academy of Sciences, 33,* 233–282.

1934

The influence of practice upon test reliability. *Journal of Educational Psychology, 25,* 321–335.

Practice and variability. *Psychological Monographs, 45*(5, Whole No. 204). Pp. 55.

1935

Some ambiguous concepts in the field of mental organization. *American Journal of Psychology, 47,* 508–511.

1936

The estimation of area. *Journal of General Psychology, 14,* 201–225.

The influence of specific experience upon mental organization. *Genetic Psychology Monographs, 18*(4), 245–355.

Review of D. H. Cooke, Minimum essentials of statistics as applied to education and psychology. *American Journal of Psychology, 48,* 557–558.

With J. P. Foley, Jr. An analysis of spontaneous drawings by children in different cultures. *Journal of Applied Psychology, 20,* 689–726.

1937

Differential psychology. New York: Macmillan. Pp. 615.

Review of G. D. Higginson, Psychology. *American Journal of Psychology, 49,* 324–325.

1938

American Council on Education Psychological Examination for College Freshmen. *Mental Measurements Yearbook*, 95–96.

Detroit Tests of Learning Aptitude. *Mental Measurements Yearbook*, 108–109.

Faculties versus factors: A reply to Professor Thurstone. *Psychological Bulletin*, 35, 391–395.

Review of S. D. Porteus, Primitive intelligence and environment. *American Journal of Psychology*, 51, 192–194.

With J. P. Foley, Jr. A study of animal drawings by Indian children of the North Pacific Coast. *Journal of Social Psychology*, 9, 363–374.

With J. P. Foley, Jr. The work of the Children's Federal Art Gallery. *School and Society*, 48, No. 1253, 859–861.

1939

Individual differences. *Fifth Yearbook, National Commercial Teachers Federation*, 26–35.

1940

Henmon-Nelson Test of Mental Ability. *Mental Measurements Yearbook*, 220–221.

The nature of individual differences (Ch. 12); Major group differences (Ch. 13). In J. P. Guilford (Ed.), *Fields of psychology*. New York: Van Nostrand. Pp. 251–284; 285–314.

Review of E. L. Smith, Tides in the affairs of men. *American Journal of Psychology*, 53, 629.

Terman Group Test of Mental Ability. *Mental Measurements Yearbook*, 250.

With J. P. Foley, Jr. The study of "populistic" painters as an approach to the psychology of art. *Journal of Social Psychology*, 11, 353–368.

With J. P. Foley, Jr. A survey of the literature on artistic behavior in the abnormal: III. Spontaneous productions. *Psychological Monographs*, 52(6, Whole No. 237). Pp. 71.

1941

Abstract of C. Burt, The factors of the mind. *Psychological Abstracts*, 15, 349.

Review of C. Burt, The factors of the mind. *American Journal of Psychology*, 54, 613–614.

Review of E. R. Carlson, Born that way. *American Journal of Psychology*, 54, 629–630.

Review of L. P. Thorpe, Personality and life. *Psychological Bulletin*, 38, 769–770.

Review of P. E. Vernon, The measurement of abilities. *American Journal of Psychology*, 54, 154–155.

With J. P. Foley, Jr. A study of spontaneous artistic productions by the insane. *Psychological Bulletin*, 38, 538–539. (Abstract)

With J. P. Foley, Jr. A survey of the literature on artistic behavior in the abnormal: I. Historical and theoretical background. *Journal of General Psychology, 25,* 111–142.

With J. P. Foley, Jr. A survey of the literature on artistic behavior in the abnormal: II. Approaches and interrelationships. *Annals of the New York Academy of Sciences, 42*(1).

With J. P. Foley, Jr. A survey of the literature on artistic behavior in the abnormal: IV. Experimental investigations. *Journal of General Psychology, 25,* 187–237.

1942

Abstract of E. Newbury, The genetics of intelligence. *Psychological Abstracts, 16,* 341.

Abstract of H. E. Rees, A psychology of artistic creation as evidenced in autobiographical statements of artists. *Psychological Abstracts, 16,* 551–552.

Review of V. Case, Your personality—introvert or extrovert? *American Journal of Psychology, 55,* 305–306.

Review of D. Wechsler, The measurement of adult intelligence. *American Journal of Psychology, 55,* 608–609.

With J. P. Foley, Jr. An experimental study of the drawing behavior of adult psychotics in comparison with that of a normal control group. *Psychological Bulletin, 39,* 462–463. (Abstract)

1943

Review of W. H. Sheldon, The varieties of temperament. *Psychological Bulletin, 40,* 146–149.

With J. P. Foley, Jr. An analysis of spontaneous artistic productions by the abnormal. *Journal of General Psychology, 28,* 297–313.

1944

Abstract of B. Morris, The aesthetic process. *Psychological Abstracts, 18,* 87.

With J. P. Foley, Jr. An experimental study of the drawing behavior of adult psychotics in comparison with that of a normal control group. *Journal of Experimental Psychology, 34,* 169–194.

1945

With J. P. Foley, Jr. Review of J. H. Sanders, Chains of shadows. *Journal of Social Psychology, 21,* 295–296.

1947

The place of experimental psychology in the undergraduate curriculum. *American Psychologist, 2,* 57–62.

1948

Individual differences (Ch. 18); Heredity and environment (Ch. 19). In E. G. Boring, H. S. Langfeld, & H. P. Weld (Eds.), *Foundations of psychology.* New York: Wiley. Pp. 393-435; 436-458.

A methodological note on the "controlled diary" technique. *Journal of Genetic Psychology, 73,* 237-241.

The nature of psychological "traits." *Psychological Review, 55,* 127-138.

Review of L. M. Terman & M. H. Oden, The gifted child grows up. *Psychological Bulletin, 45,* 363-366.

With N. Cohen & D. Spatz. A study of fear and anger in college students through the controlled diary method. *Journal of Genetic Psychology, 73,* 243-249.

With J. P. Foley, Jr. A proposed reorientation in the heredity-environment controversy. *Psychological Review, 55,* 239-249.

1949

Adaptability Test. *Third Mental Measurements Yearbook,* 302-303.

California Capacity Questionnaire. *Third Mental Measurements Yearbook,* 294-295.

Thurstone Test of Mental Alertness. *Third Mental Measurements Yearbook,* 344-345.

With J. P. Foley, Jr. *Differential psychology* (2nd ed.). New York: Macmillan. Pp. 894.

With S. Miller. Adolescent "prestige factors" in relation to scholastic and socioeconomic variables. *Journal of Social Psychology, 29,* 43-50.

1950

The concept of validity in the interpretation of test scores. *Educational and Psychological Measurement, 10,* 67-78.

The nature of individual differences (Ch. 12); Major group differences (Ch. 13). In J. P. Guilford (Ed.), *Fields of psychology* (2nd ed.). New York: Van Nostrand. Pp. 331-373; 374-412.

Review of R. Mukerjee, The social function of art. *Journal of Abnormal and Social Psychology, 45,* 569-572.

Review of N. Pastore, Heredity and environment. *Science, 111,* 45-46.

Review of G. Smith, Psychological studies in twin differences. *Psychological Bulletin, 47,* 80-81.

Some implications of cultural factors for test construction. *Proceedings of the 1949 Invitational Conference on Testing Problems, Educational Testing Service,* 13-17.

1951

Cultural factors in the concept of genius. *Yearbook, New York Society for the Experimental Study of Education,* 58-64.

With J. P. Foley, Jr. *Human relations and the foreman.* New London, Conn.: National Foreman's Institute. Pp. 251.

1952

Review of P. E. Vernon, The structure of human abilities. *American Journal of Psychology, 65*, 143–145.

With R. Y. D'Angelo. A comparison of Negro and white preschool children in language development and Goodenough Draw-A-Man IQ. *Journal of Genetic Psychology, 81*, 147–165.

With J. P. Foley, Jr. *The Human-Figure Drawing Test as an objective psychiatric screening aid for student pilots* (Proj. No. 21–37–002, Rep. No. 5). Randolph Field, Tex.: USAF School of Aviation Medicine. Pp. 30.

1953

An empirical study of the applicability of sequential analysis to item selection. *Educational and Psychological Measurement, 13*, 3–13.

The Guilford-Zimmerman Aptitude Survey. *Fourth Mental Measurements Yearbook*, 693–695.

Individual differences. *Annual Review of Psychology*, Vol. 4. Stanford, Calif.: Stanford University Press. Pp. 137–156.

Primary Mental Abilities. *Fourth Mental Measurements Yearbook*, 700–703.

Psychological traits and group relations (Ch. 3). In M. Sherif & M. O. Wilson (Eds.), *Group relations at the crossroads*. New York: Harper. Pp. 74–98.

With F. A. Cordova. Some effects of bilingualism upon the intelligence test performance of Puerto Rican children in New York City. *Journal of Educational Psychology, 44*, 1–19.

With C. deJesús. Language development and nonverbal IQ of Puerto Rican preschool children in New York City. *Journal of Abnormal and Social Psychology, 48*, 357–366.

1954

The inherited and acquired components of behavior. *Proceedings of the Association for Research in Nervous and Mental Diseases*, 67–75.

The measurement of abilities. *Journal of Counseling Psychology, 1*, 164–168.

Psychological testing. New York: Macmillan. Pp. 682.

Tested intelligence and family size: Methodological and interpretive problems. *Eugenics Quarterly, 1*, 155–160.

With J. D. Drake. An empirical comparison of certain techniques for estimating the reliability of speeded tests. *Educational and Psychological Measurement, 14*, 529–540.

With J. P. Foley, Jr., & H. Sackman. *Psychiatric selection of flying personnel: An empirical evaluation of the SAM Personality-Sketch Test* (Proj. No. 21–0202–0007, Rep. No. 6). Randolph Field, Tex.: USAF School of Aviation Medicine. Pp. 51.

1955

Review of C. J. Adcock, Factorial analysis for non-mathematicians. *Educational and Psychological Measurement, 15*, 520–521.

Review of R. J. Williams, Free and unequal: The biological basis of individual liberty. *Human Biology, 27,* 243–246.
With J. L. Fuller, J. P. Scott, & J. R. Schmitt. A factor analysis of the performance of dogs on certain learning tests. *Zoologica, 40*(3), 33–46.

1956

Age changes in adult test performance. *Psychological Reports, 2,* 509.
Intelligence and family size. *Psychological Bulletin, 53,* 187–209.
A suggested modification of T-scores: Comments on the article by D. Mahanta. *Education and Psychology* (Delhi, India), *3,* 31–32.

1957

Tested intelligence and family size: Methodological and interpretive problems. *Proceedings of the World Population Conference* (E/Conf./13/418). New York: United Nations. Vol. VI, pp. 689–702.

1958

Differential psychology (3rd ed.). New York: Macmillan. Pp. 664. (Translations: German, Italian, Portuguese, Spanish)
Heredity, environment, and the question "How?" *Psychological Review, 65,* 197–208.
Review of A. M. Shuey, The testing of Negro intelligence. *Science, 128,* 297.

1959

Differentiating effect of intelligence and social status. *Eugenics Quarterly, 6,* 84–91.
Discussion of H. Knobloch & B. Pasamanick, Distribution of intellectual potential in an infant population. *Epidemiology of Mental Disorder. Publication No. 60, American Association for the Advancement of Science,* 264–267.
Holzinger-Crowder Uni-Factor Tests. *Fifth Mental Measurements Yearbook,* 700–702.
Yale Educational Aptitude Test Battery. *Fifth Mental Measurements Yearbook,* 717–719.
With R. F. Levee. Intellectual defect and musical talent. *American Journal of Mental Deficiency, 64,* 695–703.

1960

Cultural differences. *Encyclopedia of Educational Research* (3rd ed.), 350–358.
Differential psychology. *Encyclopedia Britannica,* 367–369.
Estableciendo normas de conducta. *Revista de Psicologia General y Aplicada, 15,* 863–865.
The gifted child at forty-five: Review of L. M. Terman & M. H. Oden, The gifted group at midlife: Thirty-five years' follow-up of the superior child. *Contemporary Psychology, 5,* 46–47.
Psychological research and educational desegregation. *Thought, 35,* 421–449.

Standardized ability testing. In P. H. Mussen (Ed.), *Handbook of research methods in child development.* New York: Wiley. Pp. 456–486.
With M. J. Meade & A. A. Schneiders. The validation of a biographical inventory as a predictor of college success. *College Entrance Examination Board Research Monographs,* No. 1. Pp. 81.

1961

L'établissement de normes de comportement. *Revue de Psychologie Appliquée, 11,* 87–90.
Psychological research and educational desegregation. In J. E. O'Neill (Ed.), *A Catholic case against segregation.* New York: Macmillan. Pp. 116–145.
Psychological testing (2nd ed.). New York: Macmillan. Pp. 657. (Translations: Italian, Portuguese, Spanish)
Psychological tests: Uses and abuses. *Teachers College Record, 62,* 389–393.

1962

Intelligence. *Collier's Encyclopedia, 13,* 92–95.
The longitudinal study of populations. *Indian Psychological Bulletin, 7*(Part II), 25–28.
Mental deficiency. *Collier's Encyclopedia, 15,* 696–699.
Mongolism. *Collier's Encyclopedia, 16,* 455. (rev. 1963)
Psychological testing. *Collier's Encyclopedia Yearbook,* 515–520.

1964

Culture-fair testing. *Educational Horizons, 43*(1), 26–30.
Differential psychology. *Encyclopedia Britannica,* 419–421.
Fields of applied psychology. New York: McGraw-Hill. Pp. 621. (Translations: Chinese, Dutch, German, Italian, Japanese, Portuguese, Spanish—Spain and Argentina editions)
Some current developments in the measurement and interpretation of test validity. *Proceedings of the 1963 Invitational Conference on Testing Problems, Educational Testing Service,* 33–45.

1965

Individual differences. (Ed.) New York: Wiley. Pp. 301.
IPAT Children's Personality Questionnaire. *Sixth Mental Measurements Yearbook,* 256–257.
The Jastak Test of Potential Ability and Behavior Stability. *Sixth Mental Measurements Yearbook,* 1030–1031.
Male vs. female attitudes. In W. C. Bier (Ed.), *Marriage: A psychological and moral approach.* New York: Fordham University Press. Pp. 57–66.

1966

Differential psychology: Individual differences (Ch. 8); Differential psychology: Group differences (Ch. 9). In J. P. Guilford (Ed.), *Fields of psychology* (3rd ed.). Princeton, N.J.: Van Nostrand. Pp. 133–154; 155–173.

Psychology and guidance. In T. C. Hennessy (Ed.), *The interdisciplinary roots of guidance.* New York: Fordham University Press. Pp. 24-45.
Testing problems in perspective. (Ed.) Washington, D.C.: American Council on Education. Pp. 671.

1967

Psychological testing of children. In A. M. Freedman & H. I. Kaplan (Eds.), *Comprehensive textbook of psychiatry.* Baltimore: Williams & Wilkins. Pp. 1342-1356.
Psychology, psychologists, and psychological testing. *American Psychologist, 22,* 297-306.

1968

Applied psychology. *International Encyclopedia of the Social Sciences, 13,* 84-95.
Individual differences. *International Encyclopedia of the Social Sciences, 7,* 200-207.
A inteligência: Sua natureza e origens. *Arquivos Brasileiros de Psicotécnica, 20* (4), 11-24. (Transl. by A. M. Arruda & M. I. Garcia de Freitas)
Psychological differences between men and women. In W. C. Bier (Ed.), *Women in modern life.* New York. Fordham University Press. Pp. 42-54.
Psychological testing (3rd ed.). New York: Macmillan. Pp. 665. (Translations: Italian, Thai)
With C. E. Schaefer. A biographical inventory for identifying creativity in adolescent boys. *Journal of Applied Psychology, 52,* 42-48.

1969

Comparative analysis of Council representatives from divisions and state associations. *American Psychologist, 24,* 1115-1118.
La psychologie, les psychologues, et les tests psychologiques. *Bulletin de l'Institut National du Travail et d'Orientation Professionnelle, 2°* ser., *25*(1), 3-20. (Transl. by D. Bonora)
Sex differences in vocational choices. *National Catholic Guidance Conference Journal, 13*(4), 63-76.
With C. E. Schaefer. Biographical correlates of artistic and literary creativity in adolescent girls. *Journal of Applied Psychology, 53,* 267-273.

1970

On the formation of psychological traits. *American Psychologist, 25,* 899-910.
Correlates of creativity in children from two socioeconomic levels (Final Proj. Rep., CUE Subcontract No. 2, Contract No. OEC-1-7-062868-3060). New York: Center for Urban Education. Pp. 76.
With S. Urbina, J. Harrison, & C. E. Schaefer. Relationship between masculinity-femininity and creativity as measured by the Franck Drawing Completion Test. *Psychological Reports, 26,* 799-804.

1971

Differentielle Psychologie. *Lexicon der Psychologie, 1,* 378–388.

Focus on test construction: Review of R. L. Thorndike (Ed.), Educational measurement (2nd ed.). *Contemporary Psychology, 16,* 694–695.

More on heritability: Addendum to the Hebb and Jensen interchange. *American Psychologist, 26,* 1036–1037.

Reply to Brandt. *American Psychologist, 26,* 513–514.

Standardized tests. *Encyclopedia of Education, 8,* 391–395. (Also editorial advisor, articles on Measurement and Testing.)

What's ahead for 1972? *APA Monitor, 2*(12), p. 2.

With C. E. Schaefer. The Franck Drawing Completion Test as a measure of creativity. *Journal of Genetic Psychology, 119,* 3–12.

With C. E. Schaefer. Note on the concepts of creativity and intelligence. *Journal of Creative Behavior, 5,* 113–116.

1972

The annual convention in retrospect. *APA Monitor, 3*(11), p. 2.

The cultivation of diversity. *American Psychologist, 27,* 1091–1099.

Differential psychology. *Encyclopedia of Psychology, 1,* 273–277.

Four hypotheses with a dearth of data: Response to Lehrke's "A theory of X-linkage of major intellectual traits." *American Journal of Mental Deficiency, 76,* 620–622.

Goodenough-Harris Drawing Test. *Seventh Mental Measurements Yearbook,* 669–671.

Interpretation of heritability: A rejoinder. *American Psychologist, 27,* 975.

Personality Research Form. *Seventh Mental Measurements Yearbook,* 297–298.

Psychological testing of children. In A. M. Freedman & H. I. Kaplan (Eds.), *The child: His psychological and cultural development* (Vol. 1). New York: Atheneum. Pp. 125–151.

Psychological testing of children. In A. M. Freedman & H. I. Kaplan (Eds.), *Diagnosing mental illness.* New York: Atheneum. Pp. 265–291.

Reminiscences of a differential psychologist. In T. S. Krawiec (Ed.), *The psychologists.* New York: Oxford University Press. Pp. 3–37.

Review of R. Cancro (Ed.), Intelligence: Genetic and environmental influences. *American Scientist, 60,* 796.

Technical critique. *Proceedings of Invitational Conference on an Investigation of Sources of Bias in the Prediction of Job Performance: A Six-Year Study.* Princeton, N.J.: Educational Testing Service. Pp. 79–88.

1973

Common fallacies about heredity, environment, and human behavior. *ACT Research Report,* No. 58.

1974

Commentary on the precocity project. In J. C. Stanley, D. P. Keating, & L. H.

Fox (Eds.), *Mathematical talent: Discovery, description, and development.* Baltimore: Johns Hopkins University Press, Pp. 87–100.

Individual differences in aging. In W. C. Bier (Ed.), *Aging: Its challenge to the individual and to society.* New York: Fordham University Press. Pp. 84–95.

Unexplored correlates of creativity: Review of C. W. Taylor (Ed.), Climate for creativity: Report of the Seventh National Research Conference on Creativity. *Contemporary Psychology, 19,* 311–313.

1975

Commentary on the precocity project. *Journal of Special Education, 9*(1), 93–103.

Harassing a dead horse: Review of D. R. Green (Ed.), The aptitude-achievement distinction. *Review of Education, 1,* 356–362.

Intelligence. *Collier's Encyclopedia, 13,* 92–95. (revised)

An interview with Anne Anastasi. In A. Davids & T. Engen, *Introductory psychology.* New York: Random House. Pp. III-1 to III-4.

Mental Retardation. *Collier's Encyclopedia, 15,* 697–699. (revised)

Mongolism. *Collier's Encyclopedia, 16,* 454–455. (revised)

Psychological testing of children. In A. M. Freedman, H. I. Kaplan, & B. J. Sadock (Eds.), *Comprehensive textbook of psychiatry/II.* Blatimore: Williams & Wilkins. Vol. 2, pp. 2070–2087.

1976

Foreword. In E. Aronow & M. Reznikoff, *Rorschach content interpretation.* New York: Grune & Stratton. Pp. x–xi.

Psychological testing (4th ed.). New York: Macmillan. (Italian translation, 1981.)

1977

Discussant comments. In J. C. Stanley, W. C. George, & C. H. Solano (Eds.), *The gifted and the creative: A fifty-year perspective.* Baltimore: Johns Hopkinds University Press. Pp. 227–228, 231, 239, 242.

1978

International Primary Factors Test Battery. *Eighth Mental Measurements Yearbook,* 667–669.

Values Inventory for Children. *Eighth Mental Measurements Yearbook,* 1135–1137.

1979

Differential psychology ten years from now. In J. Lyons & J. J. Barrell, *People: The humanistic science of psychology.* New York: Harper & Row, p. 480.

Fields of applied psychology (2nd ed.). New York: McGraw-Hill. Pp. 673.

A historian's view of the nature-nurture controversy: Review of H. Cravens, The

triumph of evolution: American scientists and the heredity-environment controversy, 1900–1941. *Contemporary Psychology, 24,* 622–623.
Some reflections on the acceleration-enrichment controversy. In W. C. George, S. J. Cohn, & J. C. Stanley (Eds.), *Educating the gifted: Acceleration and enrichment.* Baltimore: Johns Hopkins University Press. Pp. 221–222.

1980

Abilities and the measurement of achievement. In W. B. Schrader (Ed.), *New directions for testing and measurement,* Vol. 5. San Francisco: Jossey-Bass. Pp. 1–10.
Anne Anastasi. In G. Lindzey (Ed.), *A history of psychology in autobiography,* Vol. VII. San Francisco: Freeman. Pp. 1–37.
Psychological testing and privacy. In W. C. Bier (Ed.), *Privacy: A vanishing value?* New York: Fordham University Press. Pp. 348–358.
Review of R. Feuerstein et al., The dynamic assessment of retarded performers: The Learning Potential Assessment Device, theory, instruments, and techniques. *Rehabilitation Literature, 41*(1–2), 28–30.

1981

Coaching, test sophistication, and developed abilities. *American Psychologist, 36,* 1086–1093.
Diverse effects of training on tests of academic intelligence. In B. F. Green (Ed.), *New directions for testing and measurement: Issues in testing—coaching, disclosure, and ethnic bias,* No. 11. San Francisco: Jossey-Bass. Pp. 5–19.
Sex differences: Historical perspectives and methodological implications. *Developmental Review, 1,* 187–206.
With K. S. Geisinger. Use of tests with schoolchildren: Final project report. JSAS *Catalog of Selected Documents in Psychology, 11,* 58. (Ms. No. 2307)

1982

Psychological testing (5th ed.). New York: Macmillan. Pp. 784.
Psychological testing. In C. E. Walker (Ed.), *Handbook of clinical psychology: Theory, research, and practice.* Homewood, Ill.: Dow-Jones Irwin. Ch. C-4.

Author Index

Subject Index